David Breakenridge Read

The Canadian Rebellion of 1837

David Breakenridge Read

The Canadian Rebellion of 1837

ISBN/EAN: 9783337186425

Printed in Europe, USA, Canada, Australia, Japan

Cover: Foto ©ninafisch / pixelio.de

More available books at **www.hansebooks.com**

LOUIS JOSEPH PAPINEAU.

CANADIAN REBELLION

OF

1837.

BY

D. B. READ, Q C.

Author of "The Lives of the Judges of Upper Canada," "Life of Lieut.-Governor Simcoe," "Life of Sir Isaac Brock."

TORONTO:
C. BLACKETT ROBINSON
1896

PREFACE.

CARLYLE, in the introductory chapter to his relation of Cromwell's first civil war, wrote: "How has pacific England, the most solid pacific country in the world, got all into this armed attitude; and decided itself to argue henceforth by pike and bullet till it get some solution?" My object in writing the History of the Rebellion of 1837 in Canada has been to endeavour to solve the same problem in relation to that colony of the British Empire. How far I have succeeded I leave to each reader's individual judgment. I have sought to make fairness and impartiality my governing principles in describing the events of the time. The History is in some measure political, but is not, I trust, written in the spirit of a partisan: *that* I have tried to avoid. I submit the narrative to my readers in the hope that they will justify my pretension.

THE AUTHOR.

TORONTO, April, 1896.

TABLE OF CONTENTS.

CHAPTER I.

Introduction—French Surrender to Lord Amherst, 1760—Terms of Surrender—Treaty of Paris, 1763—King's Proclamation Bringing into Force the Treaty—Quebec Constitutional Act, 1774—Intendant Bigot—French Laws and English Laws—Difficulty of Administration—General Murray Appointed Governor-General—Major Irving, Administrator—Sir Guy Carleton, Governor.

CHAPTER II.

Constitutional Act, 1774, Unsatisfactory to British-Canadians—Petition to Annul—American Revolution of 1776—Sympathy of French-Canadians—Clergy Opposed—American Congress Attempt to Tamper with French-Canadians—Montgomery and Arnold—Seignors and their Tenants—Canadian Merchants in London Demand Repeal of Quebec Act—Legislative Council, its Unpopularity—Haldimand Succeeds Carleton as Governor—The Militia Organization—French-Canadians Chafe Under English Rule—Du Calvet's Opinion of Canadian Sentiments—Bigots and Agitators—Treaty of Peace, 1783—America and England—Close of Haldimand's Administration—Lord Dorchester's Second Term as Governor—U. E. Loyalists—Their Appeal to Divide Quebec—Constitution of 1791.

CHAPTER III.

Provinces Divided—Legislative Assembly—Battle of Races—Papineau, Member of Assembly—Panet's Patriotic Speech—Education and Religion—Assembly's Claim to Regulate Supplies—Lord Dorchester's Instructions—French Minister Genet—Dissimulation and Treachery—Bishop Plessis' Advice to French-Canadians— Legislative Assembly Decidedly French—Judge Osgoode—French Language, its Use in Parliament—Tithes—Immigration—Sir James Craig—Acceptable to the French, but not to the English— Advises Re-Union of Provinces.

CHAPTER IV.

U. E. Loyalists—John Graves Simcoe, First Governor of Upper Canada—First Parliament of Upper Canada—Simcoe's Death— Peter Russell Administrator—British and American Insurgents—Irish Rebellion of 1798—Governor Hunter and his Administration—Discontent in Lower Canada—Governor Gore's Administration—Joseph Willcox, M.P., his Contempt of Parliament and Imprisonment—Mr. Justice Thorpe—Judge Scott— Difference of Parties on Local Government.

CHAPTER V.

U. S. Declaration of War Against Great Britain, 1812—French-Canadians and English-Canadians at One in Defending Canada— American Hopes Built on Canadian Disappointments—The War of 1812, its Lessons and Consequences—Sir George Prevost, his Administration—A Party in Opposition to Government—Louis Joseph Papineau Elected Speaker of Assembly of L. C.—His Great Ability—Sir John Sherbrooke, Governor of Lower Canada—Concessions to the Province—The Duke of Richmond Succeeds Sherbrooke—Napoleon and Waterloo—The Duke of Richmond Offends the Lower Canadian Assembly—The Duke's Death in Canada—Louis J. Papineau Delivers a Thoroughly British Speech to Electors in Montreal—Claim of L. C. Assembly—Legislative Council and Assembly at Loggerheads—Colonial Office Endeavour to Heal Differences—Constitution of 1791

Threatened—Re-Union of Provinces Agitated—Bill Brought into House of Commons—Bill Rejected—Lord Dalhousie's Administration—Governor's Refusal to Recognize Papineau as Speaker.

CHAPTER VI.

Governor Gore's Second Term—War of 1812 and Its Rewards—Slow Fulfilment—Robert Fleming Gourlay—His Life in Canada and his Trials—He was Strong, Impetuous, Honest in his Convictions—His Advocacy of Immigration—He Calls a Convention to Discuss Canadian Affairs—Indicted for Seditious Libel—Twice Tried, Twice Acquitted—Finally Expelled from the Province on Other Grounds—His Address to the King—Imprisoned in England—Return to America—Declines to Support Mackenzie's Rebellion—Subsequent Life—Sir Peregrine Maitland, Governor—His Administration—A Tory House—Liberal Measures—Barnabas Bidwell Elected to Parliament—His Subsequent Expulsion—Marshall S. Bidwell Elected—Prominent Figure in the Rebellion of 1837—William Lyon Mackenzie, his Birth, Parentage and Early Life—Mackenzie's Politics—His Arraignment of the Governor and its Consequences—His Banishment Advocated.

CHAPTER VII.

Papineau and Republicanism — Personalities — Lord Dalhousie a Soldier—Sir Walter Scott's Estimate of Him—Inaugurated Monument to Wolfe and Montcalm—His Departure from the Province—Sir James Kempt Succeeds Lord Dalhousie—Endeavours to Conciliate the French-Canadians—Petitions to the King Commending Constitutional Act of 1791, but Asking for Redress of Grievances—Sir James Kempt Receives Papineau as Speaker—Committee for Redress of Grievances—Committee of House of Assembly Disapprove Constitution of 1791—Arraignment of

Legislative Council—Council and Assembly on Granting Supplies—Sir James Kempt's Opinion of Legislative Council—Not Prepared to Revolutionize the Government—Assembly Makes Demands that Could Not be Granted—The People and the Press—Rival Factions—Riots in Montreal—The Cholera Year—Legislative Council Increased—Governor's Censure on House of Assembly for Refusing Supplies—House Asks for an Elective Legislative Council—The Legislative Council Advise the King that the Legislation of Lower Canada Assembly was Alarming—Mr. Viger, Delegate in London—Assembly Arraigns Lord Aylmer, Governor—Judges in the Assembly.

CHAPTER VIII.

Mackenzie and the Reform Party—Defects in Government—Mackenzie's Printing Office Attacked—Type Distributed and Thrown Into the Bay—Action for Damages—Mackenzie Profited by the Rash Act—Collins and the Newspaper, "The Freeman"—Collins Prosecuted for Libel—Young Men who Attacked Mackenzie's Office on Trial—Convicted—Mackenzie Did Not Countenance Prosecution—Report of Select Committee of House of Assembly—"The Advocate's" Comments Thereon Offensive and Libellous—Mackenzie Prosecuted for Libel—Appeal to the Electors—Alien Laws—Mackenzie Makes Friends of Old Settlers—Mackenzie Not Admirer of the American Constitution—Mackenzie's Address to Electors, County of York, 1827—Dr. Baldwin—Mackenzie's "Black List"—Mackenzie and Small Opposed—Sir Peregrine Maitland's Administration—Colonial System of Government—Mackenzie's Activity—Mackenzie's Thirty-two Resolutions—Grievances—Sir John Colborne, Governor—The Executive Council—Governor Responsible to English Government—Incongruous Position of Executive and Legislative Council—Colonial Despatch to Sir James Kempt—Death of George

IV.—Dissolution of House—Tory House—Reform Not a Success—Mackenzie Expelled the House of Assembly—The Election for York.

CHAPTER IX.

The Rebellion in Lower Canada—Mr. Papineau and Despotism—Despatch of Lord Stanley—The King Will Not Assent to Elective Legislative Council—In the Future Institutions of Canada May Be Modified—The Monarchical Form Must Be Maintained—Papineau's Ninety-two Resolutions—His Speech on Introducing to Assembly—The Resolutions—Resolutions Revolutionary—Mr. Morin Sent to England—No Supply Bill Passed by Assembly—Mr. Roebuck and the English House of Commons—Roebuck Champion of Lower Canada—Lord Stanley Checkmates Roebuck—Resolutions Referred to Committee—O'Connell and Bulwer Members of Committee—Hume and "Baneful Domination of Mother Country"—Report of Committee on Ninety-two Resolutions—Mackenzie in London—Agent of Malcontents in Upper Canada—Report of Committee Censured by Mackenzie's Followers—Grievance-mongers—Roebuck and Hume Favour Mackenzie and Papineau and Their Principles—"Reform Committees and Constitutional Associations"—A French Canadian Killed—His Blood Must Be Avenged—French Ascendancy in Lower Canada—Lower Canada Assembly of 1835—Papineau at the Pinnacle of his Power—Assembly Expunge Governor's Speech from Journals—Morin Moves Resolution to Consider State of Province of Lower Canada—Speeches of Papineau and Gugy thereon.

CHAPTER X.

Mackenzie's Prophecy in 1832—Papineau and Mackenzie in Concert—Reform Central Committee and Montreal Committee in Correspondence—Petitions to Home Government For and

Against a Change in the Constitution—Lord Aylmer Informs Lower Canada House that the British Government Were About to Adopt Coercive Measures to Allay Discontent—Papineau's Speech Defiant—House of Commons Appoint Special Committee to Report on Canadian Grievances—Gosford, Grey, and Gipps—Instructions to Commissioners—Lord Gosford's Address to Canadians—Montreal Constitutional Association Organizers—Concession of Lord Gosford and British Government—British Party Dissatisfied—Colonial Secretary's Concession to Mackenzie—Attorney-General Boulton—Mackenzie, Mayor of Toronto—Mackenzie Acquitted of Personal Resentment—House of 1835—Reform House—Mackenzie's Seventh Report on Grievances—Reform Party Loyal to the Crown—Lord Glenelg's Answer to Seventh Report on Grievances—Sir F. B. Head, Governor—Parliament of 1836—Governor's Speech and Assembly's Answer—Instructions of Government to Lord Gosford and Criticisms Thereon—Assembly's Answer—Papineau's Address to House—Shows Determination to Resist All Attempts at Conciliation—Dunn, Baldwin and Rolph Made Executive Councillors in Upper Canada.

CHAPTER XI.

Hon. Robert Baldwin—Conservative by Nature—Mackenzie Not the Reform Party—Reform Society of Upper Canada—Their Principles Announced—Address to Inhabitants of British North America—Governor Dissolves Upper Canada House, 20th May, 1836—Lower Canadians Distrust Royal Commission—Report of Royal Commissioners—Disappoints the Hopes of Revolutionists—Mr. Morin's Comments Thereon—"Vive Papineau; Vive la Liberté"—Death of William IV.—Ascension of Queen Victoria—Lord Gosford's Attempt to Reconcile Lower Canada—Excitement at High Pitch in Upper Canada—Upper Canada Elections of 1836—Riots and Disturbances—"Bread and Butter" Parliament—Question of Union of Upper Canada and Lower Canada Agitated—Confusion in the House—Declaration of Reformers to People of Upper Canada, June, 1837—Public Meetings—"Liberty or Death"—Plan for Revolt.

CHAPTER XII.

Movement Towards Rebellion—Armed Men—French and English Organizations in Lower Canada—Revolutionary Meetings—Inflammatory Speeches—Papineau and Dr. Wolfred Nelson—Riot in Montreal—Incipient Rebellion—Warnings of the Church—Recommends Obedience to Authority—Fire of Rebellion Stronger than Ever—Birthplace of the Rebellion—St. Eustache, St. Charles, St. Denis—Battles and Defeat of Insurgents—"The Doric Club"—Death of Lieut. Weir—Papineau's Abandonment of Insurgents and Flight to United States—His Character and Aims.

CHAPTER XIII.

Revolutionary Clubs—Council of War—Mackenzie Unfolds his Plans—How to Take Toronto and Carry Off the Governor—Hon. R. Baldwin Disclaims Knowledge of Rebellion—Jack Cade's Rebellion—Mackenzie's Similar—Mackenzie's New Constitution—Publication in Mackenzie's Newspaper—Trip to the Country to Promulgate Constitution—Mackenzie as a Recruiting Sergeant—Appointment to Meet in Toronto on 7th December—Declaration of Independence—Arms and Ammunition—Samuel Lount—Dr. Rolph Alters the Day for Rising—Disconcerts Mackenzie—His Plans Upset—Tries to Retrieve—Sir F. B. Head Reluctant to Believe There Would Be Rebellion—Col. FitzGibbon's Activity and Foresight—College Bell Rings Out Alarm—Mackenzie and Force at Montgomery's—Col. Moodie Shot—Threshold of Rebellion.

CHAPTER XIV.

Sir F. B. Head Made to Realize the Situation—Leaves Government House at Night—Makes City Hall the Headquarters, Tuesday, 5th December—Preparing for Defence of City—Picket Placed at McGill Street—Attack on Picket—Rebels Retire—Governor Sends Message to Mackenzie Under Flag of Truce—Result—Rolph and Baldwin—Wednesday, 6th December—Arms Removed to Parliament Buildings—"The Men of Gore"—Rebels' Threat to Burn Toronto—Mackenzie Urges Attack on City on Wednesday, 6th December—His Men Refuse to Move—Dr. Rolph Flees for Safety—Rebels at Yorkville—Fire Dr. Horne's House—Lount and Mackenzie Intercept Mail—Van Egmond—His Arrival in Rebel Camp—Plan to Attack City—Loyalists Force Take Rebels—Attack Rebels at Montgomery's—Dispersion of Rebels—Mackenzie's Escape—Battle of St. Eustache, Lower Canada.

CHAPTER XV.

Bishop of Montreal Deplores the Rebellion and Its Result—Sends Out Circular to his Flock—Bishop of Quebec Gives Thanks that his Diocese Not in Rebellion—American Sympathizers—Meeting in Buffalo—Rochester Follows Buffalo—Doughty Deeds in Contemplation—Mackenzie Occupies Navy Island—Provisional Government for Canada Formed—Van Rensselaer Commander-in-Chief—Proclamation to Inhabitants of Upper Canada—Loyalists at Chippewa, Sir Allan McNab in Command—Operations Before Navy Island—Burning of the Steamer *Caroline*—Evacuation of Navy Island—"Bois Blanc" Island at Mouth of Detroit River—Gen. Sutherland's Army of Invasion Occupies—Sutherland's Proclamation—Dr. Duncombe and Rebel Rising at Brantford and Scotland—Dispersed by McNab—Sutherland's Failure at Bois Blanc—Sugar Island—Van Rensselaer Occupies Hickory Island in St. Lawrence—Rebels and Sympathizers Occupy Pelee Island, Detroit River—Invaders Attacked by British Troops and Dispersed—Projected Attack on Windsor and Fort Malden—Short Hills—Hunter's Lodges—Prescott, the Battle of the Windmill—Van Shultz.

CHAPTER XVI.

American Sympathizers—Rebellion Carried On Without the Province—Foreign War Carried On by Irresponsible Americans—Determined to Avenge Prescott—Assemble at Detroit—Gen. Handy's Proclamation—Land at Windsor—Destroy Property—Met by Loyalists and Repulsed—Col. Prince—Mackenzie Dissatisfied with the American Allies—Will Rely on Himself and Canadians—Mackenzie Has no Faith in the United States—Regrets the Rebellion that he Had Stirred Up—Admits his Mistake—Should he Be Forgiven?—His Penitence Sincere—Trials, Imprisonments and Executions—Lord Durham, Governor—His Report—Constitution of 1841—Mackenzie, Papineau and Rolph Members of the Union House—Conclusion.

CHAPTER I.

Introduction—French Surrender to Lord Amherst, 1760—Terms of Surrender—Treaty of Paris, 1763—King's Proclamation Bringing into Force the Treaty—Quebec Constitutional Act, 1774—Intendant Bigot—French Laws and English Laws—Difficulty of Administration—General Murray Appointed Governor-General—Major Irving, Administrator—Sir Guy Carleton, Governor.

HE who undertakes to give an account of the Rebellion in the Canadas in the year 1837, will not do his duty fully unless he take into consideration the state and condition of things as they existed in the Colony for some considerable time before the actual breaking out of the Rebellion. Especially is this the case in regard to the Province of Lower Canada, the principal seat of the rebellion, in which a war of races has been carried on more or less ever since Canada became a British possession. The French Canadians, in what is now the Province of Quebec, are a loyal people—loyal to the British Crown. The longer they were under British rule, their allegiance from a variety of circumstances grew stronger, until they attained to the full measure of political manhood. But this was not always so. It is ever to be borne in mind that at the beginning, the French Canadians were intensely French, and that they were newly created British subjects by virtue of conquest, and the surrender of their country by a French king, who was so neglectful of his French-Canadian subjects as to withhold from them the necessary aid when most needed to successfully contend with British power.

When Lord Amherst took over the old Province from Vaudreuil, the French Commander at Montreal, in 1760, the French Commander in the interests of his people exacted from the British certain conditions and stipulations which the British Commander on his part freely accepted. The stipulations which were proposed and agreed to, or rejected, were in substance as follows:—

1. French troops to evacuate; British troops to take possession.
2. French troops and militia to go out with honors of war.
3. Same privilege granted to outer posts.
4. Militia to return to their homes without being molested.
5. The same in effect as stipulations 2, 3, 4.
6. Deserters to be pardoned.
7. French arms and ammunition of war to be delivered up to His Britannic Majesty's Commissaries.
8. Wounded or sick officers and soldiers, seamen and even Indians to be treated the same as British officers and soldiers.
9. Matter of detail as to Indians.
10. In effect the same as 9.
11. Marquis of Vaudreuil and all other officers to be masters of their own houses in Montreal, and to embark when the King's ships shall be ready to sail for Europe, and all possible conveniences granted them.
12. Marquis of Vaudreuil to be conveyed to the first seaport in France by the straightest passage. Archives necessary for Government to remain in Canada.
13. Provides for eventualities in case peace declared, and if by Treaty Canada to remain to His Most Gracious Majesty of France, then the *status quo* to be established.

TERMS OF SURRENDER.

14. Provides for deportation of Chevalier De Levis and officers to France.
15. Same as to M. **Bigot**.
16. Same as to the Governor of Three **Rivers and** his equipage.
17. Same as to soldiers and seamen.
18. }
19. } Unimportant matters of detail.
20. }
21. Provides for deporting of the Indians and other civil officers if they think fit to go, or they may remain.
22. French officers, if consent of Marquis of Vaudreuil obtained, may remain in Canada till next year to look after their families.
23. French King's Commissary may remain in the Colony till next year to settle up his affairs.
24. }
25. } Unimportant details.
26. }
27. Proposal of Vaudreuil: "The free exercise of the Catholic, Apostolic and Roman religion shall subsist entire in such manner that all the states **and** the people of the towns, countries, places and distant posts shall continue to assemble in the churches and to frequent the sacraments as heretofore, without being molested in any manner, directly or indirectly. These people shall be obliged by the English Government to pay to the priests the tithes and all taxes they were used to pay under the Government of His Most Christian Majesty."

Answer of Amherst to 27: "Granted as to the free exercise of their religion; **the** obligation of paying tithes to the priests shall depend **on** the King's pleasure."

28. The chapter, priests, curates and missionaries shall continue with an entire liberty the exercise and functions of their cures in the parishes of the towns and countries.
29. The Grand Vicars granted free exercise **of** their functions (granted, except what regards article 30).
30. If by the Treaty of Peace Canada should remain in the power of His Most Christian Majesty, His Most Christian Majesty shall continue to name the Bishop of the Colony, who shall

always be of the Roman communion, and under whose authority the people shall exercise their religion.

Answer of Amherst: "Refused."

31. Comprised in 30.
32. Community of nuns preserved in their constitutions and privileges.
33. Proposal same as 32, as to Jesuits, Recollets and St. Sulpice.

Answer of Amherst: "Refused till the King's pleasure be known."

34. Provides for preservation of movables and estates of priests.
35. The communities or orders in 33 may go to France, if they choose, in King's ships free of expense, and take their movables or sell them in Canada.
36. Permission given to French, Canadians and Acadians to go to France if they choose, and the English general to procure them a passage.
37. French and French Canadians in Canada to be allowed to retain their possessions.
38.
39. } As to Acadians and Indians.
40.
41. Neither the Acadians or French remaining in the Colony forced to take arms against His Most Christian Majesty.

Amherst's answer: "They remain subjects of the King."

42. Proposal. "The French and Canadians shall continue to be governed according to the customs of Paris and the laws and usages established for the country, and they shall not be subject to any other imposts than those which were established under the French Government."

Amherst's answer: "Answered by the preceding article and particularly the last."

43.
to } Of no political importance.
55.

The stipulations entered into between the two Commanders at Montreal were but initiatory to a treaty being afterwards concluded between the French and English nation, and culminated in the Treaty of Paris, 1763. There are 22 articles or clauses in the treaty which are of importance from a Canadian point of view. The 4th is the most important, as relating to the future government of Canada. This article, after agreeing to the cession of Canada to Great Britain, proceeds as follows: "His Britannic Majesty on his side agrees to grant the liberty of the Catholic religion to the inhabitants of Canada. He will consequently give the most precise and effectual orders that his new Roman Catholic subjects may profess the worship of their religion according to the rites of the Romish Church as far as the laws of Great Britain permit."

There were three "separate articles" having the same force as if they were inserted in the treaty and are appended to it. The 2nd of these is as follows, "It has been agreed and determined that the French language, made use of in all the copies of the present treaty, shall not become an example which may be alleged or made a precedent of, or prejudice in any manner, any of the contracting Powers; and that they shall conform themselves in the future to what has been observed with regard to, and on the part of, the Powers who are used, and have a right to give and receive copies of like treaties in another language than French; the present treaty having still the same force and effect as if the aforesaid custom had been therein observed."

A Royal Proclamation was issued by His Britannic Majesty to carry into effect the Treaty of Paris on the 7th October, 1763, and this Proclamation really formed the Constitution of the old Province of Quebec, which comprised the whole of Canada, from 1763 to 1774, when the British

Parliament passed the Quebec Act, under which Canada was governed from 1774 to 1791. An examination of the two documents, the stipulations entered into at Montreal and the treaty, reveals some marked differences. As, for instance, the 27th Proposal of Vaudreuil in the stipulations was—" that the free exercise of the Catholic, Apostolic and Roman Religion should subsist entirely, in such manner that all the states, and the people of the towns, country places and distant posts, should continue to assemble in the churches and to frequent the sacraments as heretofore, without being molested in any manner, directly or indirectly, and that these people should be obliged to pay to the priests the tithes and all taxes they were used to pay under the government of His Most Christian Majesty."

Lord Amherst seems to have been willing to grant the French Canadians the exercise of their religion, but either would not or could not impose on the people the obligation to pay tithes to the priests. This he reserved for the King's pleasure. We find that when the King's pleasure came to be expressed, His Majesty was not willing to grant the free exercise of the Catholic religion, except in a modified form: hence, in the 22nd article of the treaty it is said—" That the Roman Catholic subjects may profess the worship of their religion, according to the rites of the Roman Church *as far as the laws of Great Britain permit.*"

As under the laws of Great Britain the Roman Catholics at that time labored under many disabilities, the difference between the treaty and the stipulations become more marked.

The proposal of Vaudreuil by the 42nd article was—"That the French Canadians should continue to be governed according to the custom of Paris and the laws and usages established for the country, and that they should not be subject to any other imposts than those which were established under the French Regime."

Amherst's answer to this proposal seems to have been simply that the French Canadians should "remain subjects of the King," in other words that they were to conform to English laws. There is neither in the articles of surrender nor in the Treaty any stipulation granting to the French Canadians the ancient law, language or customs of France, or of Canada under French Government. The terms on which the evacuation was based were most liberal. It is questionable if any other power than Britain would have been as generous to the vanquished. Not only were the French officers and soldiers given free choice to return to France or remain in the colony, but free passage was granted them if they chose the former alternative. The result was that 185 officers, and 2,400 soldiers, 500 sailors, domestics, women and children, all embarked for France, and that, too, at the expense of Great Britain. Besides the soldiers and officers of the Regular Army of France, many of the French Canadian officers who had fought for France in defence of the Colony, and others, the most notable French and French Canadian people of the Province emigrated to France. It has been estimated that after this exodus no more than 70,000 people, most of whom were of French extraction, were left in the whole of Canada. M. de Vaudreuil in a letter to the French Ministry, lamenting the great loss the French nation had sustained by the cession of Canada to Great Britain, said, "With these beautiful and vast countries France loses "70,000 inhabitants of a rare quality, a race of people "unequalled for their docility, bravery and loyalty. The "vexations they have suffered for many years, more "especially during the five years preceding the reduction "of Quebec, all without a murmur, or importuning their "King for relief, sufficiently manifest their perfect sub- "missiveness."

In this letter Vaudreuil comments on the loyalty of the French Canadian people. This loyalty was loyalty to France, for which indeed they had been conspicuous, and in a degree higher than the French people had been to the Colony. To this day the French Canadians believe that if France had acted up to her duty and supplied the Colony with regular troops, in anything like the proportion required to cope with the British invading army, she would not have had to deplore the loss of a country which her subjects had originally explored, appropriated and held for one hundred and fifty years. The time had arrived however when the corruption of the French officials governing in Canada had reached such a pitch that it were better for the world that some other power should relieve them of authority. With men like Intendant Bigot in the high places of the country, the country was suffering from a disease which strong measures only could cure. It seemed not in the power or will of France to apply the necessary remedy, and thus it fell to Britain to rescue the country from the vultures that were preying on the old domain.

"The beautiful and vast countries" depicted by Vaudreuil in his letter to the French Ministers, by the cession at Montreal certainly changed owners, but in regard to loyalty it could hardly be expected that their loyalty to the French Crown could or would in a day be merged in loyalty to the English Crown.

The kind of government which superseded the French government, covering the years 1760, 1761, 1762, 1763, when the treaty was made with France, was necessarily one of military rule, and it can be easily conceived that a people wholly French could not easily become reconciled to English laws, administered by English officers, who understood neither the language, manners nor customs of France as they existed in Canada at the time of the surrender of the Colony. It is to be borne in mind, too, that until the capitulation was confirmed by treaty, it was a matter of uncertainty with the French Canadians whether after all England might not restore to France her ancient Colony. She had on a previous occasion, in 1625, taken Quebec, thereby becoming master of Canada, and after an occupation of three years, given back by the Treaty of St. Germain-en-Laye, Canada, Acadia and Cape Breton to France. Might she not now again in a spirit of generosity, or for an equivalent, surrender Canada to her ancient Mother Country? The articles of the capitulation show that there was hope left to the French Canadians that the old regime might still claim their allegiance. The 13th article of Capitulation provided for eventualities in case peace was declared, and—" if by Treaty Canada should remain to His Most Christian Majesty," the *status quo* was to remain. The Treaty of Paris was signed in September, 1763; nevertheless that did not make an end of military rule. It is difficult to conceive how any other rule would have answered the circumstances of the situation. Here was a people but recently conquered, with hardly a Briton amongst them, the Military only excepted. It would have been just as unwise on the moment to give them representative institutions as it would have been at once to have given representation to the newly conquered people of India. England did the best she could, adjusting differences through military channels, with interpreters where necessary, to aid in the taking of evidence and making the decisions of the tribunals understood. All this however was very galling to the French Canadians, so long used to the laws and customs of old France. Many of the inhabitants, where differences between them arose, constituted a tribunal of their own and submitted their disputes to this tribunal. A large number bowed themselves to Ecclesiastical authority and accepted the priest as their law-giver and judge. Thus was brought about a confidence between the Church and the people, which has ever been a leading characteristic of French Canadian polity.

The people, always restless under British rule, through agents they had in London applied to Lord Halifax, the Secretary of State, for a restoration of French jurisprudence and maintenance of the old Colonial Church establishment, complained against Martial law, and even went so far as to make demands for the maintenance intact of the Quebec See. The British Government could not yield to these demands. The King on the 17th September, 1764, made an ordinance, "that in the Supreme Court, sitting at Quebec, His Britannic Majesty was present in the person of his Chief Justice, having full power to determine all civil and criminal cases, agreeably to the laws of England and to the ordinances of the Province of Quebec." This ordinance was no doubt made by the King to encourage English immigration into the Colony. The French were not satisfied; they would like to have had control of the Province and all its resources, though but a recently subjected people.

This was the condition of affairs when, in 1764, General Murray was appointed Governor-General of Canada in place of Sir Jeffrey Amherst, then in England on leave, who did not return to the Province.

On the inauguration of General Murray the form of governing took a somewhat different shape. The purely military character of government was changed into a quasi-civil government, the Governor-General attaching to himself an Executive Council composed of twelve persons, all of whom, with the one exception, were British born. The exception was a native Canadian of no note in the Colony, t appointed, as the French Canadians considered, merely to give some colour of Colonialism to the new institution. The Canadians plainly saw in this a determined policy of the British Government to exclude them from any considerable participation in the government of the country. There can be no doubt whatever that this was the policy of the Home Government, and it is difficult to see how, at that time, any other policy would be safe, in the conservation of the country, obtained through the spilling of much British blood. The instincts of the Canadians were French to the core, and being largely in the majority and permitted to rule, the case would have been one of the conquered ruling the conquerors. From a French Canadian point of view the condition of things was very embarrassing. They sighed for their old laws and customs, which they could not have under a Council constituted for the palpable purpose of administering British law; and they could not have representative institutions, because the British Government well knew that if such institutions were granted there would be no hope for the British settlers in the Province, who, if few in number, were strong in their affections for the purely British system of government, or one as near to it as was consistent with Colonial government, especially in a Colony composed, as it was, of people nine-tenths of whom were alien to the British race. Suspicion of the loyalty of the Canadians to the King of England constantly affected the British mind in the Province. So great was s suspicion and fear of conspiracies that the Executive Council would not permit an assemblage of the French Canadians without two of the Council being present and with power to disperse the meeting if they thought fit. During Murray's time a few English settlers came to the Province, mostly artisans and adventurers on the lookout for some official position under the Government. The native Canadians were so much distrusted that Canada afforded a field for persons of this latter class—and the consequence was that the Governor became surrounded with a body of individuals who had no sympathy with the Canadians, and the Canadians had no respect for them. Besides, the new comers were all Protestants. In an estimate made by General Murray for the information of the British Government, he computed the number of Protestants in Canada in 1765 to have been 500. In the District of Montreal there were only 137 Protestants.

With a Protestant population so disproportionate to the French Catholic population, and yet the Protestants appointed to office and not the French, it was inevitable that there should not only be antagonism between the French and English Colonists, but also that religious strife should prevail. Thus we find that during the whole of Murray's administration, there was more or less of a rebellion, inactive it is true, but nevertheless a rebellion, in that part of the Province of Quebec contiguous to the towns of Quebec and Montreal, caused by religious and political differences on the part of the population.

General Murray was followed by Major Irving,* who was administrator of the Province for the period intervening between General Murray's resignation and the appointment of Sir Guy Carleton, which took place in 1766.

About this time trouble was brewing in the New England Colonies, and Sir Guy Carleton, well knowing the wishes and the interest of the British Government in view of a revolt in the Colonies, was disposed to pursue a pacific policy with the French Canadians. The French Canadians on their part knew how necessary it was for the British to secure their allegiance, at a time when Britain would require the service of every able-bodied man she could secure in the Canadian Colonies, to oppose the rising tide of American Revolution. The whole subject of the government of Canada was brought before the British Ministry. The Canadian high officials and the English high officials, civil and military, were active in endeavoring to propound some scheme by which the French Canadians would become reconciled to their position as British subjects. Some were for rigidly enforcing English law in its entirety for the governing of the Colony, with the English language alone as the official language. Some would have re-established the "Coûtume de Paris" and the old French laws in their entirety. Others were for a combination of English law and French law, an amalgamation of the English language with the French language, and a general consorting of opposing elements. To put an end to the matter, Sir Guy

*Æmilius Irving, Q.C., Treasurer of the Law Society, is a grandson of Major Irving.

Carleton repaired to London to inform the official mind of the condition of affairs in the Colony and the necessity that there was of reconciling contending interests. The law officers of the Crown, both in England and the Colony, were consulted, and the result was a partial victory for the French Canadian party. In the words of the French Canadian Historian Garneau, who glories in the triumph of his race, "The British Government deferred, till the year 1774, yielding the points at issue; and it may be said that the revolution (American Revolution) which saved the freedom of the United States, obliged, (mark the word obliged), Great Britain to leave the Canadians the enjoyment of their institutions and laws, in other words to act justly by them, in order to be able to retain for herself at least one Province in the New World."

It may be quite truly asserted by Garneau that the American Revolution had much to do in influencing the British Government to yield to Canada concessions for which the French Colonists had been long clamoring, but it ought not to be overlooked that the British party in the Province was as strongly opposed to the system of government then existing as were the French. It is evident that both parties were acting on the same lines, only in a different way and for a different object. The British party wanted a Representative Assembly on the model of the British House of Commons, in which Assembly there should be none but Protestants, as was then the case in the British House of Commons, and so would have excluded the

French Catholics from all participation in government; while the French party would have had a Representative Assembly, including the French Catholics, which, from their superior numbers, would have given them the full control of the civil and religious institutions of the Province. In short, the British party sought for British rule, while the French party were willing to submit to British form of government, but wanted actual French rule. The outcome of the whole matter was that a compromise was effected, and the Quebec Act of 1774, the first written Constitution of the Province of Quebec, was enacted by the British Parliament, which gave to the Canadians their old civil law, but in order to secure good government retained the British system of criminal law.

CHAPTER II.

Constitutional Act, 1774, Unsatisfactory to British Canadians—Petition to Annul—American Revolution of 1776—Sympathy of French-Canadians—Clergy Opposed—American Congress Attempt to Tamper with French-Canadians—Montgomery and Arnold—Seignors and their Tenants—Canadian Merchants in London Demand Repeal of Quebec Act—Legislative Council, its Unpopularity—Haldimand Succeeds Carleton as Governor—The Militia Organization—French-Canadians Chafe Under English Rule—Du Calvet's Opinion of Canadian Sentiments—Bigots and Agitators—Treaty of Peace, 1783—America and England—Close of Haldimand's Administration—Lord Dorchester's Second Term as Governor—U. E. Loyalists—Their Appeal to Divide Quebec—Constitution of 1791.

The Quebec Act of 1774 must be carefully considered in order to trace the causes which led to the Rebellion of 1837. By this Act the Province was given the laws of Canada, "Coûtume de Paris" (the custom of Paris), as the foundation of their civil law, the English law in regard to criminals being retained. The Governor of the Province was to appoint a Legislative Council of not less than seventeen, nor more than twenty-three members, to be composed of the French and English colonists. This Council was to have power to make any necessary laws, subject to the approval of the British sovereign, and the Catholic inhabitants were relieved of the operation of the

Test Act. At the outset this Act was very satisfactory in the eyes of the French-Canadians, as by it they gained the control of public affairs. It was not so satisfactory to the English settlers, who had begun by this time to pour into Canada in considerable numbers. Especially was this the case in the Ohio valley, then a part of Canada, in which region there was a population of twenty thousand English. The English settlers on the banks of the St. Lawrence, about Montreal and Quebec, were not so much exasperated with the Act, inasmuch as they were near enough the sun of the political world to enjoy the benefit of its rays.

Petitions were got up in the Colony and in London praying that the Act should be annulled. The Canadian petition was presented to the House of Lords in May, 1775, but at the instance of Lord Dartmouth was rejected.

By this time the guns of the American Revolution were being heard in New England, reverberating throughout the English-American Colonies, and extending even to the bank of the St. Lawrence and the French settlement in the Province of Quebec. Nor were there wanting sympathizers with the Revolution among the Anglo-American as well as among the French-Canadian population of the Colony. It is to the credit of the Canadian clergy and the seigniors that they did not countenance defection in Quebec. The clergy, indeed, well knew that if the Revolutionists succeeded in their rebellion against the British Government and became a separate nation, the danger of maintaining French laws and the Roman Catholic religion in Quebec would be immensely increased. The seigniors well knew that the success of the Americans implied the depriving them of the dues and exactions which they enforced on the inhabitants. The masses, however, of the French-Canadians were not unfavourable to the cause of the Revolutionists. A large number, led away by the cries of "liberty and equality," the catch-words spoken, and the drag-nets thrown out to captivate the unthinking and uneducated, were shaken in their allegiance and well nigh engulfed. After the affair at Lexington, in April, 1775, and the subsequent capture of Forts Ticonderoga and Crown Point, the Americans, in the autumn of the year, sent an army under Schuyler and Montgomery to take the fort of St. John, in the Province of Quebec. Sir Guy Carleton, the Governor, had then but 800 regular troops at his disposition, and called upon the surrounding parishes to assist in repelling the invasion. This, however, they declined to do, and remained passive.

The Chambly parishioners were actively hostile in their demonstration, and according to Garneau, the French historian, "nearly the whole militia of the district of Three Rivers refused to march at the command of the Governor, . . . the Chambly villagers joined an American detachment, under Majors Brown and Livingston, whom Montgomery sent to take a small fort there, which was disgracefully yielded up after thirty-six hours' investment by Major Stopford. Stopford struck his flag and gave up his sword to the lucky Americans, who found in the fort seventeen pieces of ordnance and much gunpowder—a warlike munition of which Montgomery was all but destitute previously, and whose acquisition now enabled him to press the siege of St. John vigorously, the men of Chambly taking part therein. Thus did the frontier contest, through the partisanship of some Gallo-Canadians, take the colour of civil law."

It is not to be disguised that there were also many of the British settlers in Quebec, and more American settlers who were favourable to the American cause, the former very much influenced by what they termed the un-British government given to the Province of Quebec, and the latter by the same spirit of revolution which animated the Colonial Americans. Thus we find that in the old French Province, more than sixty years before the Rebellion, there was, to say the least, an unsettled state of things which showed how lightly the people of that Province, or the majority of them, esteemed the Government which had been given them, by the Imperial Parliament. During the American Revolution the greatest efforts were made by the American Congress to induce the French-Canadians as a whole to declare for independence and secession from Great Britain. In this they never succeeded. The French-Canadians of the Province of Quebec were divided in their allegiance. Fathers were against sons and brothers against brothers. The allurements held out by the Americans induced some even to join their ranks, but the influence of the seigniors and clergy was sufficient to restrain the French Colonists as a people from accepting the advantages offered them by their neighbours south of the St. Lawrence.

Addresses were made to the French-Canadians by the American Congress urging them to join the Revolutionary standard. Commissioners were sent from Washington to persuade the French clergy to look favourably upon the American revolt. All was of no avail. While sundry of the French-Canadians were willing to profit by the Revolution, their leaders could not be prevailed upon to see that their condition would be improved by going over to the Revolutionists.

The defeat of Montgomery and Arnold at Quebec, and the retreat of the Revolutionary Army which had invaded Canada, strengthened the hands of the British Loyalists and the unaffected French-Canadians, and the *habitants* were able once more to sit down by their own firesides and once more enjoy the comforts of peace. The Governor was no longer prevented from exercising his civil functions, and, in 1777, was able to call together the Legislative Council, given by the Quebec Act of 1774, for despatch of business. This Council proceeded to enact measures in harmony with the design for which it was created, a design to promote and foster British influence in the Colony. The French element of the Council at first submitted with a good grace to the situation, but soon began to perceive that events were directing their deliberations into a channel not so favourable to the French-Canadians as they had hoped for.

The American Revolution was still in progress, and it became necessary to protect the militia from the seeds of rebellion which the revolting Americans were sowing in their midst.

The seigniors, members of the Council, abandoned by most of their tenants during the American invasion, were now willing to place restraints on those tenants; they were now disposed to uphold British supremacy, which in the view of many of the French-Canadians was the abasement of their race. Many ordinances were passed during the first session of the Council, lasting several days, which while fulfilling the desires of the wealthy and more aristocratic class of the community, were distasteful to the lower and middle classes and to the rural population. It was said of the seigniors that they leaned to the side of the British to protect their own interests, and this was true in more senses than one. The seigniors had use for their tenants at home, instead of encouraging their engaging in revolutionary propaganda. Their tithes and dues were the source of their income, and how could those tithes and rents be got in if the tenant was neglecting his fields and his crops in the glorious uncertainty of war?

The antagonism to the Council had gained such head, that Canadian merchants in London presented a memorial to the Colonial Secretary, demanding either the repeal of the Quebec Act of 1774 or the creation of a Legislative Assembly. The answer of the Colonial Secretary was that it would be dangerous to change the Constitution so long as the rebels were still in arms on the Colonial frontier. The Legislative Council, as created, does not seem to have been satisfactory either to the British party or to the French party. The *habitants* had not full confidence in their French-Canadian colleagues, while the French-Canadians of the Council found the Council to be too British. Governor Carleton endeavoured to be as neutral as his position would allow. Whether acting on their own opinion, or whether on the recommendation of Governor Carleton, it is not necessary to enquire, but in 1776, the British ministry for some reason instructed Governor Carleton to constitute a Privy or Executive Council, to be carved out of the Legislative Council; and Carleton, acting on these instructions, formed a Privy Council composed of five members, himself and four other members of the Legislative Council, all British in nationality and sentiment. Governor Carleton did not long remain to exercise these functions, as his services were required in other fields, and General Haldimand was appointed to succeed him in the government.

Haldimand was a man of imperious disposition—a very soldier; he could not tolerate anything akin to disaffection. In the midst of a hostile community he knew how to keep down revolution. If he was obliged to resort to what seemed arbitrary measures the fault was not his, but is to be attributed to his surroundings. His first step was to look well to the militia. He compelled these to train and place themselves in a position to resist a second invasion by the revolting Americans, which he had good reason to suspect. He was not over confident of the loyalty of the militia, and knew that the Americans were directly or indirectly tampering with the allegiance of King George's French-Canadian subjects. Full of well-founded suspicion and distrust, General Haldimand ordered many persons to be committed to prison, some of whom may have been innocent, but the majority were tainted. All this was necessary to preserve the Colony to the British Crown, but nevertheless was regarded as despotism by the French-Canadian population. Indeed it is difficult to say what conduct on the part of the British officials of whatever degree was not considered tyrannical by the French-Canadians. The history of the times abundantly proves that they were chafing under British rule, but where could they turn for relief? Their best advisers, their clergy, were able to show them that if they joined the Americans in their revolt and should gain independence, their second state would be worse than the first; and if they turned their eyes to France, there they would find a country on the verge of revolution, making herculean efforts to get rid of the monarchy and the clergy and replace them by a Republic of Reason. The French, Spanish and Americans were in alliance to overturn Monarchical and Colonial rule in America. The French-Canadians were true sons of old France, and had inherited love for the institutions of their ancestors. England had given them a Constitution, which if properly worked would, in their estimation, cure all the evils they endured, or at any rate it was better than joining themselves to a Republic such as America was likely to become, and be submerged in the gulf of democratic assertiveness. The real feelings of the French-Canadians at the time is well illustrated by Du Calvet, a prominent French Colonist, a Protestant Huguenot, who suffered imprisonment at the hands of General Haldimand. After dwelling on his personal grievances, he said: "How sad a thing it is to be vanquished; our brothers' blood shed on the field of battle cries to us from the ground; but bodily wounds, however deep, will heal in time. It is the constant pressure of the victor's hand when the struggle is over that is the 'iron' which enters the soul; and to become the bondmen of another race, itself living in freedom, is the most intolerable part of our fate. Can it be that our slackness in not holding out longer against our conquerors, has merited their contempt, as our first earnest efforts in shunning the yoke excited their ire."

The racial question here unmistakably "peeps out from the blanket of the dark," and shows the Frenchiness of the Canadian mind. Nor was this at all unnatural. A conquered people are not likely soon to forget their old nationality. It takes time to reconcile them to the new order of things. The British Government has ever been solicitous to make their lot a happy one. Leaving out the disturbances which sometimes crop up under the inspiration of bigots and agitators, the French population of the Province of Quebec are as happily situated as any people of the colony of any nation in the world. It is too early, however, to enlarge on this at this stage, as there is much more to be considered before we can fully comprehend the spirit which has constantly from the time of the conquest been giving vent to complainings at the existing state and condition of affairs.

At this period of Haldimand's administration the French-Canadian had much to disturb him on all sides. He was discontented at home, and still so kept in restraint that he could not conveniently take refuge abroad, even though

Lafayette and his followers from France, espousing the quarrel of the American Colonists in their contest with England, would fain have had them join the Revolutionary flag. General Haldimand took great care to keep the inhabitants he was sent to govern well within the lines of their allegiance. It is in a sense surprising that the French-Canadians were not caught in the toils of the rebellious Americans. They saw them, towards the conclusion of the Revolutionary War, gaining successes. Lafayette was a French hero fighting the battles of the Americans, and a French army was operating in the cause of the Revolutionists; yet, notwithstanding all this, the French Canadians as a people were never gained over to the Revolutionary cause. In the prevention of this, as has been said, much was due to the French clergy, but at the same time too much credit cannot be given to General Haldimand for his firm hand in upholding British rule in the old French Colony.

Events were now so shaping themselves that General Haldimand's official connection with Canada would be soon brought to a close. The Americans and their allies, the French, were successful in defeating General Abercrombie at Yorktown in 1783, and this led to a Treaty of Peace between England and America in September, 1783, thus ridding Canada, at all events for the present, of the meddling of the Americans in Canadian affairs, and their efforts to undermine the loyalty of the Canadians. The treaty had another beneficial effect on the Province, as it was the means of abrogating Military government in the Colony, remitting the people to their ancient condition and peaceful pursuits, thus enabling them to ponder over the past, and make comparison between the periods of turbulence and peace. As a proof that at this time the French descendants very much preferred Canada, and its Constitution, to American Republicanism, there is the significant fact that many of the Acadians, whose woes have been so eloquently described by Longfellow in his beautiful " Evangeline," came to settle in Canada upon the coasts of the Gulf of St. Lawrence.

General Haldimand's administration, after six years' good service in the Colony, was brought to a close in 1784, when he repaired to London, where he was met by Du Calvet, who did his utmost to discredit him with the British Government. This is not surprising, however, when it is considered that Du Calvet had his private grievances to avenge, on account of his imprisonment by Haldimand, as a subject in friendly intercourse with the revolting Americans.

Du Calvet was in Paris in 1783, and there applied to Benjamin Franklin, the resident Ambassador of the United States, and sought his interest to obtain payment from Congress for the equipments he had furnished the Americans, which established pretty clearly that he was more of a Gallo-American than a Gallo-Canadian. In the year 1785, Sir Guy Carleton, under the title of Lord Dorchester, was again called upon to take charge of the government of Canada, a government with which he had become familiar from his past experience in the Colony. At this time, the Legislative Council of the Constitution of 1774 was in great disrepute. Its members were divided into camps, some English, some French, some of a hybrid character, indifferent to the real welfare of the Colony, so long as they basked in the sun of Vice-Regal favour and enjoyed the emoluments attached to their official position. Matters had got to be so bad in this respect that Lord Dorchester was instructed to institute an enquiry into the whole political condition of the country, civil, military, judicial, agricultural, educational and commercial. This he set about doing on his arrival and assuming the duties of his high office of Governor General. It was found that affairs were in a very bad condition. Judges were on the Bench, some of whom would administer law according to the French system, while others contended that the Act of 1774 conflicted with previous ordinances, and ought not to be obeyed. Others again agreed that in matters of descent and property generally, the French law was to prevail, while some went so far as to contend that the Britons should have the advantage of English law, while the French-Canadians should be regulated by "La Coûtume de Paris."

In civil matters, it was found that there was a great divergence of opinion among the people. The British party wanted English law in its entirety, with trial by jury in civil cases, and the English system of conveyancing, etc.; while the French party, still clinging to their old laws of property and civil rights, would have had a change in the Constitution, a representative assembly, abolition of the feudal tenure, and other measures of a like kind, which would have given the control of the whole machinery of government to the persons most unfitted to carry out a British government in a British colony. In religious matters, the French-Canadians demanded full control, quite independent of British or any other interference. In matters of education, the Colony was sadly deficient. Before the conquest there had been the Jesuit College at Quebec, where young men received a liberal education, but that was now a thing of the past. The college existed no longer. The Seminaries in a measure supplied the place of the Jesuit College, but in a minor degree, while as to the rural population, they were wholly without education or the means of obtaining it. The consequence was that such education as there was, was confined to the few who could afford to pay for the advantages offered by the Seminaries. Some of the priests in the outer districts gave instruction to a few of their parishioners, less in secular than in religious teaching. It can easily be gathered from this how much better able the British part of the population was to administer public affairs, so that everything conspired to place the French-Canadians in an inferior position, though they were in a very great numerical majority.

The American Revolution being now over, and the Treaty of Peace between Great Britain and the United States signed, those who had been loyal to the King's cause during the Revolution were obliged to take refuge in other lands. These, who received the designation of United Empire Loyalists, flocked into Canada in great numbers. What is now called Ontario, and before that Upper Canada, was not then known as a Province. The whole territory, together with a great portion of what is now known as the United States, was called the Province of Quebec. A considerable number of the United Empire Loyalists took up their homes on the seaboard of the lower St. Lawrence River. Lord Dorchester well knew that these United Empire Loyalists would not long submit to be governed by French law, such as was then enforced in Quebec. In order to meet this emergency, an ordinance in Council was passed, which Lord Dorchester proceeded to carry out, dividing the whole of Quebec into five districts, giving to what was afterwards Lower Canada the name of the Gaspé district, and dividing what was afterwards known as the Province of Upper Canada, into four districts, under the names respectively of Lunenburg, Mecklenburg, Nassau and Hesse. This was done with the view of simplifying the government of the whole region. In 1789, the United Empire Loyalists, who had settled in the four latter districts, demanded to be governed by the English and not by the French law, which they neither cared for nor understood. The British party in the district of Gaspé, now largely composed of United Empire Loyalists, sympathising with those in the other four districts, also demanded the absolute repeal of the Constitution of 1774, and the entire suppression of French law in every part of Canada.

The United Empire Loyalists, used to representative government in the New England States, were not willing to do with less in Canada, where they had taken refuge for

PROVINCES DIVIDED.

their protection. Two parties thus arose in the Canadian Colony, the United Empire Loyalist party, and the French party, and these parties were, if possible, more English and more French than those which had preceded them. The United Empire Loyalists had been at war with their neighbours in the United States for many years, and it was not to be expected that they would willingly succumb to French rule in a British Province. How then could the Colony be governed in such a way as to satisfy the aspirations of both parties? Should British representative institutions be given to the whole of Canada, or should that part of it, the district of Gaspé, in which the French-Canadians were largely in the majority, be left to rejoice in their ancient laws, and the rest of Canada be given the English law? Here was a problem for British statesmen to solve, and Mr. Pitt, who was Prime Minister at that time, was not unequal to the situation.

He introduced a Bill in the House of Commons, to divide the Province of Quebec into two sections, to be called respectively Lower Canada and Upper Canada, on the lines previously stated. In introducing this Bill, he said that this separation will put an end to the competition between the old French inhabitants and the new settlers from Britain and the British Colonies. In imitation of the Constitution of the mother country, he should propose a Council and House of Assembly for each; the Assembly to be constituted in the usual manner, and the members of the Council to be members for life; all laws and ordinances of the Province to remain in force till altered by the new Legislature. The

Habeas Corpus to be continued as a fundamental principle of the Constitution. Land tenures were to be settled in Lower Canada by the Local Legislature. In Upper Canada, the settlers being chiefly British, all such tenures were to be in common socage. To prevent any the like dispute as that which separated the thirteen states of the mother country, it was provided that the British Parliament should impose no taxes, but such as might be necessary for the regulation of trade and commerce; and to guard against the abuse of this power, all imposts were to be levied and disposed of by the Legislature of each Province.

The Bill remained in abeyance for some time, meeting with very vigorous opposition from the British party in the Colony as well as by merchants of London, who had trade relations with Canada. It was thought by these opponents that the provisions of the Bill were entirely too favourable to Lower Canada. Notwithstanding the opposition, however, it went to a third reading, and was passed without a division by both the Lords and the Commons. This was the Constitutional Act of 1791, which for many years was the law for the government of affairs in both the Canadas. The principal features of this Act were:—

1. The English Criminal law for both Provinces.
2. A Legislative Council, the members of which to be appointed by the Crown for Life; Lower Canada to have fifteen members and Upper Canada seven.
3. A Legislative Assembly, of at least fifty members in Lower Canada, and sixteen in Upper Canada, for the time.
4. Electors to have property qualifications, two pounds sterling annual value in the rural districts, and five pounds in the towns. Tenants in rural districts paying an annual rent of ten pounds could vote.

5. All powers of legislation for the Colony to reside in the Assembly and Legislative Council conjointly, the King having a veto, and his representative a power of delaying any act he might disapprove of. The duration of each Parliament not to exceed four years; the two houses to be convoked in session once at least in every year, and all questions in debate to be decided by a simple majority vote.
6. An Executive Council, to be of Royal nomination, to advise the Governor, was instituted, with the powers of a Court of Appeal in Civil matters.

So far as the Province of Lower Canada was concerned, the different sections or parties in the Province, in order to understand the full meaning of the Act, thought it necessary to form a Club, called a "Constitutional Club," for the disseminating the requirements of the Act, and to make plain its provisions. It is always to be borne in mind that the French-Canadians were the dominant party, and that in the chief City of Montreal nine-tenths of the population were French. The political opinions of the Club may be gathered from the toasts which were drunk at a meeting of the Club shortly after the Act of 1791 was proclaimed. They were:

1. Abolition of feudal tenure.
2. Civil and Religious freedom.
3. Liberty of the press.
4. Freedom and integrity of jurymen.
5. The French Revolution.
6. The Polish Revolution.

The most noticeable toast was the first—Abolition of the feudal tenure. There can be no doubt that for many years before the Act of 1791, the feudal tenure was considered to be a real grievance by the *habitants* of the

Lower Province, and now that an opportunity is afforded, a public assembly of a quasi-national Club, regardless of ecclesiastical influence or Seigniorial power, declares for abolition of the tenure. As we proceed with the relation we will see whether or not the boon of the new Constitution given to Quebec proved a cure for the ills to which the **Province was** subject.

CHAPTER III.

Provinces Divided—Legislative Assembly—Battle of Races—Papineau, Member of Assembly—Panet's Patriotic Speech—Education and Religion—Assembly's Claim to Regulate Supplies—Lord Dorchester's Instructions—French Minister Genet—Dissimulation and Treachery—Bishop Plessis' Advice to French-Canadians—Legislative Assembly Decidedly French—Judge Osgoode—French Language, its Use in Parliament—Tithes—Immigration—Sir James Craig—Acceptable to the French, but not to the English—Advises Re-Union of Provinces.

THE dividing of the old Province of Quebec, and the establishment of the two Provinces of Upper and Lower Canada by the Act of 1791, was thought by the English people to mark an epoch in Colonial history, inasmuch as the Provinces now established were given Legislative Assemblies, which was considered by many to be equivalent to giving the right of self-government to the Colonies. The French-Canadians had clamored for a government which should enable them to manage their own affairs, but had they got it? Were they even able to work out their destiny by this toy, so comely to look at, but difficult to manage? The first difficulty they met with was the constitution of the Assembly. By virtue of their great numbers, they had the power to exclude wholly from this branch of government everyone who was not in accord with French-Canadian sentiment. This course, however, if adopted, would not only have been ungracious, but would have shown the on-looking world how incapable they were of driving the car of state. The mass of the French-Canadians were devoid of that education which fits a man for parliamentary service. There were educated men among them, chiefly of the seignior, notary and *avocat* class, but the rural population had not had the means of storing their minds with the knowledge necessary for representatives of the people. The want of such men could only be supplied by drawing on the British element for legislators, in sufficient numbers to at least fulfil the duties of one of the four wheels of the coach, and thus prevent a breaking down of the equipage.

It was felt that the experience of the Anglo-Canadians would be of service in the guiding of the chariot of state, until such time as sufficient knowledge could be gained to enable them to conduct affairs unaided.

In the first Assembly under the Act, the majority of whose members were French-Canadians, there were nevertheless fifteen members of British origin, who owed their election to French-Canadian support. This support was generously given, but whether or not it was as generously received the reader must judge. There may be a great divergence of opinion on this as on other matters which affect the relations existing, or which did exist, between the different races in the Province of Quebec.

When the Assembly met, and it became necessary to elect a Speaker, the question at once arose whether the Speaker should be English or French. The British party wanted one of their race elected Speaker, while the other party wanted a French-Canadian. Much discussion took place in the House over this matter, the British contending that in a British Province there should be a British Speaker, and one who spoke the English language, and the French-Canadians contending that the very object of the Imperial Parliament, in granting a Representative Assembly to the Province of Quebec, was to give the French-Canadians control over, at least, this branch of the Legislature and that the Speaker should be of their race, whether he could speak English or not. The speaking part of his functions could be accomplished through an interpreter.

The battles of the races waxed hot and furious. M. Papineau, a member of the Assembly, and father of that Louis Joseph Papineau so celebrated in the history of Canada as leader of the Rebellion of 1837, emphasized his adherence to the interests of the French-Canadians by declaiming: "Is it because Canada forms a part of the British Empire that Canadians who speak not the language in use on the banks of the Thames, are to be deprived of their natural rights?" Thus we have the race and language question cropping up for the first time in a Canadian Representative Assembly, and who so likely to have raised the question as a Papineau, the ancestor of that great man who for national love sacrificed much, rebelled fiercely, suffered much, but at the last died a peaceful death at his home, Montebello, on the banks of the Ottawa, a faithful subject of the Queen.

Speaker

The French-Canadians in the House generally favoured the election of a French-Canadian Speaker, but one among them, more liberal than the majority, impressed with the importance of maintaining the English character of the Assembly, was very outspoken in his opposition to the sentiments expressed by the French majority. This member was Mr. P. L. Panet, who said: "Is not this country a British possession? Is not the English language that of the Sovereign and the British Legislature? Ought we not, then, to speak English in British legislational halls, whether located in London or Quebec?"

It was in vain that the British party in the House, augmented by the support of M. Panet, heroically fought against a French-Canadian being elected to preside over the Assembly. Mr. J. A. Panet, a namesake, if not a relative of the M. Panet who had taken a part with the English side, was duly nominated and elected to the Speakership by the proportion of two to one of the members in a full House. Mr. J. A. Panet could speak both languages, English and French, so no harm was done, except showing the cleavage between the two races, English and French.

An equally difficult question as that of the election of Speaker engaged the members at this first attempt at legislation, in the beginning of the representative period in the Province of Lower Canada. This was, how were the minutes of the proceedings of the House to be kept? In French or in English? Again the parties divided, each according to his nationality espousing the French or English side, with as much zest and vigour as in the old days before the American Revolution, when the Colonial New Englanders and the French assailed each other, as they felt in duty bound, to mark the enmity which existed between their respective parent states. In this case a compromise was effected and the minutes ordered to be kept in both languages.

A fruitful subject of discussion during the first session, which lasted into 1792, was the subject of education. The Jesuit Estates—what should be done with them? And the Convents, the Recollets and Ursulines—what was to become of them? Were they to be razed to the ground, or to be preserved? These are subjects, however, which cannot be said to have had any direct bearing upon the Rebellion of 1837. They had their day, and may be suffered to pass into oblivion. The Rebellion of 1837 was neither an educational or religious war, hence we are relieved from considering these questions, foreign to the matter in hand.

Another and much more important question, in a political sense, than either education or religion, next disturbed the Legislative Assembly. The French-Canadians were fully alive to the fact that unless their Assembly could obtain full control of taxation and finance, the Act of 1791 would be of but little value to them; so they at once set their faces against any part of the supplies for the support of Government being provided for by the Imperial Government. One of the most, if not the most important resolutions of the House in the first session, was that in which the House declared that the voting of subsidies belonged exclusively to them, and that no supply bill could of right be amended by the Legislative Council in any way.

It looks strange to us at this day, so well have we become acquainted with the British Constitutional form of government, that it should have been found necessary to raise such a question in the Assembly. But we must remember that in 1792, Colonial Government had not, nor indeed had the British Parliament itself, attained that pitch of excellence which is exhibited at the present day. At that time Colonial rights were hardly regarded. The Royal prerogative held sway over all the British Dominions. The British Government, at the very time the Assembly's resolution was passed, was furnishing part of the funds for carrying on the government of the Province, and demanded, in return, a controlling and active part in the administration of the affairs of the Colony.

Nor was this altogether unreasonable, when we consider that if a different course had been pursued at that time, the British part of the population would have thought themselves entirely forsaken by the parent state. British emigration would have been discouraged, if not altogether prevented, and that which was supposed to be a British Colony handed over to the alien race who could never forget the laws, the customs, the language and the religion of their ancestors.

Lord Dorchester, who was never at any time an unpopular Governor, resumed the office in 1793, armed with new powers for the endeavour of pacifying the French-Canadians. He came to the Colony with instructions from the Home Government that the two Seminaries of Quebec and Montreal, as well as the religious communities of women, should remain in perpetuity, being administered in accordance with the rules of their foundation.

Lord Dorchester realized his position and responsibility, at a time when the spirit of Revolution was abroad. France was in a condition of wild delirium over her success in getting rid of her king, by regicide, and was, as she vainly imagined, the instrument by means of which all monarchies were to be felled to the earth and the brazen idol of Republicanism set up in their place. In the year 1793, she had as her Minister in the United States a fit emissary of such a government, built on treachery, dissimulation, fraud, massacre and murder. Genet was this man. France had declared war against England, and Genet did his utmost to embroil the United States in the war, and would have succeeded, if President Washington had not, with firm hand, opposed his schemes.

Genet next intrigued with the French-Canadians. He sent emissaries among them with the purpose of undermining their allegiance. Lord Dorchester was on the watch tower. In the session of 1793, he directed the attention of the Legislature to the organization of the Militia, and, to thwart the design of Genet, induced the Legislature to pass an Act authorising the Executive to suspend the operation of the Habeas Corpus Act, and thus obtained a ready means of disposing of any agents that the French Minister might send into the Province, to propagate Revolutionary notions.

The session of 1793 was a long one, lasting from November to June. It was a stormy session, and resulted in the passing of only six acts, which goes to prove that the legislators of that day were in no special hurry to get through with their business. The Governor, in proroguing the session, cautioned the members, when returning to their homes, to diffuse among the people a spirit of loyalty, and the avoidance of all traitors and traitorous conspiracies.

M. Plessis, the then parish priest of Quebec and afterward bishop, on a public occasion took particular pains to admonish his flock that gratitude as well as interest should prevail with them to be loyal to the British Crown. His words were: " Our conquerors, regarded at first with a jealous eye and lowering brow, inspired in us feelings only of detestation or aversion. We could not be persuaded that a race of men, strangers to our soil, to our language, to our laws, to our worship, could ever be willing to render to Canada an equivalent to Canada for what it lost by changing its masters. Generous Nation! which has made us aware by so many evidences how ill founded were our prepossessions. Industrious nation! which has developed the earth's fecundity and explored its hidden riches. Exemplary nation! that in critical times, taught the attentive world wherein consists that liberty which all men desire to obtain, but so few know how to keep in proper bounds. Pitying nation! which has just welcomed, with so much humanity, the most faithful, yet worst used subjects of that realm to which ourselves once belonged. **Beneficent nation**! which daily gave **us men of** Canada **fresh** proofs of its liberality. No, no, your people are not enemies of our people, nor are **ye** despoilers **of** our property, which rather do your laws protect; nor are ye foes to our religion, to which **ye** pay all due respect. Pardon us, then, for that our first distrustfulness of a foreign race, whose virtues, being as yet unexperienced by us, we had not the happiness to know; and, if after being apprised of the overthrow of the monarchy and the abolition of the only right of worship in France, and after experiencing for thirty-five years the gentleness of your domination, there remain among us some natures purblind enough, or of such an evil disposition, as to revive past antipathies, or awaken in the popular mind disloyal wishes to revert to French supremacy, let Britons be assured that such beings **are rare** among us; **and** we beg that what may be true of the malcontent few, **will** not be imputed to the well-disposed many."*

These were noble words from such a distinguished man as M. Plessis. The sentiments thus expressed were the sentiments of the best disposed of the French-Canadians, but there was then, as there ever has been in Canada, both French-Canadian **and** English-Canadian, a class of men, who, not content with the great privileges they enjoy under the British system of government, stretch out their hands for Republicanism, whose **name sounds so** well to many ears, but to others **is but as** sounding brass **or** a tinkling cymbal. But in the words of M. Plessis, "We **beg that**

* This refers to the emigrant nobles and priests driven from **France by the** Revolution, who sought refuge in England and her Colonies.

what may be true of the malcontent few, will not be imputed to the well-disposed many."

In 1795, the Seigniorial question was again to the front, owing to the fact that many of the old French Seigniories had fallen into the hands of Britons, who were not satisfied with the old tenure and the old scale of rents.

The French-Canadians, always attached to their old laws and customs, to the contribution of just so much corn to the Seigniorial Mill, to the exact payments demanded by the Seigniorial system, to the established rents under the old laws, would not hear of a change being made. Despite the efforts of the English Seigniors, all of which were directed to an increase of charge, the old *habitants* would not move an inch. The House of Assembly, reflecting their opinions, refused to alter the terms of land holding, thus disappointing the hopes of what the French-Canadian called the avaricious landlord.

The Second Legislative Assembly was more pronouncedly French than the first. The course taken by the English members of the First House in regard to the exclusion of the French language, their vote on the Speakership, and on other questions which the French-Canadians claimed were antagonistic to their interests, impelled the Electorate, so largely French-Canadian, to exclude from the halls of Parliament many of the English members to whom they had formerly given their support. Mr. Panet was again elected Speaker by a large majority of the votes of the House.

General Prescott was Governor when the second Parliament assembled. It was indeed convened by him. The name of Prescott is familiar to most Canadians, from the fact that Prescott, in the County of Grenville, where the Battle of the Windmill, in 1837, was fought, is so named to commemorate him.

Perhaps the most important of the political acts of Governor Prescott, was that he obtained from the Parliament an Act vesting the Executive Council, or any three of its members, with the power of ordering the arrest of parties accused or merely suspected of treason or seditious practices. Nor was this power untimely conferred, for the French Republic had been continuously industrious in spreading Republican notions in Canada. Many of the *habitants*, allured by the successes that the French troops had gained in Spain, Austria and Italy, were disposed to be rebellious. The French Minister to the United States had boldly advised the Canadians to throw in their lot with the French Republic, which intended to invade the Colony and raise troops there to fight the battles of the French against the English.

It was at this time that a man named McLane came into the Province of Lower Canada and, visiting Quebec, was detected making drawings of the fortifications. He was arrested, tried and condemned to death as a traitor.

A general feeling of uneasiness among the officials prevailed in Canada. Many of the *habitants* were suspected of Revolutionary tendencies, which caused the Governor to tighten the reins of government. There were not wanting those who insisted that there was no cause for uneasiness, and who asserted that this uneasiness was brought about by self-interested hangers-on of the Government, who instilled such notions into the minds of their superiors for the purpose of profiting by their suspicions.

The Crown lands afforded a fine field for the exploitation of enterprising Englishmen, and not a few of them were tempted to engage in speculation in wild lands. The Land Board, at this time, was made up of members of the Legislative Council, and we have seen how largely the British interests predominated in that body. Judge Osgoode was a member of the Council and consequently of the Land Board. The Imperial Government warned Governor Prescott to allow nothing to take place in this department which might irritate the French-Canadians, and when Judge Osgoode espoused the cause of the British claimants, he was immediately brought into collision with the Governor. It was not convenient, at this time, that important political differences between high government officials should be allowed to pass unnoticed, and the breach between the Governor and the Judge was summarily healed, by the removal of both from the scene of conflict. The Governor was recalled and Osgoode resigned his position.

These events occurred in the years 1798 and 1799. It is a singular fact, of apparent inconsistency, that while there were undoubtedly French-Canadians who were made uneasy by the French Revolution, Sir Robert Shore Milnes, who succeeded General Prescott as Governor, on opening the session of Parliament in 1799, was able to thank the Canadians for moneys they had subscribed to defray the cost of the war of Britain against the French Revolutionists.

During the session, one of the members of the Legislative **Assembly** named Bone was expelled from the House **for** swindling, notwithstanding which he was twice subsequently returned by **the** electors, and was only finally rendered ineligible **by an** Act of the Parliament **of 1802.**

The subject **of** language was one **which** very much concerned the British inhabitants of **Lower** Canada at this time. In this second Parliament, one-fifth of the members were British, and four-fifths French and French-Canadian. The English members, not **being** able to speak **the** French language, **were** not able to make themselves understood by the **other** members of the House. Hence, their presence there was of very little benefit to themselves or their constituents. Still, the English representatives were not without influence with the Government, which influence reacted to a certain extent in the legislative body. The English representatives were all State officials, three **Judges,** four Executive Councillors and other office holders. They may also be said to have been the Government. They were able to induce the Legislature to pass an Act for the foundation of a Royal Institution of learning, and to endow the same with **Crown** lands. The appointment of the President **and Directors** of this body was placed in the hands of **the Governor,** Sir Robert **Shore Milnes. The** Governor was very well known to very much favour the existing party, and it was now hoped that by diffusion of knowledge, by means of the English language, throughout the Province, under control of the Royal Institution, the much desired object, English government and institutions would be obtained.

Two colleges, one for Quebec and the other for Montreal, were accordingly established to make the system complete. Unfortunately, in carrying the scheme into operation, the Protestant Bishop was appointed President of the Royal Institution. This was quite sufficient to prevent the French-Canadians from giving the Institution or the Colleges any support whatever. They became alarmed lest their faith and their language should be sacrificed to the evil designs of the English party. There was no use for colleges or schools without scholars. With the Canadians standing aloof the experiment was a decided failure, and the English idea and the English language received a blow from which it took some years to recover.

Another subject which agitated the people about this time was the creation of new parishes. The Executive attempted to lay out new parishes. To this the Church took exception. The Roman Catholic Church, in the Province of Lower Canada, has always maintained that, under the Treaty, the ecclesiastical authorities, and they alone, have the right to set apart parishes; that the State has no control whatever over them; that a disarrangement of them would seriously interfere with the system of levying tithes; that, at all events, their retention is necessary to preserve the status of the Roman Catholic Church in the Province. There was a man in the Government service, who held his post for many years, who was always ready to combat this ecclesiastical pretension. That man was Mr. Ryland, the Secretary of the Province. Mr. Ryland was a man of great influence, and, had his advice been followed, the Church in the Province of Lower Canada would have been shorn of much, if not all its power. He would not only have done away with tithes, but with the licensing of priests by the papal authority and every other semblance of ecclesiastical jurisdiction.

We have now arrived at the year 1804, and find the racial differences not only not lessened but, if anything, increased. British merchants were commanding the trade of Canada. With British merchants, other Britons, of the agricultural and artisan classes, were taking up their positions in the Province. It may be that it was in consequence of this immigration we hear more of the racial difficulty than before. With population comes taxation. The public necessities of the Province required that taxes should be levied in some shape to meet the expenditure. The question was, what form should this levying of imposts take? Should the tax be levied on land or goods, in other words, a land tax or a commercial tax? The British merchant was very averse to a tax being levied on his goods, thus increasing the price to the consumer. The French party, on the other hand, were equally opposed to levying a tax on land, which was for various reasons not adapted to new countries. The Assembly, largely French, favoured the taxation of commerce.

As was often the case in Lower Canada, when questions of this nature arose, and there were radical differences between the parties, appeals were made to the British Government and to the British Parliament. The Colonial Office was deluged with petitions urging the different views. The question was an important one as settling, once for all, the future government of the Province in the matter of taxation.¹ As was more frequently the case than otherwise, the French-Canadians got the ear of the British Ministry. An Act of the Assembly for levying the required tax on goods was assented to by the Governor, no doubt under instructions from the Imperial Government, and all French Lower Canada was jubilant. The *habitant*, always docile to his religious superiors, ready to pay a tax to the Church, escaped the unpleasant duty of a tax to the State, and was happy. The Church was happy because the *habitant* was pleased and was not rendered less able to pay his tithes.

But what of the British residents? Sour and discontented, they submitted because the higher authority so decreed, but rage and chagrin rankled in their breasts. The Quebec *Mercury*, the organ of the British party in the Province, was moved to say, "This Province is far too French for a British Colony. After forty-seven years' possession, it is now fitting that the Province become truly British."

Whether or not it was to emphasise the opinion of the English inhabitants, so expressed in the *Mercury*, or for other reasons, Sir James Craig was sent out to Lower Canada as Governor in time to open the Parliament of 1808. There has perhaps never been a Governor of Canada who had the misfortune to so thoroughly antagonize the French-Canadian party as Sir James Craig.

A military man, with no experience in the Senate, he was essentially a man of war and not of peace. The new Governor had not been long in the Province before he waged war upon the Assembly, and showed his want of confidence in the Militia by having erased from its rolls several of the most important officers. Mr. Panet, who had the confidence not only of this Assembly, but of the two previous Assemblies, and was their Speaker, met with the displeasure of the Governor because he was, or was supposed to be, one of the proprietors of a newspaper, *Le Canadien*, published in the French interest. This newspaper was very outspoken in its comments on Government and Government placemen, which brought it into disfavour with the reigning powers. There was nothing treasonable in *Le Canadien's* utterances, but it was sufficiently abusive to earn the resentment, not only of the Governor and those surrounding him, but of a majority of the British population.

The first session of the Assembly, under Sir James Craig's administration, was a stormy one. The Governor, the Legislative Council, and the Assembly were at logger-heads. Sir James, a Briton, believed it his duty to act as a Briton, and always favoured the Council, the majority of whose members were British, as against the Assembly which was French-Canadian. The session only lasted thirty-six days, and, for all the good that was effected, might as well have never been called. The Governor, in proroguing the Assembly, which he also dissolved, after lecturing the members in a style more appropriate to a despotic Sovereign than a Constitutional Governor, wound up his speech by saying to the House, "You have wasted by fruitless debates, excited by private and personal animosity, or by frivolous contests upon trivial matters of form, that time and those talents, to which, within your walls, the public have an exclusive title."

As if to add fuel to the fire, the Governor took occasion to discriminate between the Council and the Assembly, by telling the Council that the meagre result of the sessional labours did not lie at their door. There were only five bills passed during the whole session, of which three were renewals of former Acts.

The British party, in the principal towns in the Province, were delighted with the rating the Governor had given the Assembly, which tended to widen the breach between the Governor and the French-Canadians. *Le Canadien*, in relation to the Governor's speech, said: "The King's Representative has power by law to dissolve the House when he thinks fit to do so, but he has no right whatever to make abusive remarks, such as his harangue contained, upon the action of the Legislature, a body which is absolutely independent of his authority. The respect due to this branch is as sacred and as inviolable as that due to His Excellency himself, and those reflections became him all the less, that upon the Governor is the duty specially imposed of paying due respect to that branch of legislature as well as to all other parts of the Government."

As was to be expected, the strong language used by the Governor was resented, not only by the French-Canadian organ of French-Canadian opinion, but by the Assembly. This branch of the Legislature, at the succeeding session, declared the Governor's strictures a breach of privilege and dangerous to the liberties of the people. The Deputies, members of the Legislature, thought that the Governor's action was prompted more by the officials surrounding him than by his own natural impulses. It now became quite evident to the Assembly that they must bring these officials under their influence and control. The way to effect this was to make the placemen dependent on the Assembly for their salaries. Hitherto, they had received their income from the English exchequer, or from sources entirely independent of the Representatives of the people in Parliament. The embroglio between the Governor and the Assembly was in the end productive of good, as it caused the Assembly to declare that it was now prepared to assume the whole cost of civil government.

There had before this date been established in the Province a Court, called the Court of King's Bench; Monsieur De Brune was judge of that Court and partial to the Government. He was also a member of the Assembly. This body, in order to get rid of him, humble the Governor, and assert their complete independence of office holders, declared that Judge De Brune should be expelled the House. Sir James Craig thereupon in turn became incensed at the House and their proceedings, stigmatized the act of the Assembly as unconstitutional, and prorogued the Legislature. According to the Constitutional system, then in force, the Governor was right and the Assembly wrong. It may have been a mistake that judges should engage in politics and be elected members of the Assembly, but there was no law against it at that time; and the Assembly had no more right to expel Judge de Brune than they would have had to expel any other member of the Legislature.

The repeated causes of difference between the Governor and the Assembly, together with the apparent disposition of the members of that body to oppose everything British, or British-Colonial, so influenced the Governor that he thought the time had come to apprise the British Government that Canada was on

RE-UNION ADVISED.

the brink of a volcano. He saw, or affected to see before him the spectre of a Revolution, in imitation of the Revolution in France, if of smaller dimensions, and in communicating with Lord Liverpool, the British Minister, denounced the French-Canadians, in no stinted terms, as unworthy of confidence; that they were ignorant, disloyal, enemies of Britain, and in every way disreputable; that a mistake had been made in entrusting the destinies of Lower Canada to an Assembly whose constituents were French or French-Canadian and so entirely opposed to British interests. Sir James even went so far as to advise the British Government to suspend the Constitution and to reunite the Provinces of Upper and Lower Canada, and in this way give the British portion a commanding influence.

The advice tendered by Sir James Craig was not acceptable at that time to the British Government, though it was followed at a subsequent period. Sir James Craig's administration was brought to a close just before the breaking out of the war of 1812. It may be said of it that it was of a stormy character and fittingly ended in the foreshadow of a war, which was destined to try the loyalty not only of the French-Canadian, but of every subject of Canada.

CHAPTER IV.

U. E. Loyalists—John **Graves** Simcoe, First Governor of Upper Canada—First **Parliament** of Upper Canada—Simcoe's Death—Peter Russell Administrator—British **and** American Insurgents—Irish Rebellion of 1798—Governor Hunter and his Administration—Discontent in Lower Canada—Governor Gore's Administration—Joseph Willcox, M.P., his Contempt of Parliament and Imprisonment—Mr. Justice Thorpe—Judge Scott—Difference of Parties on Local Government.

THE Constitutional Act of 1791 had been obtained principally through the exertion of the United Empire Loyalists. After the Treaty of Peace of 1783, between Great Britain and the United States, had been declared, numerous loyalists of the American Colonies, some compelled by force, some voluntarily, turned their backs forever on the revolted Colonies and hewed out for themselves homes in the wilderness of Canada. At the time of the passing of the Act of 1791, there were not more than twenty thousand inhabitants in that part of Canada forming Upper Canada, and these mostly United Empire Loyalists, men who had sacrificed everything they possessed in defending the cause of the King in the New England and other States of America.

In the period between 1783 and 1791 the Loyalists in Upper Canada had, with almost superhuman labour in cutting down large forest trees, removing great boulders, putting up log houses and log barns, managed to make settlements on the St. Lawrence west of Cornwall, on the Bay of Quinté, in the Niagara district and London and Western districts. These settlements were far removed from each other, and there was but little intercourse between them, but such as there was, was of the most friendly character.

There was one man in the British House of Commons at the time of the passing of the Imperial Act of 1791, who was able to give Mr. Pitt, the Prime Minister, very valuable advice and assistance in the passing of that Act. This was John Graves Simcoe, who in time became the first Governor of Upper Canada.

John Graves Simcoe had gone through the Rebellion of the American Colonies, and had acquitted himself with honour in command of the Queen's Rangers, that corps which performed such eminent service to the Crown in more than one campaign in the struggle which the Americans successfully made for their independence. On the defeat of the British under Cornwallis at Yorktown, a defeat largely brought about by French aid to the Americans, Colonel Simcoe was made prisoner, paroled and returned to England. When it became necessary to appoint a Governor to the newly created Province of Upper Canada, what better selection could be made than to send to the

Province the man who above all others enjoyed the confidence of the population of Upper Canada, the greater number of whom had been with him and many had even served under him throughout the American Revolutionary war.

Colonel Simcoe arrived out from England in 1791, and in passing up the St. Lawrence was received at Johnstown by quite a number of U. E. Loyalists with a salvo of artillery from a gun taken from the old French fort on an island down the river. On his arrival at Kingston, the first Government of the Province of Upper Canada was organized, with a solemnity befitting the occasion. In the church in this town was read and published His Majesty's Commissions, one appointing Lord Dorchester Captain General and Commander in Chief, and the other Col. Simcoe Governor of the Province of Upper Canada. According to the Royal instructions the Governor was given an Executive Council composed of five members.

In July, 1792, the Executive Council met at Kingston, when the following gentlemen were appointed members of the Legislative Council: Robert Hamilton, Richard Cartwright and John Monroe. It is to be presumed that the Governor took counsel with his new Councillors, all of whom were prominent men in the Province, as to the future government of the country. Governor Simcoe, however, combined strength with judgment. He might consult others, but he was guided by his own opinions.

When he came to select a capital for the Province he considered that Newark, now Niagara, was the proper site. Fort Niagara at that time on the opposite, or American side, of the river was in possession of the British, retained by them after the Treaty of Peace of 1783 as a hostage for the performance of certain articles of the treaty by the Americans. Pitching his tent at Newark, he was under the protection of the old Fort, and could look around him with security and contentment. When he afterwards discovered that it was the intention of the British Government to hand this Fort over to the Americans, he no longer thought Newark a fit place for the seat of government. Hence it was that in 1793 the seat of government was removed from Newark or Niagara to Toronto, newly christened York by him in honour of the successes of the Duke of York, on the continent, in the French war.

The Constitution of 1791, which Governor Simcoe was called upon to administer in Upper Canada, was in the main the same as the Constitution of Lower Canada. There was, as we have seen, an Executive and Legislative Council, and there was also a Legislative Assembly of sixteen members. Governor Simcoe had a much easier task in governing Upper Canada under this Constitution than had the Governors of Lower Canada.

In the Province of Lower Canada there was a mixed community, while in the Upper Province the population was composed of United Empire Loyalists, not only with not a drop of French blood in their veins, but men who, when residents in the New England States, before the American Rebellion, had been in constant warfare with the French-Canadians.

The Legislative Assembly of Upper Canada occupied its early days in passing Acts for the material advancement of the Province. There was none of that bickering, occasioned by racial and other causes, which affected the body politic in Lower Canada. During Simcoe's time there was but little political discussion in the Province; the people had neither time nor inclination to discuss political subjects. There was but one newspaper in the Province, and that was the official gazette, published once a week, which generally contained foreign news a month or two old. As to home matters, the people were mostly concerned about how to secure houses and homes for themselves in the new country. The representatives in the Assembly reflected the wishes of the people, and the Governor was sufficiently occupied in exploring the country, tranquillizing the Indians and establishing a cordon of his old veterans of the Revolutionary war along the rivers and lakes of the frontiers of the Province, ready to resist any future depredations that the Americans might attempt to make on the Province committed to his charge.

How well Governor Simcoe administered the affairs of the Province may be gathered from the histories of the time. A reading of the Smith manuscripts, which will be found in the Public Library at Toronto, will convince the reader that his government was a paternal one. He looked upon the United Empire Loyalists as his children, and the widows and children of the United Empire Loyalists as his wards. In 1806, at which date he had been promoted to the rank of Major-General, that he enjoyed the confidence of the sovereign to the full is evidenced by the fact that on his return to England he, conjointly with Lord St. Vincent, was placed in command of an expedition to thwart the designs of Napoleon Bonaparte, who had threatened to invade Portugal with an army of thirty thousand men. He was taken ill on the voyage to Portugal and he was obliged to return to England. On the 7th February, 1807, the *Upper Canada Gazette* published the following notice as a communication from London:—

"LONDON, November 6th, 1806.

"Governor Simcoe, we regret to state, died on Tuesday last, at Topsham in Devonshire."

In Exeter Cathedral, a monument, with the following inscription, was erected to his memory:—

"Sacred to the Memory
of
John Graves Simcoe,
Lieutenant General in the Army and Colonel of the 22nd Regiment
of Foot,
who died on the 25th October, 1806,
Aged 54 years ;
In whose life and character the virtues of the Hero, the Patriot and the Christian were so eminently conspicuous, that it may be justly said, he served his King and his country with a zeal exceeded only by his piety toward God."

The Ontario Government has voted a substantial sum towards the erection of a monument to Governor Simcoe's memory in Toronto, made by him the capital of the Province.

Major General Peter Hunter, the successor of Governor Simcoe, assumed the government of the Province in August, 1799. The intervening period, between the departure of Governor Simcoe and the arrival of Hunter, was filled by the administration of the Honorable Peter Russell, as senior member of the Council. Nothing of a startling nature occurred during the administration of Mr. Russell. As President of the Council, it fell to his lot to issue or order the issue of grants of land. There is a tradition that he had favourites, and that in the exercise of his office some of those favourites profited by his care of their interests. A playful saying, which passed current for many years but has now passed into oblivion, was that grants of land were made which might read—"I Peter Russell grant to you Peter Russell." There was little, if any, foundation for the pleasantry. It arose from the fact that it was claimed that his position as a private citizen conflicted with his official duty when he became a purchaser of public lands, and gave an opportunity to his opponents to lay on him the reproach of an unfaithful trustee. There were no political opponents in those days, in a party sense, as there were no defined lines between political parties. There were, however, land opponents. Every one was on the look-out for lands, and if one man crossed the path of another he was an opponent. President Russell had no doubt opponents of this class, who gladly utilized the humorous idea of Peter Russell granting to Peter Russell.

By the time General Hunter was installed in office as Governor of the Province, a considerable trade had sprung up between the settlers in Upper Canada and their American neighbours. It was much cheaper for the merchants of Upper Canada to get in goods from Albany and New York, than from England by the route of the St. Lawrence. There were no canals in those days, and the rapids of the St. Lawrence offered an almost insurmountable barrier to the importation of goods by that channel. With the importation of American goods, there came into the country a large number of Americans, spying out the richness of the land. The American immigrant was welcome, so long as he conformed to the laws and institutions of the country, but panoplied with the coat of republicanism, he found it difficult to divest himself of republican prejudices, and it was not long before he attempted to use his persuasiveness to make the Canadians believe that they were terrible sufferers from the want of republican government. Thus it is that trade and commerce between old countries and new frequently induces an undermining of the new edifice, to gratify the whims of denizens of the old.

The American import of goods was thought better than the import of American men. Out of the goods there could be collected a revenue, but not out of the men. The Canadian Parliament, to provide for the expense of civil government, during the first years of General Hunter's administration, passed laws to levy a tax on American goods. The levying a tax on goods involved the appointment of collectors and ports of entry, all of which tended to strengthen the country, the revenue financially, and the collectors and ports of entry acting as watchmen and watch towers in defence of the Province. While Canada, and especially Upper Canada, was importing goods from the United States, she was active in importing men from England, Scotland and Ireland. The Irish Rebellion of 1798 was the cause of a large number of the men of the land of the shamrock leaving the old land for the new. Upper Canada afforded a fine field for the labourers and men accustomed to hard work to better their condition. England and Scotland, (England less than Scotland) contributed their quota of emigrants, so that by the time that Governor Hunter was half through his administration, he was able to report that Upper Canada was being settled by a hardy class of Britons, as a counterpoise to the enterprising American citizens who were getting a foothold in the country.

At the period of which we are writing, the first germ of discontent made itself manifest, in the same quarters and from the same cause as had occurred in Lower Canada, that is in the Legislative Council. This body, consisting of five members and the Governor, virtually ruled the

Province. The Assembly could pass Acts, but the Council could reject them, and thus stifle public opinion. The Province had not indeed got a Constitution under which, as in England, there was an Executive responsible to the Crown. Barnacles had attached themselves to the Governor and Council, in the shape of needy adventurers out of employment. It was quite evident that in the near future some one, more independent than his fellows, would make an assault on the Government, and the Governor himself might not escape. The explosion, however, was reserved for the reign of a future Governor. General Hunter's administration on the whole was beneficial to the Province. A reference to the statute book will show that the material, if not the political interests of the Province had been well looked to, and that peace and contentment rested with a large majority of the people.

Governor Hunter was recalled to England in 1805, Alexander Grant, President of the Council, taking his place for a short period, and being succeeded by Francis Gore as Lieutenant-Governor. Governor Gore first met the House of Assembly at the opening of the third session of the Fourth Parliament, on the 2nd February, 1807. In his address to the House he asks the Assembly to unite with him in sentiments of loyalty and gratitude, while reflecting on the very liberal supplies annually afforded to the Province, by the bounty of the parent state, for its necessary expenditure, and to consider whether the mother country ought not in some measure to be relieved from the expense of civil government.

The Governor is said to have been a man of generous disposition, easily influenced by others. There were not wanting then in Upper Canada plenty of men willing to give their services to the Governor for a consideration. When such men got into the Governor's confidence, he became surrounded by a party who manifested too plainly the insolence of office not to become a mark for men of independent thought. Joseph Willcox was a man of the latter class. He was an Irishman, and in addition to a sharp tongue, wielded a vigorous pen. He established, or had established for him, a newspaper called the *Upper Canada Guardian* for the avowed purpose of acting as a counterfoil to the *Canadian Gazette*, the Government organ.

This may be said to have been the first step in forming a new or reform party in the country. Mr. Willcox was enabled to obtain a seat in the Legislature, and become a thorn in the side of the Government party. On the 18th February, 1808, it is recorded in the Journals that Captain Cowan, a member of the Assembly, stated on the floor of the House that an honourable member, Joseph Willcox, had made use of language out of doors derogatory to the honour and integrity of the House, and nearly in these words: "That the members of the House of Assembly dared not proceed against him. He was sorry they did not. It would have given him an opportunity of proving they had been bribed by General Hunter, and that he had a member of the House ready to come forward to give testimony to that effect."

This rash charge, made by Mr. Willcox, was taken into consideration by the House, and on the report of a Committee and vote of the House, after hearing evidence *pro* and *con.*, it was unanimously resolved, "that Joseph Willcox be committed to the common jail of the District (Home), and the Speaker do issue his warrant for that purpose."

Mr. Gore, the Governor, did not fail to do justice to General Hunter, his predecessor, at the same time exposing the total ignorance of Mr. Justice Thorpe, who was a firm ally of Mr. Willcox in his crusade against Governor Hunter, and who had listened to idle stories about the Governor, which were not by any means credited by the respectable people of the Province. In a communication made by Governor Gore to Mr. Windham, Secretary of State, under date of the 29th October, 1806, the Governor thus wrote: "Judge Thorpe has not been in this Colony much more than twelve months, he only saw Lieut.-Governor Hunter at Quebec a short time before his death, whose character and memory he has endeavoured, both in private and public, to degrade, and can only know by report many of the circumstances he thinks proper to allude to, respecting the Government of this Province. . . . It is but justice to General Hunter's character, whom I had not the honour of knowing, to say, that as I am able to judge, his conduct was firm and decided to the promoting of the good of this country."

Mr. Willcox and Justice Thorpe were so intimately connected with the political affairs of the Province at the period of which I am writing, 1806-1807, that it is necessary to give some consideration to these two gentlemen, the one a member of Parliament and the other a judge, more particularly as the latter, at all events, had the opportunity and the inclination, both of which he exercised to the fullest extent, to excite the people to discontent and incipient rebellion. It is not by any means certain that either gentleman was an advocate of a separation of the Colony from the Mother Country, but their acts were such, that considering their official positions, the more unthinking of the people might easily be led to believe that such was their design. There were a good many Americans in the Province, who were but too willing to point to the conduct and sayings of those prominent individuals, as indicative of a desire on the part of the Colonial authorities themselves to change their allegiance.

Judge Thorpe, from the time he came to the Province to the time he left it, was at perpetual war with the Colonial authorities, and made himself most obnoxious to them. An examination of the correspondence, letters, papers and other documents, official and non-official, which are on file in the archives at Ottawa, and copies of which are to be found in the library of the County of York Law Association at Toronto, will enable a tolerably fair estimate to be made of the character of this gentleman, both as a judge and as a citizen. In truth he was much more of a politician than a judge, and had a natural bent for intrigue. If, after his appointment to a judgeship in the Colony, he had confined himself to official duties, he would have saved himself a great deal of trouble, the Government a great deal of annoyance, and the Province a great deal of discontent, a discontent roused by him to promote his own ends. It is to be presumed that the Government of England, in sending him out in the capacity of judge, considered that he was fitted for the office. His letters and correspondence show that he, at least, thought himself fit for the position he occupied, and that he was worthy of a higher position than that of puisne Judge of the Court of King's Bench, to which he was appointed. He had not been long in the Province when he aspired to be Chief Justice of the King's Bench, or failing that, the head of a Court of Chancery, which he wished to see established.

On the 5th March, 1806, Judge Thorpe wrote to his friend Edward Cooke, Under Secretary of State, a letter in which is contained the following passage, from which it is clear that he was apprehensive that Judge Scott would be promoted to the Chief Justiceship instead of himself: "Unless you wish to entail misery on the new Governor (Mr. Gore) let no representation induce Lord Castlereagh to do anything for Mr. McGill or Mr. Scott, until the Governor knows them and the present state of this Province.

"Mr. Allcock is appointed to Lower Canada. He became Chief Justice of this place from the seat I now fill on the Bench, but I do not press that as an inducement for Lord Castlereagh to place me there; I hope the knowledge I have shown in my profession, the exertion I have made for the Government, and the confidence the public have of my ability and integrity, will have its full weight with His Lordship, but if anything should induce him to disgrace me, by sending any one over me, I only beg you will intercede to have me removed, for to remain would kill me."

The judge speaks of the confidence "the public have of his ability and integrity." This confidence was imparted by political speeches made by him to Grand Juries when on circuit. In these speeches he was evidently paving the way for a candidature to the Legislative Assembly. In his remarks in making his address to juries, he had no scruple in attacking the Government in their administration, and not content with that, arraigned their capacity for governing at all. At the assizes of the London District he was favoured with an address from the Grand Jury of that District, and in answer he said among other things:—

"The act of governing is a difficult science, knowledge is not intuitive, and the days of inspiration have passed away; therefore when there was neither talent, education, information, or even manner in the administration, little could be expected and nothing was produced. But there is an ultimate point of depression as well as exaltation from whence all human affairs naturally advance or recede. Therefore, proportionate to your depression, we may expect your progress in prosperity will advance with accelerated velocity."

These addresses of the judge to Grand Juries and replies elicited by him were during the month of September, 1806, and evidently bore fruit. It is recorded in the journals that at a meeting of freeholders, held at Moore's Hotel, on the 20th October, 1806, for the purpose of considering of a proper person to represent them in Parliament, William Willcox, Esquire, in the chair, it was resolved unanimously, that Mr. Justice Thorpe be requested to represent the counties of York, Durham and Simcoe, in the place of the late lamented William Weeks, Esquire, deceased. Justice Thorpe accepted the nomination thus tendered, and was elected member of the House of Assembly. It is quite clear that Judge Thorpe was elected by the democracy of the counties named, that is by those who had been drawn into the belief that the Government of Upper Canada was too exclusive and not sufficiently democratic.

Mr. Thomas B. Gough was the opposing candidate, and after his defeat, under date of January 8th, 1807, he issued an address to the electors thanking them for the support they had given him, though unsuccessful, and said: "You went to the hustings, gentlemen, under the banners of liberty, loyalty and union, with hearts animated with pure love of King and Constitution, and many of you have proved your attachment thereto by shedding your blood in their support; but your opponents were preceded by the standard of discord, anarchy and rebellion, which in another part of the Empire has led thousands to a premature death," etc., etc.

To this address of Mr. Gough, the supporters of Judge Thorpe made answer, in which they defended themselves against the charge of discord and anarchy, referred to the loyal flags carried by them, inscribed with the King's Crown and initials G. R., "Freedom of election," the crown and harp, surrounded with the words "The King, the People, the Law, Thorpe and the Constitution," and then resolved: "That we know no discontented demagogues, nor if we did could not be deluded by them. Many of us have fought, bled and sacrificed our families and properties for the British Government; we have exerted and ever will exert ourselves to preserve the freedom of election from all undue influences, and to the last moment of our lives shall be ready to support our King and Constitution."

These deliverances abundantly prove that the real cause of difference between the parties was not on account of the Home Government, but rather the local Government of the Province. Proof also is afforded that Judge Thorpe had among his supporters United Empire Loyalists and others who claimed to be as loyal as those who were content with the existing order of things. There were many of the U. E. class who felt themselves under obligation to Judge Thorpe, for exertions he had made in their behalf at a former period, to obtain their grants for land, as compensation for the loss they had sustained in the service of the Crown.

Governor Gore had not so high an opinion of Judge Thorpe as had the electors of York, Simcoe and Durham.

In a conversation which he had with the Governor's Secretary on the 31st October, 1806, Judge Thorpe placed before him a list of certain grievances which he thought affected the body politic, the character of some of which may be gathered from the comments thereon made by the Governor and forwarded to England. The Governor said : "Truth is always consistent, but what can be said of a man who in the course of one conversation asserts that the people are so discontented, that it has been said, 'two hundred Americans might take the Province,' and a little after, that the 'people were extremely well disposed, and that the smallest coincidence with their wishes would do a great deal.' The plain English of all this is, let me dictate to you, and everything will go well. I, the people, though not the actual language is in reality a characteristic motto of Mr. Thorpe and every other factious demagogue."

To return to Judge Thorpe as a member of the Legislative Assembly. On the 9th February, 1807, a petition was presented to the House by electors of the Counties of Durham, Simcoe and East Riding of York against his return as member of those counties and riding, on the ground that he was ineligible, being a Judge of the King's Bench, "that the election of a judge to be a member of the Assembly was unconstitutional, inasmuch as being an attempt to clothe, arm and blend in one person the conflicting powers, authorities and jurisdiction of its legislative functions." On the 10th of February, 1807, the prayer of this petition was rejected by the House. Thus we have the spectacle presented of the Upper Canada Assembly recognizing the right of a judge to sit in Parliament, while in Lower Canada that right was denied to Judge de Bonne, who was expelled the Legislature. In Upper Canada the judge allowed to retain his seat was a violent opponent of the Government, while in Lower Canada the judge was a supporter of the Government, a French-Canadian, and expelled by the votes of his compatriots. Who then were the Liberals—the Parliamentary representatives of Quebec, or those of Upper Canada?

It is not necessary to discuss Mr. Thorpe at any greater length. His conduct was sure at some time to bring upon him the displeasure of the Governor and his Council, and even the Home Government.

On the 19th June, 1807, Lord Castlereagh, Prime Minister, addressed to Lieut.-Gov. Gore a letter in which he said, "The various particulars which you have stated of Mr. Justice Thorpe's having exceeded his duties as a judge by mixing in the political parties of the Province and encouraging an opposition to the administration, afforded such well grounded reasons for believing that his continuance in office would lead to the discredit and disservice of His Majesty's Government, that I am commanded to signify to you His Majesty's pleasure that you suspend Mr. Thorpe from the office of judge in Upper Canada, and measures will be taken for appointing a successor."

In the same communication Lord Castlereagh took occasion to say that he might be able, "to recommend

Judge Thorpe to some other professional situation under an assurance that he will confine himself to the duties of this profession hereafter, and abstain from engaging in Provincial party politics."

The careers of Joseph Willcox, sheriff, and of Judge Thorpe as politicians were of an extraordinary character. Both were officials of the Government, and yet were strong adversaries of that Government. Both came from the Old Country, no doubt to improve their positions, and yet waged war with the Colonial authorities. It is too late in the day to recognize in the old Canadian Colonial Government, under the Act of 1791, a system of government most conducive to British liberty. The acts of both Justice Thorpe and Mr. Willcox may have been instigated by a desire to improve the system of Colonial Government then existent, but unfortunately in their case, especially in the case of the former, they had the appearance of being instigated by personal ambition and party spite. If Judge Thorpe had been made Chief Justice it might have been that his better nature would have dominated, and himself and the colony spared much anxiety and political excitement. The country survived the judge's deposition. Governor Gore, whom he made his enemy, in 1811 left the Province for England on temporary leave of absence, leaving the affairs of the Province in charge of Major General Brock, who had too many military duties to attend to to concern himself about political affairs, except so far as was necessary to maintain the honour and dignity of the Province.

CHAPTER V.

U. S. Declaration of War Against Great Britain, 1812—French Canadians and English-Canadians at One in Defending Canada—American Hopes Built on Canadian Disappointments—The War of 1812, its Lessons and Consequences—Sir George Prevost, his Administration—A Party in Opposition to Government—Louis Joseph Papineau Elected Speaker of Assembly of L. C.—His Great Ability—Sir John Sherbrooke, Governor of Lower Canada—Concessions to the Province—The Duke of Richmond Succeeds Sherbrooke—Napoleon and Waterloo—The Duke of Richmond Offends the Lower Canadian Assembly—The Duke's Death in Canada—Louis J. Papineau Delivers a Thoroughly British Speech to Electors in Montreal—Claim of L. C. Assembly—Legislative Council and Assembly at Loggerheads—Colonial Office Endeavours to Heal Differences—Constitution of 1791 Threatened—Re-Union of Provinces Agitated—Bill Brought into House of Commons—Bill Rejected—Lord Dalhousie's Administration—Governor's Refusal to Recognize Papineau as Speaker.

WITH the opening of 1812, war's alarm is sounded and British, British-Canadians and French-Canadians march shoulder to shoulder to the conflict. The Americans may have secured their independence with the aid of Lafayette, but notwithstanding the seeds of dissension which had been sown among them by interested republicans from across the border, the Canadians of all classes were determined to defend their country to the last extremity.

The United States Government declared war against Great Britain on the 18th June, 1812, relying no doubt on the assistance they might expect to get from France in 1812, as they had previously had in the war of the Revolution, as also, because they were aware, as Mr. Robert Christie has well said in his History of Lower Canada, "that recent events had soured the temper of the great body of the French-Canadian population, and the American Government built upon the circumstance, expecting that far from opposing, they would hail the invaders of Canada as their deliverers."

That they built their hopes of conquering Canada on an insecure foundation, so far as assistance from the French-Canadians was concerned, is made manifest from the alacrity with which the French-Canadians pledged the resources of their Province for the public defence. The session before the actual declaration of war by the United States was opened by the Governor, Sir George Prevost, on the 21st February, 1812. The Parliament at once set about preparing for the defence of the Province. Twelve thousand pounds were granted for drilling the local militia, twenty thousand pounds for incidental measures of defence, while a further sum of thirty thousand pounds was placed at the Governor's disposal should war be declared between Great Britain and the United States.

Taking into account the fact that the total revenue of the Province was seventy-five thousand pounds, charged with the expenses of the civil list of fifty-nine thousand pounds, the war defence fund was a splendid contribution by the Province of Lower Canada. More than this, when it became known at Quebec on the 24th June, 1812, that Congress had actually declared war, a Provincial Statute was at once passed to legalize the issue of army bills, to the amount of two hundred and fifty thousand pounds, in order to replenish the public exchequer, and an annual grant of fifteen thousand pounds made for five years, to pay whatever interest might accrue. On the 6th July, 1812, the whole Militia of the Province had been directed to hold themselves in readiness to be embodied, while the flank companies of the Montreal Militia were formed into a battalion and armed.

These acts of public spirit and beneficence afford an object lesson to all, that it is not safe to trust to political differences which exist, and will doubtless continue to exist in Canada, as a permission to foreign nations to make war upon a peace-loving people. In the war of 1812, the Canadians, French and English, acquitted themselves nobly, and under skilful commanders were able to transfer their country to their descendants unscathed, purified by the blood of patriotic men of both nationalities, shed in its defence.

It should be noticed that Sir George Prevost, the Governor General and Commander-in-Chief, throughout the war had, by his liberality towards the French element in Lower Canada, aroused the ire of the ultra-British element of that Province. In acting as he did, however, he had a purpose in view, in which he succeeded. This was to gain the entire confidence of the French-Canadians, so necessary at a time when every man was required to do his part in defence of the Province.

During the war domestic strife was buried in the performance of public duty. The war ended in 1814. As may be supposed, the Canadas, Upper and Lower, were much exhausted by the strain that had been placed upon them. Leaving out of account the lives that had been lost in the struggle, there was much else to mourn over. Fields were untilled, houses were unbuilt, improvements neglected, and the country generally deprived of nourishment, the product of honest labour.

It behooved, then, the survivors of the war to set about building up what had been pulled down, and to place their country in a position to compete with other nations in progress and advancement.

Both the Provinces of Upper and Lower Canada had shared in the perils of the war. It will now be our task to see how they vied with each other in their onward march in the paths of peace and development. We have seen in previous chapters that before the commencement of the war, there was a wide difference of opinion among the inhabitants of Lower Canada as to the excellence of the Colonial administration of government, and that in Upper Canada there had begun to be formed a party in direct opposition to the Government.

In the session of the Lower Canada Legislature, which assembled on the 16th January, 1817, M. Panet having been called to the Upper House, Mr. Louis Joseph Papineau was elected Speaker of the Assembly. Louis Joseph Papineau's father had been an ardent supporter of the British Government in its rule over Lower Canada. He himself was no less an admirer of the British system of government, but was at the same time opposed to the Colonial government, which was not in his opinion a fit representation of the mother government. He held indeed that it was a government which had to be pruned of its useless branches, or else the trunk would fall to the ground. The members elected to the Legislature were of his opinion and shared his sentiments, which, added to his commanding ability, signalled him out as the most worthy successor of M. Panet, but lately appointed to the Legislative Council.

Sir John Coape Sherbrooke had at this time succeeded to the Governorship of the Province. He made himself very popular in Lower Canada by the lively interest he took in the affairs of the Province. Early frosts having destroyed the wheat crops of the Province, so that starvation threatened many parishes, he took the responsibility of advancing from the public chest a sum of nearly fifteen thousand pounds for the relief of the distressed. The Assembly on its meeting made this good to him, and at the same time acceded to his recommendation to vote £1,000 per annum to Mr. Speaker Papineau during that Parliament.

In this way complete harmony was established between the Governor and the Assembly. In the meanwhile much progress was being made in Lower Canada in the development of civil government. The Colonial office had by this time become convinced that it was necessary to make some concessions to the popular feeling of the Province. Sir John Sherbrooke, on opening the Provincial Legislature of 1818, was enabled to inform the Assembly that its former offer to defray the expenses of the civil list had been accepted by the Home Government. The Assembly welcomed this concession as a great boon, and voted three thousand pounds towards the expenses of the civil government. By this means they acquired some control over Government officials, who, hitherto basking in the sunshine of Government favour, were becoming arrogant and offensive to the French-Canadian part of the community.

Before the close of the year, Sir John Sherbrooke returned to England on the plea of ill health. His departure was signalized by a most ostentatious show of regret on the part of the people of the Province, both French and English. Though in the estimation of the British part of the population he had leaned more than was to their liking to the French-Canadians, they nevertheless did him honour. As a soldier he had distinguished himself in the British service in India, and had served under Wellington in the Peninsula. The British inhabitants of the Colony were too generous to allow even a fault of administration, if it were a fault, to prevent them doing honour to His Majesty's Representative in a Province which ever since its inauguration had, owing to racial difficulties, been a source of constant concern to those clothed with authority, both at home and in the Colony.

Sir John Sherbrooke was succeeded in the government by the Duke of Richmond, who came to the Province with the prestige of having been Lord Lieutenant of Ireland. This is the same Duke of Richmond, who the night before the battle of Waterloo, gave a ball at Brussels, which was attended by the flower of the military then at Belgium's capital and in its vicinity, awaiting the attack of Napoleon Bonaparte on the allied forces of Britain and Prussia, who were combined in defending the liberties of Europe. Many a brave heart that beat strong that night, beat no more after the sanguinary engagement at Waterloo.

This was the ball that Byron has commemorated in the well-known lines in "Childe Harold."

When he arrived in Canada as Governor-General, the Duke was accompanied by Sir Peregrine Maitland, his son-in-law, who had been appointed Lieutenant Governor of Upper Canada.

The people of Lower Canada thought that in being honoured with a Duke for ruler they had been ushered into the presence of Royalty itself. The Duke endeavoured to make himself and his administration agreeable to the people he had come to govern. He brought with him to the Province a large retinue, and was disposed to rule the country in truly princely fashion. The French-Canadians, who predominated, were disappointed in their expectations of the Duke in the matter of government, and were struck with amazement at this extravagant pretension. The Duke was not a thrifty man; on the contrary, he had by lavish expenditure well nigh impoverished himself, and from a French-Canadian point of view would impoverish the Province of Lower Canada if the native element did not interfere on behalf of the Province.

On the meeting of the Assembly on the 12th January, 1819, that body was startled at finding that in the estimated expenditure of the year sent down by the Government there was a large increase over previous years. The Duke was soon apprised that the Assembly could not justify to their constituents any increase whatever of the expenditure. On the contrary, the Assembly was for a rigid economy and decrease of expenditure. The Assembly was not in a mood at this time to leave the making of the civil list to the Government of the day. They were contending for a complete control of the list, even so far as to fixing the amount to be paid to each individual engaged in the civil service. This was too serious a claim for the Government to submit to with equanimity, and on a subsidy bill passing the Assembly in the shape that that body demanded, namely specifying the sum to be paid to each officer of the Governor for his services, the bill was promptly rejected by the Legislative Council who declared, "that the mode adopted in it (the Legislative Assembly) was unconstitutional, unparalleled and incompatible with the rights, even in direct violation of the prerogatives of the Crown." This language seems strange at the present day when we know that the popular branch of the Legislature has absolute control over the public expenditure.

It had been the settled policy of the British Government to maintain a check on the French-Canadians, through the agency of the Legislative Council. Thus, Lord Bathurst, in the previous year, 1817, discussing the matter of the finances of Lower Canada with Sir James Sherbrooke, the then Governor, had said: "The necessity of a concurrence of the whole Legislature in a money grant is the only tight curb which can be put on the action of the Assembly. You will agree with me in opinion, that now more than ever, it should not be relaxed or abandoned."

The Duke of Richmond approved of the action of the Legislative Council in thwarting the Assembly's bill of supplies and on proroguing Parliament took occasion to censure the Assembly, while commending the Council for the steps taken by that body in rejecting the supply bill. To the two bodies he said: "As for you, gentlemen of the Council, I must say you have not disappointed my hopes, and I beg to return you my thanks for the zeal and alacrity you have shown in all that more immediately belongs to your body, but it is with much concern I feel myself compelled to say, that I cannot express to you, gentlemen of the Assembly, the same satisfaction, nor my approbation of the general result of your labours (at the expense of so much valuable time), nor yet of the principles upon which they rest, as recorded in your journals. . . . The bill of appropriation which you passed, was founded upon such principles that it appears, from the journals of the Upper House, to have been most constitutionally rejected."

This address of the Duke gave great offence to the French-Canadians. The distinguishing between the relative merits of the Council and Assembly expressed in the address was well calculated to annoy the sensitive French-Canadians, and they were loud in their condemnation of the ducal utterances.

Notwithstanding the Duke's lecture, he was willing to accord to Lower Canada his meed of praise for their loyalty to the Sovereign of Great Britain. He wrote to Lord Bathurst, Colonial Minister, that the people of Lower Canada were satisfied with their Constitution; and that perfect reliance might be placed in their loyalty, should the United States ever invade the Colony.

The Duke of Richmond lost his life in Canada. He died at Richmond, a village not far from Ottawa, where he succumbed to injuries brought about by the bite of a tame fox. His body was interred at Richmond, and was afterwards removed to the citadel of Quebec, where his bones now repose. His reign was a short one, brilliant in the eyes of the English-speaking inhabitants of the Province, but too magnificent to be altogether satisfactory to the French-Canadians. Owing to his sudden death the administration of the government devolved on the senior member of the Council, who dissolved the Assembly on the 9th February, 1820.

It was found on the meeting of the next Parliament that the French-Canadian element in the Province had by their votes resented the insult, or supposed insult, offered to the members of the last Assembly, and that the *habitants* had returned to the new Assembly a majority of members who had declared themselves opposed to the Executive Council.

The demise of George III., news of which reached Quebec in April, caused another dissolution of the Parliament, followed by an election held under the administration of Lord Dalhousie, appointed to succeed the Duke of Richmond as Governor of the Province. This election was chiefly remarkable for a speech delivered to the electors of the West Ward of Montreal by Mr. Louis Joseph Papineau, which shows how Mr. Papineau then appreciated his status as a British subject, and for the comparison he made between British rule and French rule. Mr. Papineau said: "Then," (referring to the French regime) "trade was monopolised by privileged companies, public and private property often pillaged, personal liberty daily violated, and the inhabitants dragged year after year from their homes and families to shed their blood from the shores of the great lakes, from the banks of the Mississippi and the Ohio, to Nova Scotia, Newfoundland and Hudson Bay. Now, religious toleration, trial by jury, the Act of Habeas Corpus afford legal and equal security to all, and we need submit to no other laws but those of our making. All these advantages have become our birthright, and shall, I hope, be the lasting inheritance of our posterity. To secure them, let us only act as British subjects and free men."

How strange do these words sound in our ears, knowing as we do that before two decades were over, Papineau was a leader in rebellion against the Government of the country. Papineau was the undoubted leader of the French party in the Province of Lower Canada. He had been elected Speaker in the last Assembly. He was now again elected to the House, notwithstanding the opposition of the Government party.

Every new Governor who came to Lower Canada was furnished with instructions to carry out the same course as his predecessor; that course was to resist all attempts on the part of the Assembly to obtain control of the civil list, the public expenditure of the country. The address of Lord Dalhousie on opening the Legislature elicited from the Assembly a clear exposition of their position in regard to the civil list. They claimed absolute and unequivocal control over the entire list, not recognizing the Government's claim to share in the control of any part of it. They claimed that the Governor had no constitutional right to dictate to their body how the civil list should be made up, or for how long a time voted. They demanded that the appropriations should be annual, and not for the life of the Sovereign, as was contended for by the king's representative. They insisted that they, and not the Governor or Council, had the right to initiate the bill of supplies.

As might be supposed, these claims of the Assembly were all rejected by the Legislative Council, as wholly untenable and unconstitutional, if not revolutionary. The Council not only rejected the civil list prepared by the Assembly, and voted by that body, but in doing so proclaimed their right to exercise a full and entire control over the public expenditure. They said "That the Council had an incontestible right to join in voting the supplies; that the right extended to the option of accepting or rejecting the ways and means devised by the Assembly and sent for the consideration of the Council; that any grant of money without the Council's concurrence was in itself literally null; that the Council would entertain no enumeration of supplies till such were first demanded by His Majesty's representative, nor if it were divided into chapters and items, nor if the civil list were not fixed for the whole reign of the king. Finally, that the Council would pay no heed to any bill of supply initiated by the Assembly, unless it were one relating to payments for its own maintenance, as a constituted body, or else to meet some unforeseen and urgent call upon it."

There was thus a complete issue between the Assembly and the Council. The Council would not yield to the Assembly, nor the Assembly to the Council. The Governor sided with the Council, as he could not help doing, carrying out the general instructions he had received for the performance of his duty as chief executive officer of the Colony. As has been said before, it was the constant policy of the Colonial office to keep control over the disbursements necessary to be made in the management of the affairs of the Province, and this was done through the channels of the Lieutenant Governor and Legislative Council.

The Council did not hesitate to accuse the Assembly of sedition and seditious practices, for their attempts to resist the demands of their honourable body, and the Governor was inclined to share with the Council the sentiments which they entertained towards the popular branch.

This state of things could not be allowed to continue for a very long time. The friction between the Assembly and the Council had now reached that stage that some remedy must be found to cure the evil. The Colonial office set about the task. In discussing the matters of differences between the Council and the Assembly it was found that they were irreconcilable. It was further found that differences had sprung up between Upper Canada and Lower Canada arising out of the claim of

Upper Canada to a larger portion of the customs revenue than Lower Canada was willing to concede. The only cure of these differences seemed to be a revocation of the Canadian Constitution of the year 1791, and the re-union of the Provinces. The British Government resolved to execute this project and introduced to the Parliament a bill to effect that object, but this coming to the ears of the French Canadians they strongly remonstrated, and the bill was withdrawn.

The circumstances connected with this attempt at re-union of the Provinces might almost be called romantic. The idea of such a re-union had for some time engaged the attention of the Colonial office in London, but did not come to a head till 1823. The Anglo-Canadian population of the Province had the ear of the Governor, and brought such influences to bear that the measure had the almost undivided support of the British party of the community. The object in view was, by a union with Upper Canada, to neutralize the attempts being made by the French-Canadians to render the carrying out of the existing constitution impracticable. Now there was at this time in the Province of Lower Canada one man who had great influence with the British residents, as well as with the British ministry. That man was Mr. Ellice, the seignior of Beauharnois, who had for a wife a daughter of Earl Grey.

In 1820, Mr. Ellice had almost persuaded the British Cabinet to propose the measure to the British Parliament.

The measure itself was one which could not help meeting violent opposition from the French-Canadian party in the Province, as soon as it became known such a bill was to be introduced into the House of Commons. It gave to Lower Canada a smaller representation than to the Upper Province, notwithstanding the large majority of French-Canadians over the Anglo-Canadians in the former Province. It vested in the Council the privilege of taking part in the discussions of the Assembly, thus giving to that body a mixed nominative and elective character. It abolished the use of the French language in the debates and public acts of the Legislature, and limited the religious liberty and rights of the Catholic Church, or let it rather be said the rights and privileges claimed by the Catholic Church. It retained the right of the Assembly touching the disposal of revenue derived from taxes.

When this measure was introduced to the British Commons there was in England a Mr. Parker, a trader, who in his ventures in trade, had become acquainted with the French-Canadians' susceptibilities; he was then living in retirement in England. He lost no time in acquainting the Colonial office that such an act would be most obnoxious to the French-Canadians, and imputed its introduction to the work of Mr. Ellice. He only asked time for Canada to be heard from. The Colonial office was deaf to his remonstrances, but the measure coming before the Commons, Sir James McIntosh and his political friends espoused the cause of the French-Canadians, and the bill was shelved for a year at all events.

When it became known in the Province that such a bill had been introduced, the excitement of the French-Canadians knew no bounds. It expressed itself in meetings got up to oppose the bill, in public and private remonstrances, and in petitions, containing 60,000 signatures, sent to the Colonial Office and the British Parliament, couched in respectful language but loudly protesting against the proposed legislation. These petitions were confided to Messrs. Papineau and Neilson, who went to England to lay them before the proper bodies. This was during the recess of the Lower Canadian Assembly. In its next session that body proceeded at once to pass strong resolutions against the measure.

As to Upper Canada, it was also strongly opposed to the union. The people of that Province, on the whole, were contented with the Constitutional Act of 1791. There were some discontented spirits of the Thorpe type, but the majority were content to live under the Constitution, though perhaps they were not given by it that measure of liberty enjoyed in the old land, and which new-comers to the Province, not distinguishing between a parent state and a colony, would have wished to see in the Province.

Even the Legislative Council of Lower Canada joined in hostility to the Bill, and sent addresses to Messrs. Papineau and Neilson for transmission to the King and House of Parliament against the measure. This was the only occasion for a long time in which the Legislative Council and the Assembly, though for entirely different reasons, met on common ground. The Councillors were opposed to the bill because, if it passed, their hold on the Government would be disturbed; the Assembly, because the passage of the bill would have threatened their very existence. Thus opposed, the measure for a time received its quietus in the House of Commons, but only for a time, as at a later day it was revived in a different form, and at length gained the assent of the British Parliament.

The next session of the Lower Canada Legislature met in November, 1823. Lord Dalhousie then found it to be his duty to inform the Chambers that the Receiver-General was a defaulter to the extent of £96,000, equal to two years' revenue of the colony.

It was found on enquiry that the officer in question had been appointed to his responsible office without any security having been exacted for the faithful performance of his duties. His appointment was by the Home, not the Colonial Government. Here was a fresh grievance made to hand, justifying the Colonial Assembly in the war they had made on the Colonial Government in regard to the appointment of Colonial officials. The Assembly, as we have seen, was constantly demanding the control of the civil list, the appointment of officers to carry on the government, their incomes and tenure of office; while this was as constantly resisted by the Legislative Council and the Governor, acting no doubt under instructions of the Colonial Office. The defalcation of the

Receiver-General being brought under notice of the House, a committee of that body declared the Home Government responsible for the malversation in office of the functionary.

As was to be expected, this mishap again brought up the question of the civil list. When the estimates were brought down, the Assembly, under the leadership of Mr. Papineau, rejected the Government proposals, and demanded a reduction of twenty-five per cent. in all salaries, which not being acceded to, they stopped the supplies and left the Government to carry on public affairs as best they could. This was a sorry position for the Government. The moneys they ought to have received from the Receiver-General unaccounted for, the Colonial treasury empty, and the Assembly unwilling to come to the rescue, there was nothing for it but that the Governor prorogue Parliament, which he did on the 9th of March, 1824.

Soon after the close of the session, Lord Dalhousie returned to England. In the ensuing summer the Provincial Parliamentary election was held, and served only to increase the number of members elected in opposition to the Government. This election took place under the presidency of Sir F. Burton, who took the place of Lord Dalhousie in the administration of the government while the latter was absent in England. It was hoped now that with the change of Governors there would come a change of policy. Sir F. Burton did the best he could to reconcile the Assembly to the Government and partially succeeded. He even so far conceded to their demands as to submit a civil list and estimates in such a shape that the Assembly could criticize its items, and allow or reject them as circumstances might require.

Lord Dalhousie returned to his official duties as Governor in January, 1826, and the temporary peace which reigned during Sir F. Burton's administration was broken up soon after Lord Dalhousie returned to the Government. There was, however, a lull during the first session after his return. The Colonial Office in June, 1825, by a despatch to the acting Governor Burton gave him to understand that what he had done in regard to the estimates, recognizing some right of control in the Assembly, might be allowed for that session but must not occur again. Lord Dalhousie being made aware of those instructions had no alternative but to carry out the policy of the Home Government. The Assembly in its next session attempted to pass the supplies in the same manner as under Sir F. Burton, but met with a rebuff, the Legislative Council absolutely refusing to sanction them in that form. The result was that the supplies were not granted.

The next day after the refusal of the supplies Lord Dalhousie prorogued Parliament, and in addressing the two Houses, following the example of the Duke of Richmond on a former occasion, he made it a point to discriminate between the two Houses, the Legislative Council and Assembly.

"I have come," said he, "to bring to a close this session of the Provincial Parliament, being convinced that nothing likely to promote the public interest can now be expected from your deliberations. To you, gentlemen of the Legislative Council, who have attended to your duties in this session, I offer my thanks on the part of His Majesty, as an acknowledgment of the regard which by your presence you have shown to the welfare of your country, and also of that proper respect which you have manifested to the Sovereign from whom your honours are derived. Gentlemen of the Assembly, it is painful to me that I cannot speak my sentiments to you in terms of approbation and thanks. Many years of continued discussion of forms and accounts have proved unavailing to clear up and set at rest a dispute which moderation and reason might have speedily terminated."

This address by the Governor of course gave offence to the Assembly and members of that body. Mr. Papineau, in the lead, thought it necessary to issue a counter-address to the electors, censuring the Governor and justifying their refusal of supplies. The newspapers at this period became very violent in their language, the Government and Opposition papers hurling epithets at each other with a freedom worthy of Billingsgate fish-wives. Some of the French-Canadians affected to believe that the Government contemplated reducing the compatriots to the position of slaves worse than Spartan helots. These patriots were not content to use the Provincial press for the airing of their grievances, but must forsooth send forth their fulminations from foreign soil. It is in evidence that the patriots aforesaid were at the time not actually resident in the Province, but rather that they had betaken themselves to the State of New York. There they established a newspaper, at Plattsburgh in that State, and gave it the name, *L'Ami du Peuple*, a favourite name for those who place their faith in democracy and republican government. Here is a specimen of the writing in that paper: "Canadians, chains are forging for you; it now appears that you are doomed to annihilation, or to be ruled with a sceptre of iron. Your liberties are invaded, your rights violated, your privileges abolished, your reclamations contemned, your political existence threatened with utter ruin. Now is the time to manifest your strength, to display your energy, and to convince the Mother Country and the horde which, for half a century, has played the tyrant's part among your homesteads, that if ye be subjects, ye are not slaves."

It would be interesting to know whether the editor of *L'Ami du Peuple* was an American or a Gallo-Canadian—more probably the former, a wolf in sheep's clothing. Past action and subsequent events prove that the border men of the United States are ever too ready to foment the troubles of the dissatisfied citizens of Canada, hoping to profit by their success.

Lord Dalhousie's prorogation of the Parliament was followed by a dissolution of the Assembly. It was an appeal to the electorate to confirm or condemn the withholding of the supplies. It shows how strong was the faith of the Canadian people in their leaders that the French-Canadian representatives to Parliament were sent back to the House, the majority against the Government being increased rather than diminished. This by no means proves that the Governor was wrong and the constituent body right. As a matter of fact, the Governor was right, as he was but carrying out the policy of the Home Government and the instructions of his superiors. The *habitants*, however, were not concerned about Home Governments and instructions. All they knew or cared to know was that the system that prevailed and the Colonial administration of affairs were not in accordance with the principle that majorities should govern. The *Canadian Spectator*, a Lower Canada journal, commenting on the elections, while they were still in progress, said: "The elections are nearly over; the friends of our King, country and Constitution have achieved a signal victory. The functionaries of Lord Dalhousie and his whole government system have been practically condemned generally and formally."

It is difficult to understand how the *Spectator* could call the opposers of the Government friends of the Constitution, when we reflect that the Governor was only performing his duty in carrying out the Constitution. If the Constitution were at fault, it was not his fault. However, the turn the elections had taken afforded a good opportunity for uttering a philippic against the Governor, and it was seized upon with avidity. One cannot but express a feeling of sympathy with the Governor. Here was an officer of much distinction placed in the position of governing a Province under a Constitution which subjected him to the appearance, if not actuality, of always being at war with the people, while it may be that his sympathies may always have been with those who were clamorous for reforms in the government. Lord Dalhousie's subsequent administration in India shows that he was a man most worthy of his Sovereign's favour.

Lord Dalhousie was not the people's favourite, their compatriot Papineau was. The time had now come to try a fall with this gentleman. In the new House the question of Speakership necessarily arose. The Governor would have preferred that Papineau of all men should not have been elected President of the Assembly. The Governor's wishes, however, were not in the least regarded. The Assembly, rightly, no doubt, considered themselves an independent body, and in making choice of the mouthpiece of the House cast their votes almost unanimously for Mr. Papineau. Mr. Papineau with several others had since the prorogation of the House issued a manifesto on public affairs, in which, not content with giving voice to his political opinions and condemnation of the Government, he very unadvisedly made a bitter and unwarranted personal attack upon the Governor. In his individual capacity Lord Dalhousie could have overlooked this attack, but as His Majesty's Representative in the Province he felt bound to resent it in the most marked and public manner. The Governor now regarded Mr. Papineau as a fomenter of discord, as a disturber of the public peace, as an enemy seeking to destroy the props by which the Government was upheld. When the House presented Mr.

Papineau to the Governor as their Speaker, on His Excellency going down to open Parliament, the Governor refused to recognize him.

The Assembly returned crestfallen, but not beaten. They in confidence determined that if the Governor desired to address the House should do so with Papineau as their Speaker, or not at all. The Governor absolutely refused to open Parliament while Papineau was Speaker, and no compromise being effected or offered immediately prorogued the House, the British part of the population highly commending him for this act of firmness in dealing with the leader of what was considered by them a rebellious party.

These proceedings produced a large crop of addresses to the British Parliament and to the Home Government from the partisans of both sides of the House. The French-Canadians were accused of sedition, the Government party of tyranny. Violent diatribes were renewed in the public press, and the Province was in the throes of a political revolution. Agents were sent to England by both parties to represent their various views to the British Government.

When the addresses were laid before the House of Commons there opened a field day for the discussion of Canadian affairs. The Canadian Constitution and its administration came under review in the Commons in a manner refreshing to those who were desirous of ripping to pieces the Colonial system. Mr. Hume was specially aggressive; he warmly espoused the cause of the French-

Canadians. Mr. Hume was seconded by Mr. Labouchere, a member of the Commons of French descent. His attack was more on the administration of the Constitution than on the Constitution itself. He said: "I look upon the act of 1791 as the Magna Charta of Canadian freedom. I am of the opinion that if the intentions of Pitt and his coadjutors had been better followed out by those who came after him and them, Lower Canada would have attained to that height of prosperity they destined for that Province; and that it would at this hour be in the enjoyment of the concord and tranquillity its connection with Britain must have assured."

Mr. Huskisson, Government Minister, recognizing that there was a crisis in Lower Canada, felt it necessary to propose that a Committee of the House should be nominated to enquire into the condition of the two Canadas. He, at the same time, took occasion to defend the Constitution, though he did so in a rather apologetic manner. He said: "There may be many defects in the Colonial Constitution; but this was inevitable at the epoch of the initiation; and it is not at all to be wondered at, that imperfections should exist in that Constitution, although it was drawn up by the greatest contemporary statesman of Britain."

The Committee appointed on the motion of Mr. Huskisson had before it the various addresses to Parliament, and besides a petition from traders in London asking for a re-union of the Provinces of Lower and Upper Canada. After due deliberation the Committee reported, but in such a manner as to be satisfactory to no one. Lord Dalhousie condemned it as being too favourable to the French-Canadians, while the French-Canadians, thankful for some concessions, were not contented because they did not get more. The result was that nothing came of the report. Matters were left to drift along in the old way. The Colonial office exercised supreme control. Lord Dalhousie left the Province and was appointed Commandant of the forces of India. The Lieutenant Governor of Nova Scotia, Sir James Kempt, was transferred to Lower Canada and the wheels of government once more set moving under his administration.

CHAPTER VI.

Governor Gore's Second Term—War of 1812 and Its Rewards—
Slow Fulfilment—Robert Fleming Gourlay—His Life in Canada
and his Trials—He was Strong, Impetuous, Honest in his
Convictions—His Advocacy of Immigration—He Calls a Convention to Discuss Canadian Affairs—Indicted for Seditious
Libel—Twice Tried, Twice Acquitted—Finally Expelled from
the Province on Other Grounds—His Address to the King—
Imprisoned in England—Return to America—Declines to Support Mackenzie's Rebellion—Subsequent Life—Sir Peregrine
Maitland, Governor—His Administration—A Tory House—
Liberal Measures—Barnabas Bidwell Elected to Parliament—
His Subsequent Expulsion—Marshall S. Bidwell Elected—Prominent Figure in the Rebellion of 1837—William Lyon Mackenzie,
his Birth, Parentage and Early Life—Mackenzie's Politics—His
Arraignment of the Governor and its Consequences—His Banishment Advocated.

In the year 1811 Lieutenant Governor Gore left Upper Canada for England on temporary leave of absence. He did not return to the Province till after the war. Governor Gore had not been long in the Province, after his second assumption of the duties of government, when he found that the body politic was in a less friendly frame of mind than he had anticipated. The loyalists of the Province had nobly acquitted themselves in the war which their kinsmen of the United States had waged against them, but the honours and rewards, which they believed themselves entitled to, were slow in coming, and might possibly never reach them. The Volunteers and Militia had been promised grants of land, but for some reason the patents were withheld, and the people murmured and denounced the Government in no stinted terms. Besides this there was no longer that large expenditure of money which had been made during the war. The people would almost rather the war had continued than to find themselves reduced to a comparative state of poverty by the peace. There was no immigration, no trade, no commerce. The people would gladly have welcomed immigrants from the country with which they had been at war, rather than to be without their capital and their enterprise. The Government had set its face against grants of land being made to Americans, and indeed was opposed to Americans even being admitted into the country.

This was the state of things when the Legislature met in 1817. The Assembly after meeting lost no time in going into committee to take into consideration the state of the Province. The feeling which prevailed among the people in regard to the matters of which they complained had its reflex in the Legislature. Resolutions on these subjects were submitted to the House, and the Government was about to be called to account. This did not suit the views of the Lieutenant Governor or his Council. In reviewing the proceedings of the Lower Canada Legislature, we have seen how common it was for a Governor when the Assembly became too independent or outspoken to prorogue, and in some instances to dissolve the House.

Governor Gore followed this precedent in Upper Canada. When he found that the Assembly had the temerity to threaten to probe into the affairs of government, he prorogued the House in a curt speech of three paragraphs.

The members of the House of Assembly of Upper Canada were not the men to submit to be treated contemptuously by any man, though that man should occupy the position of Governor of the Province and be the Monarch's Representative. It no doubt galled the Governor to find the people's agents so independent, but then it is to be remembered they were independent in a good cause. The lands which they had fairly earned by their services in the war were withheld. The Clergy Reserve lands, one-seventh of the lands of the Province, were withheld from settlement. Favourites of Government and the ruling party were accused of securing grants of wild lands, holding them for speculative purposes. The settlement of the country was retarded and there was great discontent.

At this time there crossed the sea for Canada, a Scotchman, the son of a lawyer (but not himself bred to the law), who took advantage of a proclamation inviting emigrants to settle in Upper Canada, for the improvement of their condition.

Robert Fleming Gourlay, born in Fifeshire between 1780 and 1784, was a remarkable man. Endowed with great natural abilities, he had not arrived at the age of twenty-one years when he was employed by the Government to enquire into the condition of the English poor and suggest a remedy for prevailing distress. This was in about the first year of the century, when great poverty afflicted the people of the British Isles.

He made a report, which led to a bill being introduced in the House by the President of the Board of Agriculture, which, however, was thrown out.

After this Gourlay seems to have taken up the rôle of agitator in his own land, and took up the cause of the people against the landlords and the Church. In 1808, according to his own statement, he took up the cause of the farmers against the Lairds of Fife. In 1809, he published an appeal for Parliamentary reform, and in 1815, attacked the Church property, demonstrating, to his own satisfaction, at least, that Church property was the property of the people, and in the same year, as he says, posted the Bath Society as rogues for deserting the commutation of tithes. He rented a farm from the Duke of Somerset in Wiltshire, and seems to have been an advanced student of agriculture and to have been fairly prosperous.

Having acquired some land in Upper Canada, in 1817, he determined to make a visit to the country, intending to be away about six months. Arrived at Quebec he travelled through Upper Canada and New York State, and resolved to establish a land agency for his own benefit and promote emigration. He had not been long in the Province before he became convinced that the existing system of government, or rather the administration of it, retarded the settlement of the Province. The govern-

ADVOCATES IMMIGRATION.

ment of the Province, which was largely in the hands of the original settlers, was opposed to free grants. If immigration increased there would be a demand for grants of Crown lands, while those who had the control of public affairs preferred to have control of the lands also, and sell their own lands to the people who came to the country with means to buy, which was not the class of immigration Gourlay had in view.

There were many land agents in the Province, many of whom were employed to look after soldiers' claims, and U. E. rights, as they were called. This consisted in securing for the United Empire Loyalists the lands to which they were entitled under King George III. bounty for losses occasioned by the War of the Revolution. Mr. Gourlay was shrewd enough to observe that this kind of business might be made remunerative. He set about acquiring a knowledge of the national resources of the Province and the wants and wishes of the people. He prepared, at the cost of much labour, a compilation called "Statistical Account of Upper Canada, with a view to a grand system of Emigration." This book of several hundred pages must have cost him much time as well as labour. He was indefatigable. Some people might say, and some people did say—as is generally said of men with an idea—that he had a "bee in his bonnet," especially on this subject of emigration.

When he found that the Governor had prorogued the Legislature, and for the reason, as was thought, that the Assembly was too free in criticizing the land policy of the

Government, Gourlay conceived the idea of calling delegates from all parts of the Province to meet in convention "to deliberate upon the propriety of sending commissioners to England to call attention to the affairs of the Province." If Mr. Gourlay had been a man of judgment, or had understood the people of Canada, he could not have done a more harmful thing to himself or his reputation than propose a convention. The very name of "convention" was odious to Canadian ears. It was a mode of procedure so much in favour with the rebels in the Colonies before the American Revolution of 1776 that anything in the shape of convention or congress was considered insulting to a Canadian community, and their promoters hostile to the best interests of the country.

Mr. Gourlay, in promoting his immigration scheme, addressed to the farmers throughout the country a circular containing a number of queries with a view of ascertaining the probabilities of success, if immigrants on his recommendation should determine to take up lands in the Province. One of the questions calculated to bring answers that the people favoured emigration was this: "What in your opinion retards the improvement of your township in particular or the Province in general, and what would most contribute to the same?" This was a very innocent question, but was construed by the Government as intended to invite a reply that the want of immigration and the mismanagement of the public lands were the cause of Upper Canada's backwardness. The Government must look into this. Here was a new-comer interfering with the province of Parliament, proposing conventions, suggesting deliberations as to the propriety of sending commissioners to England to call attention to the affairs of the Province, and criticizing the Governor and the Government party on the land policy. This stranger in the land must be got rid of in some way, and it did not seem necessary to be very particular as to the way to go about it.

The convention, the idea of calling which arose in the fruitful brain of Mr. Gourlay, was actually held. This in itself shows what influence Mr. Gourlay had obtained with the masses. The convention, or Gourlay's circular, seconded by the writings of the Scotch immigrant in the public press, produced the hoped-for effect, so far as the Assembly was concerned. At the next meeting of the Legislature, in 1818, a resolution for an enquiry into the affairs of the Province was carried in the Assembly, but before the resolve of that body reached the Executive, the Governor again hastily prorogued the House.

The outcome of the convention was that the militia embodied during the war got their patents. Mr. Gourlay, in continuance of the proceedings of the convention, published the draft of a petition to the Crown, to be adopted by the people as far as they thought proper. Never choice in his language, and often offensive, this petition had in it the following passage : " Corruption indeed has reached such a height in this Province that it is thought no other part of the British Empire witnesses the like. It matters not what characters fill situations of public trust at present ; all sink beneath the dignity of men and have become vitiated and weak."

This language, to the minds of the Executive Government, afforded an opportunity for indicting Mr. Gourlay for seditious libel : accordingly he was twice indicted, but on each occasion acquitted. An Act, however, was seized upon to enable his enemies to attain their object. He was arrested, brought before two members of the Assembly under an Act of 1804, aimed at persons, not being inhabitants, who should give cause to suspect that they were endeavouring, or about to endeavour to engage in sedition, and providing for their expulsion from the Province.

By these members of the Assembly he was ordered to leave the Province, and, choosing to disregard their order, Gourlay was arrested and confined in the jail at Niagara for eight months. Weak in body, the heat and confinement seemed to have partially affected his mind. He was prevented from having free consultation with friends and brought at last into Court in August, 1819, where he appeared indifferent to what was going on. As was said by the witnesses at the Parliamentary enquiry afterwards held, his speech was incoherent, and he appeared in a great measure unconscious of what was going on around him. This was attributed to his physical condition, brought about by his confinement. However this may be, the unfortunate Gourlay was convicted and sentenced to banishment from the Province.

Gourlay now made his way back to England, his mind full of resentment at the wrongs he had suffered. Arrived

RETURNS TO ENGLAND.

there he found his affairs in disorder. In his absence his landlord, the Duke of Somerset, had preferred a claim for rent, although Gourlay claimed that when he left England the Duke owed him some hundreds of pounds. The action of the Duke so oppressed Gourlay's wife, whom he had left in care of his farm, that she gave it up, and Gourlay found himself banished from Canada and homeless in England. Nevertheless, his indomitable heart was not yet broken. He sought redress in law through that most tedious Court of that day, the Court of Chancery. Six years were consumed in bills, interrogatories, references, and all the endless proceedings of the Court of that period. In the end Gourlay got judgment, but did not get his costs. A most barren result, as no doubt the costs consumed all that was gained by the judgment.

During this time, Gourlay had proceeded to petition Parliament with regard to his treatment in Upper Canada, but no attention was paid to his complaint. He had confided one petition to Mr. Brougham to present, and conceiving that Mr. Brougham had neglected his case, the man seems to have become desperate. He made a premeditated assault on Mr. Brougham in the lobby of the House, was at once arrested and committed by the Speaker and the House to confinement during the session of the Parliament for his contempt. On Parliament rising, he was released from the custody of the Sergeant-at-arms, only to be arrested again and committed to the House of Correction, in default of bail, as a dangerous person of unsound mind. Here he remained for nearly four years, making endless appeals to the public through the press, and publishing an appeal to the nation of some two hundred pages.

Gourlay had many friends in his own country, and had a friend in the House in Mr. Hume, then a prominent Reformer. Through the efforts of friends, he was at last released from confinement in March, 1828, and went to Scotland, where he resided till November, 1833, tortured as he says by unsettled affairs. He then set sail again for the New World, landing in New York in December of that year. On board ship he indited the following address to his creditors:

"NOTICE TO CREDITORS.

"THE PACIFIC—AT SEA, Nov. 9, 1833.

"I hereby intimate that I have sailed for America, not to evade payment of debts, but that all may be paid in full, for which funds are more than sufficient.

"Witness my hand,
"ROBERT GOURLAY,

"*Late of Leith, subject of the King, now Robert Fleming Gourlay of the ocean and subject of Neptune!*"

Arrived in New York, he opened communication with his Canadian friends, who invited him to return to the Province, in which there was a large class which still maintained feelings of animosity to the Government of the Province. Gourlay, however, refused all their overtures, and in fact exhibited a profound distrust of the leaders of the Reform party. Following his own course, he addressed a series of remonstrances to the Lieutenant Governor, Sir John Colborne, and his successor, Sir Francis Bond Head, and to the Duke of Wellington, then at the head of the Home Government, in his addresses to the latter urging an enquiry into the affairs of the Colony, as well as reparation of his own wrongs. During the year 1835, he addressed several communications to the Duke, urging that the Canadians should be given the right to legislate for themselves, in all matters, civil and religious. He expressly explained that he had no desire to see the Colony separated from the Empire. Gourlay was in fact always a constitutional agitator, and his writings show he had no sympathy with those who incited revolt or sedition. His last address, prior to the breaking out of the Rebellion, was to Her Majesty Queen Victoria, then lately come to the Throne, in October, 1836, urging her to visit the Colony in person, and free it from the existing abuses of government.

In 1837, when William Lyon Mackenzie was leading the armed revolution, he was informed that Mackenzie wanted his assistance in the movement headed by him. He communicated with Mackenzie, and urged him to abandon the course he was pursuing. He reminded him that there were constitutional means for reform in Canada, and (Mackenzie's movement having at the time met with a check), assured him that had he succeeded, so far from rejoicing, he would have turned his back on America forever. He had, it is true, been in sympathy with Mackenzie until about 1829, when, as he says, "finding he had no stability, he cut correspondence with him." In 1834, Mackenzie wrote to him in New York. Gourlay would have no dealings with him, and said that while he had "no bad feeling personally towards him, he wished to have no correspondence with him on political subjects." Mackenzie writing twice to him again, he peremptorily desired him to desist. In his methods entirely differing from Mackenzie, Gourlay was always a loyal subject. Amid all his trials and losses, and although his mind was at times clouded, possibly by the troubles he had endured, he never lost faith in Canada, or in the Empire. His differences were in truth more with the administration of affairs in Canada by the ruling party there, than with the Home Government.

In 1841, after the fall of the Rebellion, Gourlay petitioned the Canadian House of Parliament, gave a detailed account of his sufferings, and demanded redress. The petition was referred to a select Committee which reported —"That the Petitioner's imprisonment in 1819 was illegal, unconstitutional, and without the possibility of excuse or palliation."

The Government felt that Gourlay deserved better treatment than he had received during his short career in Upper Canada, and Sir Charles Bagot, while Governor of the Province, offered him a pension of fifty pounds, from the civil list. Gourlay considered himself insulted by this offer : he refused to accept any grant made on the score of compassion, and declined to accept the pension.

What he wanted was not a state pension, but full indemnity for the wrongs that had been inflicted on him, acknowledged to be such by the Legislature. He continued his addresses to the Government and to the Legislature, but they, feeling that they had endeavoured to make compensation and that their efforts had not met with success, did no more for him. He returned to Scotland, where he lived till 1863, when he died at the ripe age of eighty.*

To return to chronological sequence, we find that Alexander Smith was Administrator of the Province in the spring and summer of 1818, and was followed by Sir Peregrine Maitland, who was Governor of the Province in succession to Governor Gore. He opened Parliament on the 12th of October, 1818.

Mr. Gourlay's imprisonment occurred during the early administration of Sir Peregrine Maitland. The population of the Province at this time was about one hundred and twenty thousand, and was steadily increasing. Sir Peregrine, on opening the eighth Parliament, in January, 1821, was enabled to congratulate Parliament that the current of immigration was now setting steadily into the Canadas. In contrast with Lower Canada, the Upper Province presented an entirely different aspect. In the former the Executive was stoutly opposed by the

---

* "The Banished Briton and Neptunian," published by Gourlay in 1843, is the principal authority for the facts relating to Gourlay's connection with Upper Canada.

9

Assembly, while in Upper Canada, the Governor, the Council and the Assembly were in complete accord. The House might be called a Tory House, and yet the statutes show that the Assembly thoroughly appreciated the wants of the people, and even their prejudices were considered. Several acts of a liberal character were passed. Certain persons in the Province had endeavoured to persuade the electorate that it was the purpose of Parliament to endeavour to exact tithes, for the support of a Protestant clergy. Parliament, however, soon undeceived the people by passing an Act declaring—"That no tithes should be claimed, demanded or received by any ecclesiastical parson, rector, or vicar of the Protestant Church within the Province."

There were at this time agitators in the Province, willing to set afloat any tale, to deceive credulous people as to the administration. The truth seems to have been, that the new settlers in the Province were imbued with the idea that the old settlers had too many favours from Government, and these agitators continually worked, so that whenever these old settlers held office, they should be worked out from that office, for the accommodation of the new comers. That, however, was not the idea of the United Empire Loyalists, who, it must be admitted, had the principal control of affairs. Their opinion on this subject may perhaps be best gathered from an address of the House of Assembly to the Governor, when referring to Mr. Gourlay and his proceedings. "We remember," said they, "that this favoured land was assigned to our fathers as a retreat for suffering loyalty, and not as a sanctuary for sedition. We lament that the designs of one factious individual [Gourlay] should have succeeded in drawing into the support of his vile machinations, so many honest men and loyal subjects of His Majesty."

If there was one class of men that the United Empire Loyalists abhorred more than another, it was the American, who leaving the United States, had come to Canada to there make his home. The schoolmasters, the singing men, the quack doctors and the peddlers, who were in the habit of invading the Province, were looked upon with suspicion, not because of their professions or trade, but because of their continual endeavours to undermine the loyalty of the settlers, and to convert them to Republicanism.

The first session of the eighth Parliament was prorogued by Sir Peregrine Maitland on the 14th April, 1821, and the second session opened in November, 1821. In the recess between the two sessions a vacancy occurred in the representation of the Counties of Lennox and Addington.

Barnabas Bidwell was then a resident of those counties. He had been Attorney-General of the State of Massachusetts, and had been indicted for some offence in that state and fled to Canada. He taught school for some time in the village of Bath. A lawyer by profession, and gifted of speech, he had no difficulty in ingratiating himself with the electors. When the election to fill the vacancy came to be held, he was put forward as a candidate for the suffrage of the constituents, and was elected member of Parliament. It is but fair to say, that the majority of the electors did not know that Mr. Bidwell was a fugitive from justice, and for those who had heard it so stated he had a ready explanation, which was that his political enemies there had got up an accusation against him for misapplication of public moneys, but that he had not been convicted of that offence. The fact was that Mr. Bidwell had fled the country on account of a warrant having issued for his apprehension.

Whether innocent or guilty of the charge it was not necessary to enquire, as he was a foreigner, foreign-born, and owed allegiance to the United States. His election was petitioned against on this ground, and he was expelled the House.

Barnabas Bidwell had allied himself with the party of Reformers which had by this time sprung into existence, and as he could not be a member of the Legislature himself, Marshall S. Bidwell, his son, ran for the same constituency and was elected. An attempt was made to unseat him also, but the attempt failed, and he became a prominent politician and one of the most shining lights of the Reform party.

Marshall S. Bidwell was technically a British subject, having been born in Massachusetts before the revolt of the American colonies. He had not held office under the United States Government, and had not taken the oath of allegiance to the Government. Nevertheless, he was a Republican at heart, and would have been glad if Canada could have been prevailed upon to cast in her lot with the United States. Mr. Bidwell was a man much respected by those who knew him, was a profound lawyer, and well qualified to hold the highest position in the state. His Republican proclivities, however, operated to his disadvantage, and he ultimately left the Province, residing many years in New York, where he practised his profession with great success. He died in the land of his birth, mourned by many friends, amongst whom may be classed those who knew him best in Canada.*

At or about the same time that Robert Fleming Gourlay emigrated to Canada, William Lyon Mackenzie, a young man of Scotch birth, the son of Daniel Mackenzie, of Dundee, Forfarshire, crossed the Tweed and took up his abode in England. Mackenzie was an active, pushing young man, and going out into the world to make a living at an early age, he did not neglect any opportunity to strengthen both body and mind for the arduous duties of life. His mother was a woman of great force of character and resolute will. An ardent Presbyterian, she doubtless instilled into her son's mind that love of independence which was a characteristic of his life. Or was it that, left without the care of a father when but a month old, deprived of the restraining influences of the head of

---

* Mr. Bidwell died in 1872. He is buried in Stockbridge, Massachusetts. The following inscription on his tomb is supplied by the Rev. Arthur Lawrence, the Rector of the Episcopal Church there:

"He hath showed thee, O, Man, what is good;
And what doth the Lord require of thee
But to do justly, and to love mercy,
And to walk humbly with thy God."

the family, a fond and widowed mother allowed him a latitude which subsequently affected his erratic and restless life? Unfortunately, Mackenzie's independence of character was always swayed by his extreme and restless disposition.

Mrs. Mackenzie, the mother, was left in rather straitened circumstances on her husband's death, in 1795. Notwithstanding this, she strove to educate her son. He had not only home, but school education. Her circumstances compelled the mother to allow her son William to "gang his gait," and strike out for himself. He first entered a counting-house in Dundee. After being there for a short time he entered into the employ of a wood merchant. In the year 1814, when only nineteen years of age, he went into business for himself, keeping a general shop, with a circulating library, in a small place called Alyth, near Dundee. He was a great reader, and naturally joined the book business with his general store keeping. His business not being profitable, he crossed the Tweed in 1817, and went to England, where he became managing clerk to a canal company in Wiltshire. It would be interesting to know if at this time he made the acquaintance of Gourlay, for we find him in Wiltshire about the same time. After leaving Wiltshire he was for a brief period in London; he then made a flying visit to France, and, in 1820, being then twenty-four years of age, he emigrated to Canada. Comparing dates, it will be seen that this was but a short time after Gourlay had gone through his trial experience, and had been banished the Province.

The sound of Gourlay's voice still echoed in the ears of the people of the Province, but was soon to be stilled by the more potent voice of *this* his countryman, who had come to Canada prepared to show the people the way they should walk.

Sir Peregrine Maitland was doomed to have his administration clouded by the aggressiveness of this intruder upon the public peace of the Province. It cannot be said that these aggressions were not in some measure good for the future of the Province, but a scrutiny of the list of those who had been in the Province for years before either Gourlay or Mackenzie set foot on her soil, will show that there were many men, quite as well qualified as either the one or the other of these gentleman for reforming the laws, manners and customs of the Province. It was galling to these to find comparative strangers entering upon a crusade to change the institutions of the country.

Mackenzie had not been long in the Province before he undertook the office of General Censor. This was about the year 1824. He had occupied his time between his arrival in 1820, and 1824, in selling drugs and general merchandise, at one time in Toronto, then Dundas, and then Queenston. He was for fifteen months in the general store and book business with Mr. Leslie, in Dundas. The style of the firm was: "Mackenzie & Leslie, druggists and dealers in hardware, cutlery, jewellery, toys, confections, dye stuffs, and paints," and in their posters, the business was said to be carried on "at the Circulating Library, Dundas." It is probable they divided the business according to their respective tastes, Mr. Mackenzie taking to himself the profits of the "Circulating Library" part of the business, and Mr. Leslie the general, but more profitable part of the venture.

Altogether the businesses in which Mr. Mackenzie had engaged were not unprofitable, and if his restless nature had not prevailed on him to leave the counting desk for the life of a journalist and politican, he would without question have been among the foremost in commercial life.

While still at Queenston, in 1824, he abandoned the business in which he had been engaged, and, on his own account, and wholly unaided, he established and published a newspaper, giving it the name of *The Colonial Advocate*. As its very name implies, Mr. Mackenzie had constituted himself the champion of Colonial rights. The building is still standing in which this first newspaper, in the modern sense of what a newspaper should be, was published. It is a brick building, on the main street of Queenston, at the foot of the hill. It is now without a roof, but it is still known as the "Printing House." Thus does tradition keep in remembrance the occupation of William Lyon Mackenzie, the greatest agitator that ever Upper Canada has had within her limits.

The reason Mr. Mackenzie had for establishing this paper was that, at that time, there was really

WILLIAM LYON MACKENZIE.

no independent organ of public opinion in the Province. There was the *Upper Canada Gazette*, published at York, by Mr. Fothergill, the Government printer; but that was an official paper, principally used for official notices, with now and then a guarded reference to political events, but in its general character absolutely and essentially a Government organ.

Mr. Mackenzie held views in some respects similar to those entertained by Mr. Gourlay, especially on the subjects of immigration, and the monopoly of public lands. There were two other subjects which gave him much concern. These were the Clergy Reserves, and the Provincial University. Neither of these subjects need have disturbed him in his daily round or prevented his sleeping at nights. Before he started *The Colonial Advocate*, the people were alive to the necessity of a change in the distribution of the revenues of the Clergy Reserves, which were claimed to belong exclusively to the Church of England. One-seventh of the lands of the Province had been set apart by the Constitutional Act of 1791, for "the support and maintenance of a Protestant Clergy." The term, "Protestant Clergy," opened a very wide field for political discussion and difference of opinion. While adherents of the Church of England, who were the minority of the population, contended that the revenues were dedicated to their Church, all other Protestant denominations contended they were entitled to a share. If the revenues were to be divided between all Protestant Churches, of which there were many, the income would have been filtered away, no one receiving the benefit intended by the grant of the lands by the king.

Mr. Mackenzie well understood the prejudices of the majority of the people on this question. There were many, who although supporters of the Government on other questions, were ready to cast in their lot with the opposition, if any agitation were commenced, leading to an issue on this particular subject.

The Constitutional Act had wisely provided that the Colonial Parliament might, at any time, vary or altogether repeal the law which had devoted one-seventh of the Crown lands and their revenues to the support and maintenance of a Protestant Clergy. There was thus a ready-made opportunity for an agitator to get up an excitement on this important question. Mr. Mackenzie was not the man to lose the opportunity.

In the first number of the *Colonial Advocate*, distributed broadcast through the country, free of expense, he expressed a hope that a law would be enacted "by which the ministers of every body of professing Christians, being British subjects, should receive equal benefits from the Clergy Reserves."

In the same number of the journal, Mr. Mackenzie assailed the Governor, Sir Peregrine Maitland, the Executive Council, and the Legislative Council. The latter he represented as being "always selected from the tools of servile power."

As viewed nowadays, there was probably not much in Mr. Mackenzie's expressions which would be regarded as a political crime. There was nothing clearly indicated by his writings, further than that he was a Radical reformer, and as such desired to catch the ear, and it may have been with a view at some future time to capturing votes of the people. It is fair to presume that Mr. Mackenzie, in establishing a newspaper, printing it at his own expense, and distributing it all over the Province, had some object in view other than pure patriotism and a desire to sacrifice himself on the altar of liberty. It was his privilege to criticise the Government and its acts; if he had confined himself to this and not assailed the Governor, no doubt his effusions would have gone unheeded. But when he went so far as to arraign the Governor and to declare that the Legislative Council was "always selected from the tools of servile power," these tools could not be expected to view with equanimity the actions of this man, a comparative stranger in the Province, and but little known to the ruling dynasty.

It was left to the organ of the official party to take up the cause of the Government, and to mete out such punishment to him as he seemed to deserve. The organ referred to suggested that Mr. Mackenzie should be banished the Province, and that the whole edition of his newspaper should be seized and suppressed. However, the advice came too late. The offending edition of the *Advocate* was not seized, since it had already been distributed throughout the Province; neither was Mr. Mackenzie banished the Province, and it is quite sure that if he had been expelled he would have soon found his way back again. Mr. Mackenzie was as agile as he was clever, and it would have been found pretty difficult either to have kept him behind bolts and bars in the Province, or if sent out of the country, to keep him from wandering back again to his "printing house" in Queenston. At any rate, here he was to be found, after the sentence of banishment was pronounced against him by the organ of the official party, periodically sending out the *Advocate* and his fulminations among the people.

The paper had not got further than its fourth number when Mr. Fothergill, the Government printer, undertook to describe him in the *Gazette* as a thorough-going Democrat and a disloyal subject. This was a grave charge to bring against a Mackenzie of the Mackenzies, and more than he could submit to without reply. In the *Advocate* of the 10th June, 1824, he took Mr. Fothergill to task for the supposed libel on his character. Mr. Mackenzie was a Democrat, but certainly not, at this time at least, a disloyal subject. He certainly opposed the local Government, but his disloyalty to the Empire at that time could not be proved. In his reply to Mr. Fothergill, he said: "I will refer to every page of the four numbers of the *Advocate* now before the public; I may ask every impartial reader; nay, I may even ask Mr. Robinson* himself, whether they do not, in every

---

* Mr. Robinson was the Attorney-General, afterwards Sir John Robinson, Chief Justice of the Province.

line, speak the language of a free and independent British subject." . . .

In another place he said: "It may be proper that I should for this once add a few other reasons why disloyalty can never enter my breast; even the name I bear has in all ages proved an insurmountable barrier." He then gives his reasons, protesting the loyalty of all the Mackenzies, reflecting on the horrors of alliance with a foreign power, and the fearful responsibility of him who goes in battle array against the heritage of his ancestors. Prophetic thought! How lightly it was regarded in Mackenzie's future action.

Notwithstanding the differences between Mr. Fothergill and Mr. Mackenzie, Mr. Fothergill soon afterwards from his place in Parliament gave credit to Mr. Mackenzie for the accuracy with which he reported the proceedings of the Assembly in the *Advocate*, and even went so far as to get a sum of money placed in the contingency account of the House expenses as some remuneration to him for this service. The item passed the House, but was afterwards struck out by the Lieutenant-Governor.

In July, 1824, the general election was held for the return of representatives to the House of Assembly, when the Government party was defeated and a majority returned who were in favour of the Reform party. There were twenty-six new members elected to this House, the majority of whom were for reforming the Government. Marshall S. Bidwell was returned as a member for Lennox and Addington, his colleague being Peter Perry. These were no doubt doughty champions of reform, but, on the other hand, the old party sent many able men to the House, among whom were John Beverley Robinson and Archibald McLean, Chief Justice of the Province. A return of a majority opposed to the Government in those days did not necessarily cause a change of Government. This was a defect in the Constitution of which the Reformers loudly complained. The complaint was a just one, but such was the form of Colonial government at the time. The Constitution of both the Provinces of Upper and Lower Canada was founded on a similar principle, the mainspring of which was the retention by the Imperial Government of power to regulate Colonial affairs through a Governor and Legislative Council. The people had only a semblance of power in the Assembly, which was constantly subject to the control of the Government and Government appointees.

CHAPTER VII.

Papineau and Republicanism — Personalities — Lord Dalhousie a Soldier — Sir Walter Scott's Estimate of Him — Inaugurated Monument to Wolfe and Montcalm — His Departure from the Province — Sir James Kempt Succeeds Lord Dalhousie — Endeavours to Conciliate the French-Canadians — Petitions to the King Commending Constitutional Act of 1791, but Asking for Redress of Grievances — Sir James Kempt Receives Papineau as Speaker — Committee for Redress of Grievances — Committee of House of Assembly Disapprove Constitution of 1791 — Arraignment of Legislative Council — Council and Assembly on Granting Supplies — Sir James Kempt's Opinion of Legislative Council — Not Prepared to Revolutionize the Government — Assembly Makes Demands that Could Not be Granted — The People and the Press — Rival Factions — Riots in Montreal — The Cholera Year — Legislative Council Increased — Governor's Censure on House of Assembly for Refusing Supplies — House Asks for an Elective Legislative Council — The Legislative Council Advise the King that the Legislation of Lower Canada Assembly was Alarming — Mr. Viger, Delegate in London — Assembly Arraigns Lord Aylmer, Governor — Judges in the Assembly.

GLANCING back at the history of the events happening just before the nineteenth century entered upon its third decade, one is struck with the progress which public men in Lower Canada, especially Mr. Papineau and others of the Liberal party, were making towards that kind of government then called Republican, but now rather constitutional, as opposed to the mixed form of government of a limited monarchy. Mr. Papineau started out well as a politician, applauding the British Government, and the Colonial Government instituted in Canada, but was now opposing, not only measures taken by that Government within the limits of its jurisdiction, but in a most violent manner assailing the Governor sent out to carry out the will of the Imperial power.

When a man descends to personalities, he weakens his arguments, and he is sure to bring on himself the indignation of the better class of people. The French-Canadians of the higher classes, and all English-Canadians, were indignant with the Speaker-elect for his unmerited abuse of Lord Dalhousie, the retiring Governor, in 1828. Lord Dalhousie was a soldier who had seen much service under Wellington before coming to Canada, and on the occupation of Bordeaux by a division of the British army, under that great Commander, was left Commandant of the Garrison.

Sir Walter Scott in his "Life of Napoleon," referring to that occupation, said of Dalhousie: "If excellent sense, long experience, the most perfect equality of temper and unshaken steadiness be necessary in so delicate a trust, the British Army had not one more fit for the charge."

It would thus seem that Lord Dalhousie succeeded in his governorship of Bordeaux, but in the opinion of Mr. Papineau and the *habitants* who followed his lead, he entirely failed in the government of Lower Canada. It was Lord Dalhousie who inaugurated the movement for the erection of the monument to Wolfe and Montcalm, in Quebec, and under his auspices subscriptions were obtained from the military and civilians in the Province, for the accomplishment of that object. The subscribers to the fund were nearly all British and British-Canadians, not French-Canadians. One would have thought that the noble act of the Governor, in thus commemorating the French Commander Montcalm, in conjunction with the hero Wolfe, would have at least animated Mr. Papineau and softened his feeling towards Lord Dalhousie.

Lord Dalhousie had the satisfaction of knowing that he left Canada sincerely regretted by those whose opinion he most valued. The manly character of the Governor is seen in a reply to an address he received at Three Rivers previous to his departure. He said: "I have never varied from the course of my duties, so far as I could comprehend those of the representatives of our most gracious Sovereign, in the distant colonies of the British Empire. I have studied to walk the path of honour as a man and as a soldier. I have above all things studied to do justice with impartiality, without any respect of persons. I have disregarded popular clamour and the slander of wandering scribblers. My sense of duty has never been influenced by such common weapons, and I leave them behind me, utterly inoffensive. The favourable opinions expressed in the language of this address are to my mind the highest reward of public life; they are lasting and imperishable to me and to those who shall follow me to sustain my name. I can leave no better record to guide the young to a close as honourable as that which you now testify to me."

Sir James Kempt succeeded Lord Dalhousie as Governor-General in the autumn of 1828. Sir James' instructions were to pursue a more conciliatory policy toward His Majesty's Lower Canadian subjects. At the same time he was not to loosen the reins of Imperial control by negativing the powers and duties of the Legislative Council. To satisfy the French, he ordered the prosecutions for libel, which had been commenced under his predecessor, to be discontinued. He also warned the press that the ribaldry and license in which they had indulged should cease. In this regard he was more attentive to the ministerial than to the opposition press. Both parties had gone beyond the bounds of decency in criticising the acts of opponents, but it was thought wise to leave the opposition press to the discipline of their leaders and the agents of the French party, who had returned from England, whither they had gone to present petitions to the Imperial Government and Parliament, praying for redress of grievances.

One of these petitions may be given as a sample of the whole. It was signed by the greatest number of the *habitants*, at the instigation of their leaders, and may be presumed to pretty well represent the grievance-mongers' complaints.

" *To the King's Most Excellent Majesty :*

"We, your Majesty's faithful and loyal subjects, inhabitants of your Province of Lower Canada, most humbly supplicate your Majesty to receive graciously this, our humble petition, which we now lay at the foot of your Imperial throne, with hearts full of gratitude and inviolable attachment to your Majesty's paternal Government.

"Among the numerous benefits for which the inhabitants of Lower Canada are indebted to your Majesty's Government, there is none that they more highly prize than the invaluable Constitution granted to this Province by the Act of Parliament of Great Britain passed in the thirty-first year of the reign of our beloved Sovereign, your august father, of ever-revered memory.

"Called by that Act to the full enjoyment of British constitutional liberty, and become the depositaries of our own rights under the protection of the Mother Country, we contracted the solemn obligation of preserving inviolate this sacred deposit, and transmitting it to our descendants, such as it was confided to us by the great men who then presided over the destinies of your powerful and glorious Empire.

"Deeply impressed with a sense of this obligation, alarmed by the abuses which have crept into the administration of the Government of this Province, and suffering under the evils which weigh on its inhabitants, we entertained an anxious hope that the House of Assembly, in the session of the Provincial Parliament called for the despatch of business on the twentieth of November last, would take into consideration the state of the Province, and adopt efficacious measures to obtain the remedy and removal of these abuses and evils. We had a sure reliance on the well-tried loyalty and disinterested zeal of our Representatives, but we had the mortification of seeing our hopes frustrated by the refusal, on the part of His Excellency the Governor in-Chief, to approve of the Speaker elected by the Assembly, and by the Proclamation of the twenty-second of the same month of November, proroguing the Provincial Parliament. In these circumstances, deprived of the services of our Representatives, suffering under great evils and threatened with others still greater, we humbly implore the protection of your Majesty, the source of all grace and of all justice.

"The enlightened and patriotic statesman, who devised our Constitutional Act, and the British Parliament by which it was granted, intended to bestow on us a mixed Government, modelled on the Constitution of the parent state: the opinions publicly expressed at the time in Parliament and the Act itself, record the beneficent views of the Imperial Legislature ; a Governor, a Legislative Council and an Assembly were to form three distinct and independent branches, representing the King, the Lords, and the Commons ; but the true spirit of that fundamental law has not been observed in the composition of the Legislative Council ; for the majority of its members, consisting of persons whose principal resources for the support of themselves and of their families, are the salaries, emoluments and fees derived from offices which they hold during pleasure, they are interested in maintaining and increasing the salaries, emoluments and fees of public officers, paid by the people, and also in supporting divers abuses favourable to persons holding offices. The Legislative Council, by these means, is in effect the Executive power, under a different name, and the Provincial Legislature is in truth reduced to two branches, a Governor and an Assembly ; leaving the Province without the benefit of the intermediate branch, as intended by the aforesaid Act : and from this first and capital abuse, have resulted, and still continue to result, a multitude of abuses, and the impossibility of procuring a remedy.

"We acknowledge that the Legislative Council ought to be independent, and if it were, we should not be entitled to complain to your Majesty of the repeated refusals of that branch to proceed upon various bills, sent up by the Assembly, however useful and even indispensable they might be ; but considering these refusals as the natural results of the composition of that body, and of the state of dependence in which the majority of its members are placed, we are compelled to consider its acts as the acts of the Executive Government ; and we most humbly represent to your Majesty, that the Legislative Council of this Province, the majority of which is composed of Executive Councillors, Judges and other persons dependent on the Executive, have, year after year, rejected such bills, refused and neglected to proceed on several other bills sent up by the Assembly, for the remedy of abuses, for encouraging education, promoting the general convenience of the subject, the improvement of the country, for increasing the security of persons and property, and furthering the common welfare and prosperity of the Province particularly.

"Various annual bills granting the necessary sums for all the expenses of the civil government of the Province, but regulating and setting limits to the expenditure.

"For affording a legal recourse to the subject having claims against the Provincial Government.

"For regulating certain fees and offices.

"For enabling the inhabitants of the towns to have a voice in the management of their local concerns, and a check on the expenditure of moneys levied upon them by assessment.

"For facilitating the administration of justice throughout the Province, for qualifying and regulating the formation of juries and introducing jury trials in the country parts, and diminishing the expenses occasioned by the distance of suitors from the present seats of justice.

"For providing a new and sufficient gaol for the district of Montreal.

"For qualifying persons to serve in the office of justice of the peace.

"For continuing the Acts regulating the militia of the Province.

"For increasing and apportioning the representation in the House of Assembly equally among the qualified electors throughout the Province, particularly in the new settlements and townships.

"For the security of the public moneys in the hands of His Majesty's Receiver-General in the Province.

"For the independence of the Judges, by securing to them their present salaries, upon their being commissioned during good behaviour, and for providing a tribunal for the trial of impeachments by the Assembly, so as to ensure a just responsibility in high public officers within the Province.

"For appointing and providing for an authorized agent for the Province, to reside in England, and attend to its interests there."

If the two first paragraphs of that petition expressed the true sentiments of the French-Canadian population of Lower Canada, there ought not to have been a rebellion in that Province, for they undoubtedly, in an unnecessarily pointed manner, lauded the Constitution which had been given by the Act of 1791, acknowledged that the population were "in the full enjoyment of British Constitutional liberty," and that "they had become the depositaries of their own rights under the protection of the Mother Country."

It is a singular commentary on this petition of the people, that the people's House were presenting a very different view of the situation. At or about the same time a Committee of the House of Assembly proposed and the House adopted the following resolutions:

"1. That it is the opinion of this Committee, that from the instant when by the capitulations, the inhabitants of Lower Canada became British subjects, they had a right to the benefit of the representative system and to the liberties and political rights of Englishmen.

"2. That it is the opinion of this Committee, that the provision of the Act 31st Geo. III, Chap. 31, which invests his Majesty with the power (at once extraordinary, unusual and contrary to the pinciples of the British Constitution,) of composing according to his pleasure, one entire branch of the Provincial Legislature, is incompatible with the principles of free government.

"3. That it is the opinion of this Committee, that experience of more than forty years has demonstrated that the Constitution and the composition of the Legislative Council of the Province were not, and are not, adapted to assure contentment and good government to this Province, nor, therefore, to favour the development of its resources and its industry."

The Legislative Council was always the *bête noir* of the French party. It disturbed their work by day and their sleep by night, and yet how could the British Parliament, as it were in a day, give to its Canadian subjects the same measure of liberty that had taken it hundreds of years to establish? The House of Assembly of Lower Canada seemed to forget that the government of Canada was Colonial, not Imperial, nor as yet advanced to the full measure of manhood.

Sir James Kempt's first official act, after he assumed the duties of his office, was to recognize Mr. Papineau as Speaker of the House of Assembly, which was convened shortly after his arrival. It may be said, generally, of the whole of Sir James Kempt's administration that it was eminently conciliatory. He endeavoured in every way to reconcile the differences existing between the Council and the Assembly. It was his happy privilege, in a week after the opening of the session of Parliament, to lay before that body a message from the Imperial Government, which it was announced went a long way in granting the reforms which the Assembly had asked for.

The message, in fact, proposed a compromise between the Assembly and the Government. The Assembly, after referring the message to a committee, for consideration, arrived at the conclusion that the compromise offered by the Home Government would prove nugatory, and passed a series of resolutions which were embodied in an address to the Imperial Parliament, which, at their request, was transmitted by the Governor to England. This address asked for several redresses, among others—(1) That the judges be independent and secluded from the political business of the Province. (2) Responsibility of public officers. (3) Independence of support from public revenue. (4) Application of Jesuit estates to educational purposes. (5) Removal of obstruction to land settlement.

When Sir James Kempt opened the second session of Parliament he congratulated the House on substantial progress having been made in the trades, commerce and general improvement of the Province, and he assured them that the petition would be submitted by the British Ministry to Parliament, although they had not been able, up to that time, to do so.

" There was one incident which occurred during this session, which goes to show that there was, in the minds of supporters of the Government, a suspicion that the leaders of the French-Canadian party were imbued with rebellious designs. Mr. A. Stuart was a prominent member of the Assembly and supporter of the Government. It so happened that Lord Dalhousie, during his term of office, for reasons satisfactory to himself, had recourse to the old militia ordinances, passed for the protection of the Province. The House had resolved that these ordinances were still in force. They were thought to be too stringent in their operation, and were but poorly obeyed. Mr. Papineau, speaking to a motion for an address to the King, on the subject of these ordinances, and to harmonise some difference of opinion as to whether they were abrogated or not, said: "If the House yields to the desires of the inhabitants, then these ordinances are abrogated, for when all the people in a country unanimously repudiate a bad law, there is no possibility of executing it, therefore I say, the laws in question are already abrogated." Whereupon Mr. A. Stuart exclaimed, "This is rebellion."

This session of the Legislature may be considered a memorable one, as in granting supplies the Assembly declared they only did so conditionally that the grievances of which they complained should be redressed, the grievances being mostly those specified in the petition of which mention has been made. The Legislative Council were much agitated over this method of granting supplies, with the condition attached, but finally, in order to conciliate the Assembly, passed the bill, with a majority of one, the minority strongly protesting against the Act. Sir James Kempt was the means of bringing about this temporary peace, and thought he had succeeded in harmonising the contending branches of the Legislature. The sequel will show that his expectations were wholly fallacious.

A despatch from the Colonial Minister apprised him that the question was being considered by the Imperial Government, whether or not it might be possible to reconstitute both the Executive and Legislative Councils. The despatch asked for Sir James' opinion in the matter. The Governor replied that the Legislative Council was composed of twenty-three members, twelve of whom were placemen; and in religious profession, sixteen Protestants and seven Catholics; **that the** Executive Council had nine members; **that** only one of them could be said to be independent of the Government, and all were Protestants but one.

The Governor further stated that although he thought more independent members, **than those in** the Legislative **Council, might be gradually introduced, he,** nevertheless, **was of opinion that no** organic change in the Constitution of the Council was desirable. The opinion of the Governor, so expressed to the Home Government, proves that however desirous he may have been to modify existing institutions, and in every way to improve the existing order of things, especially in the Legislative Council, he was not prepared to radically change the existing form of government.

The French-Canadians, on the other hand, were determined, if possible, to get rid of the Council, root and branch. So soon as it came to their ears that Sir James Kempt had sent a despatch to England, pronouncing against any organic change in the Council, the *habitants* in those counties and parishes about Montreal, which afterwards were most open in promoting the rebellion, viz., Richelieu, Verchères, St. Hyacinthe, Rouville and Chambly, met at St. Charles in public meeting, and protested against the action of the Governor, adding that, " if the Executive and Legislative Councils were not to reformed, the most serious disorders might be expected to ensue."

Sir James Kempt, like many another Governor before him, became convinced that, notwithstanding concessions, the majority of the population of Quebec were determined to force a conflict with the British Government, a conflict in which he did not care to engage. He accordingly retired from the Government.

Sir James Kempt was succeeded by Lord Aylmer, who opened his first session of the Colonial Parliament in January, 1831. Lord Aylmer came to the Parliament at a most critical time in the administration of the affairs of the colony. He had to face a powerful opposition to the Government, one that was more powerful than at any former period. The malcontents were getting the upper hand, almost to the point of revolt. The British Government would fain have quieted the people by even more concessions than those already made. Lord Aylmer informed the Parliament that the Government of the Empire were willing to give over to the colony full control over all revenues levied in the Province, on condition that a civil list of £19,000 a year were granted to His Majesty for life. It was thought that the French-Canadians would be satisfied, and all apprehensions as to the future would be thus allayed. This was not to be so. The Assembly was unwilling to accept this overture of peace and good will, or to be satisfied with anything less than the abolition of the Council, which the British Government still esteemed the safeguard of British dominion in the Province.

The more advanced of the French-Canadian party boasted, that situated as they were, in a province bordering on the American Republic, England, to avoid complications, would in the end grant them all that their most extreme wishes could desire. Things were going from bad to worse, and the Assembly began to browbeat the Governor, and finally decided to refuse all supplies until the public income, without excepting any part of it whatever, should be put under the control of their House, till the judges were finally excluded from the Council, and the Council reformed in all other respects. These demands were so opposed to the instructions of the Governor, and so far outside of the Constitution, under which he held his commission, that they could not possibly be acceded to. The constant demands made on the Imperial Government, added to reiterated complaints made to the Governor, induced him to think that the French-Canadians had other designs than mending the Constitution. When a committee of members of the House of Assembly placed in his hands a petition to the King, asking for further concessions, he enquired of the committee if there were not something behind, and desired to know if the petition contained all that they sought or were likely to seek to obtain. The committee could not but perceive that the Governor more than suspected that influences were at work to thwart, or make wholly unworkable, the office which he held under the Crown. And, indeed, he was not far astray in his conjectures, as there were at that time a number of ardent young men in the Assembly who were forcing their leaders to make unlimited demands on the Imperial authorities, with the purpose of throwing the country into a state of revolution, from which they hoped to derive benefit to themselves and the French-Canadian people.

During all this period one is struck with the fact that many reforms were gradually being made under the tutelage of the British Government; and this in spite of, or perhaps indeed on account of the ceaseless clamour for immediate action on the part of the French-Canadians and the Colonial Assembly. Impatience seemed to characterize all the proceedings of those who were moving against the Government in Lower Canada. This was owing, possibly, to the impulsive nature of the French-Canadian people, especially their young people, which kept the whole Province in a state of excitement, and which neither the Government nor the elders of the Province were in the least able to control. The newspapers of the Province were inspired to spare neither the Governor or Council in their most offensive criticisms. At the same time they proceeded to overload the Assembly, the people's House, with praise and laudation.

A Parliamentary election was always a time of excitement in the Province of Lower Canada. This was especially the case in 1832, when was held the first general election under Lord Aylmer's administration. The rival factions had been goaded on to a state of frenzy. Parties met in the streets of Montreal, fought, bled and killed. Three men lost their lives in the riots that took place, and two were wounded. The military were called upon to quell the disturbance, which they did effectually, and, as it would appear, very distastefully to the French-

Canadian faction. The French-Canadians succeeded in having the colonel and captain of the troops which were called upon to perform their duty arrested. They were under arrest, however, for a few hours only and then were admitted to bail.

The affairs of shooting the citizens engaged in the riots created a great sensation among the *habitants*. "Were the citizens to be shot down by the soldiers of the king? Never." "Aux armes, citoyens, aux armes!" was the battle cry. It was with the greatest difficulty that the public feeling was appeased. These occurrences took place in 1832, the year of the introduction of the Asiatic cholera into Canada. The cholera itself, terrible as it was, more than three thousand persons dying of it in Quebec, was powerless to stay the political conflagration which raged in the Province. The *habitants* assembled in great numbers to denounce the Government and the military. To pacify the French, eight French-Canadian members were added to the Legislative Council. It was thought this would satisfy the French-Canadian element, but all in vain. The Governor, not wishing to offend the Legislature, passed over the insults that had been heaped upon him and his Government. In his address to the Assembly, when he met the Legislature a second time, in 1832, he proved how able and willing he was to sink his private feelings in the fulfilment of duty and obligation to the Crown.

In the performance of the service, which he was required to render, however, he had to communicate to the

Assembly the intelligence that the Home Government treated the refusal of the supplies, at the last session, as equivalent to a declaration that the Government must cease, if it was to depend on Colonial sustenance. The King would, therefore, apply other funds, which he had in his disposition, to meet the public expense.

This determination of the British Government did but add further fuel to the flames. The districts about Montreal were again in a condition nigh bordering on rebellion. A meeting of the whole House of Assembly was called for the 14th January, 1833.

After consuming a month's time in discussing grievances, the House, by a resolution of a considerable majority, addressed the King, praying that he would reconstitute the Legislative Council as an elective body. This may be regarded as another proof that the French party were aiming at complete control of the Province.

On this occasion the Council acted with great dignity. In place of exchanging ungraceful compliments with the Assembly, they addressed themselves to the King, pointing out that the evils flowing from the legislation of His Majesty's French-Canadian subjects were alarming; that a state of prosperity was being turned into a state of ruin; that the races, French, French-Canadian and English, were divided; that the trade and commerce of the country was being seriously affected; that the Elective Council was but another term for an additional Elective Assembly, and that if the 150,000 subjects of his Majesty of British birth and descent in the colony were to be made secure, it was absolutely necessary that the existence of the Council, as then constituted (a nominative and not an elective body), should be maintained.

The Council further informed the King that His Majesty's subjects in Upper Canada would not look calmly on and see Republican institutions introduced into Lower Canada, but would resent it, even if it brought about fraternal war. However well the Council may have thought they were serving British interests, by plain speaking, their address was not so well received as they had expected. Nothing better illustrates how completely the Council were, at the home office, considered to be the King's servants, than the reply made by the King to their address. His Majesty could not help commending their loyalty and attachment to the Constitution. He took occasion, however, to rebuke them for not confining themselves to more temperate language in their references to the Lower Canadian Assembly. He said : " His Majesty cannot but wish that the Council had abstained from using, with reference to the other branch of the Canadian Legislature, language less temperate in its tone than is consistent with its own dignity, or calculated to maintain or restore a good understanding between the two bodies. More especially His Majesty laments the introduction of any words having the appearance of ascribing to a class of his subjects of one origin, views at variance with their allegiance."

It is to be borne in mind that when this reply was written, Mr. Viger, the Lower Canadian Assembly's representative in the capital of the Empire, was in London, and that his presence there added much to the strength of the Gallican party in the Province of Lower Canada. Mr. Viger was too loyal a French-Canadian to be within hearing of the King's ministers and not impart to them sentiments not far different from those expressed in the King's reply to the Legislative Council.

If the sailor King could have lived to the time of the actual rebellion in Lower Canada and to receive the report of High Commissioner the Earl of Durham on the affairs of Canada, made to his successor, Her Most Gracious Majesty Queen Victoria, in 1839, he would have had cause to commend the Legislative Council, not for a part only, but for the whole of their address to the Sovereign.

The Earl of Durham frankly admitted that he, in common with the people of England, had been deceived in regard to the true condition of affairs in Lower Canada, and had wholly misunderstood the causes of the differences which had existed in the Province. He said: "I expected to find a contest between a Government and a people. I found two nations warring in the bosom of a single state, a struggle, not of principle, but of races."

Reference has been made to the insults which the Lower Canadian Assembly, in their own way, heaped upon the Governor of the Province. Lord Aylmer did not deserve this at their hands, as he was conscientiously desirous of promoting the interests of the French-Canadian, as of other subjects of the Crown. Here is a specimen of the Assembly's deliverance, on a subject which really was of little importance in itself, but was regarded by the people's House as a great breach of their privileges. A vacancy occurred in the representation of the County of Montreal, on the 24th November, 1833. The Speaker's warrant for a new writ of election was issued on the 27th of the same month. The Governor, owing to the special circumstances under which the vacancy occurred, conceived it to be his duty before issuing the writ of election, to refer the matter to the Colonial Office, and so informed the Assembly by message, stating at length the reasons that had prevented him from issuing the writ, and that he was awaiting instructions from his superiors in England.

The communication between England and her Colony was not at that time as rapid as the present. To give time for the Home Office to deliberate on the matter, and to inform the Governor of the result of their deliberations, necessarily consumed some time. The Assembly, on the 5th March, addressed the Governor on the subject of the delay. Lord Aylmer informed the House that no answer had yet been received from the Colonial Office to his application for guidance. His message to the Assembly was delivered on March 8th, and was at once referred to a Committee of the House. The Committee, with great precipitancy, considering the more important business that was then engaging the attention of Parliament, reported that—"His Excellency had, in violation of the Constitution and laws of the

Province, and in infringement of the privileges of the House, for a long time, and until the present time, prevented the County of Montreal from being represented. Under these circumstances, which must put an end to every feeling of good understanding between His Excellency the Governor-in-Chief and the House of Assembly, the House ought perhaps to suspend all further proceedings, and all communication whatever with His Excellency, until he has made reparation for this breach of its rights and privileges. The only circumstance which may induce them to defer the communication of such a determination to the Commander in Chief, is the indispensable necessity of passing a bill with the view of preventing, as far as human means may permit, by a proper system of quarantine, the return of the cholera morbus, or to diminish its ravages, if it breaks out afresh in this Province, as there is but too much reason to fear."

The *Quebec Gazette*, published at the time, refers to the expulsion of Mr. Mondelet from the House for accepting the position of member of the Executive Council, which was the very same thing that Mr. Panet had done with the approbation of the House, and relates how the Governor had been assailed with addresses for information, and the palpable object and character of some of those addresses. "How very strangely the warrant for a writ for the west ward of the City of Montreal was delayed, on the ground of danger of riot, and the magistrates and the military, while an immediate issue of the writ, calling on the very same electors to act in the immediate neighbourhood of the same magistrates and military, is urged and made a subject of disrespectful expressions and accusations against the Governor. A just ground for putting an end to the whole business of the country and throwing everything into confusion, were it not for fear of the cholera." And adds—" Well, we are glad the cholera has at last been found good for something."*

A fruitful subject of discussion in Lower Canada, which came to a head during Lord Aylmer's administration, involved the right of the judges of the Province, or any of them, to sit or vote in the Legislative Council. The practice had been for the Crown to nominate the judges, or some of them, to the Legislative Council, and, as the judges were mostly of British origin, the French-Canadian party made of this one of the grievances they were subjected to. The judges in the Province held their office during pleasure. The British Government was of opinion this ought not to be. Not only was it contrary to the English system, but the judges, by being made subject to the whim or caprice of the Assembly, for the annual vote of their salaries, were thus deprived of their independence.

The Assembly, in order to incapacitate the judges from sitting or voting in the Executive or Legislative Council, on the 10th April, 1832, passed an Act, designed to accomplish that purpose. When the Act came to be submitted to the British Government, it was found to be wanting in the essential element of creating a fixed salary for the judges. Viscount Goderich, Colonial Secretary,

* Christie's Lower Canada, Vol. III, p. 501.

thereupon addressed a despatch to Lord Aylmer, in which he informed him of the King's command to acquaint the House of Assembly, that His Majesty was not only prepared, but was most desirous to co-operate with them in the enactment of the law, which should render the tenure of the judicial office dependent on the good behaviour of the judges, and the salaries independent of the future votes of the House of Assembly. The Governor communicated a copy of this despatch, which was found to contain a clause announcing to Lord Aylmer that with no ordinary feelings of regret he was informed that His Majesty would not be advised to assent to the particular Bill passed by the Assembly. The despatch was not a bald one, but entered minutely into the whole question covered by the Bill, and fully explained why it was necessary that the judges should not be made subject to an annual or uncertain vote for their salaries. It said,— "The Bill does not make a fixed and permanent provision for the maintenance of the judges. I observe that the enactment itself amounts to nothing more than a declaration that the judges shall be paid out of those collective funds of which the House of Assembly have, or claim to themselves, the right of appropriation. Such a provision will not supersede the necessity of an annual vote of the House to sanction the payment of the judges' salaries, nor authorize the Governor to issue his warrant to the Receiver General for the sums, in the event of such a vote being withheld. The popular branch of the Legislature would, therefore, retain the power of diminishing the official incomes of the judges, or of stopping the payment of them altogether, and would thus exercise an influence over the Bench, subversive of that sense of independence of all parties in the state, so requisite in the members of a body, whose high office it is to ascertain and protect the rights of all with strict impartiality. The British Parliament have studiously divested themselves of all such means of controlling the freedom of the judges."

The conclusion to be drawn is, that while the Assembly and their electors were clamorous to have the judges independent of the Crown, they were quite willing to have them dependent on the Legislature. This is not, however, surprising, as all the energies of the French party in the Province of Quebec were directed to making, not only the judges, but everybody and everything, dependent on that branch of Parliament controlled by themselves.

CHAPTER VIII.

Mackenzie and the Reform Party—Defects in Government—Mackenzie's Printing Office Attacked—Type Distributed and Thrown Into the Bay—Action for Damages—Mackenzie Profited by the Rash Act—Collins and the Newspaper, "The Freeman"—Collins Prosecuted for Libel—Young Men who Attacked Mackenzie's Office on Trial—Convicted—Mackenzie Did Not Countenance Prosecution—Report of Select Committee of House of Assembly—"The Advocate's" Comments Thereon Offensive and Libellous—Mackenzie Prosecuted for Libel—Appeal to the Electors—Alien Laws—Mackenzie Makes Friends of Old Settlers—Mackenzie Not Admirer of the American Constitution—Mackenzie's Address to Electors, County of York, 1827—Dr. Baldwin—Mackenzie's "Black List"—Mackenzie and Small Opposed—Sir Peregrine Maitland's Administration—Colonial System of Government—Mackenzie's Activity—Mackenzie's Thirty-two Resolutions—Grievances—Sir John Colborne, Governor—The Executive Council—Governor Responsible to English Government—Incongruous Position of Executive and Legislative Council—Colonial Despatch to Sir James Kempt—Death of George IV.—Dissolution of House—Tory House—Reform Not a Success—Mackenzie Expelled the House of Assembly—The Election for York.

As in nature and the life of man, so in the political life of a nation, there are periods of gloom and of brightness, sunshine and shade, of storm and of calm. The period in the life of Upper Canada between the years 1824 and 1830 may justly be called the stormy period, and William Lyon Mackenzie was the stormy petrel which followed in the wake of the ship of state, foreboding wreck for it at every turn.

What may be termed a Reform House was elected for the Parliament which commenced its first session in January, 1825. There was a considerable majority of the members of this House who adopted the principles, or some of the principles, espoused by Mr. Mackenzie. Prominent among the Reform members were the well-known names of Rolph, Perry and Bidwell. Those in the Province, opposed to the policy and procedure of the Government, were much elated at the success they had, for the first time, attained in the political development of the Province.

Mr. Mackenzie, by his writings, had contributed not a little to the success of the Reform party, if that may be called a success which placed a number of gentlemen in a House of Assembly, the principal function of which was to pass resolutions, without power to carry them into effect. The defect in the colonial system of government was that the Legislative Council, composed of Government nominees and Government place-men, could, when so disposed, block all legislation that did not accord with their views, or, it may be, conflict with their interests. It was not the fault of the men who constituted either the Executive or Legislative Council that they owed no responsibility to the people's House. These men were given their places by the higher or sovereign power of the State, and under the Constitutional Act, which they were bound to respect. If they erred at times, it was nothing more than human, and they might well have been spared the virulent attacks made upon them by

Mr. Mackenzie in his paper, *The Colonial Advocate*. This weapon, in the hands of Mr. Mackenzie, enabled him, metaphorically speaking, to throw vitriol into the face of the officials of the Government, calculated very seriously to disfigure them in the eyes of the inhabitants of the Province generally.

The officials had no means of parrying the attacks made upon them, unless they had recourse to the law courts, which would have been tiresome and expensive. Fifteen ardent young men, the most of them officials, or the sons of officials, in the month of June, 1826, determined to punish Mr. Mackenzie for the offences, many and oft-times committed by him, in libelling themselves, their sires, or immediate relatives in the columns of the *Advocate*. In broad daylight, they visited Mr. Mackenzie's printing office, at the corner of Caroline and Palace Streets (the latter now Front Street), in the City of Toronto, and distributed some of the type over the floor of the office, as freely as Mr. Mackenzie had distributed his paper through the length and breadth of the Province. Other types they threw into the bay, broke a new printing press that they found in the building, and committed havoc generally. All this was done to resent the calumnies of Mr. Mackenzie. It was a very foolish act on the part of these young men, for even supposing that Mr. Mackenzie had been more vituperative than he need have been, or even more censorious of the official conduct of the fathers or kinsmen of the young men than the circumstances and condition of things demanded, a destruction of his property, besides making a martyr of the individual attacked, would compel the law officers of the Crown, however unwilling, to take action against the offenders.

One of the first results of this attack of the young men was that one of the party of assault, Mr. Lyons, who held the office of private secretary under Governor Maitland, was dismissed from his position, no doubt with a view to pacifying public opinion. Mr. Mackenzie commenced a civil action against the perpetrators of the trespass on his property. The case went to trial, and the offenders were mulcted in $2,500 damages, which was, however, raised by private subscription of their friends. This destruction of Mr. Mackenzie's property gained for him considerable sympathy from the non-official class in Toronto (York). The official class, on the other hand, rather gloried in the act, and the Governor, or Government, condoned the offence by rewarding the offenders. Mr. Lyons, who lost his position as secretary, was appointed to the office of Registrar of the Niagara District. Mr. Samuel Peters Jarvis, another of the rioters, obtained an Indian Commissionership. Mr. Charles Richardson, student in the office of the Attorney-General, was given the office of Clerk of the Peace for the Niagara District, no doubt recognizing his services to the Crown. That these young men should have been promoted, rather than degraded, on account of this illegal act of theirs, in destroying Mr. Mackenzie's property, shows very clearly that Mr. Mackenzie was regarded by the ruling powers as a nuisance, which they would be glad to get rid of by any means.

Mr. Mackenzie, for his part, rather prided himself in being considered a nuisance by the officials. It seems to have been his mission in life always to have been at war with the official class. Mr. Macaulay, afterwards Chief Justice, was a practising lawyer in York at the time of the press destruction, and endeavoured to bring about a settlement of Mr. Mackenzie's claim, without a trial at law. A passage in his letter to Mr. Small, who acted for Mackenzie, to this end, shows that he considered Mr. Mackenzie was not blameless in the matter, and that if there was no legal justification, there was at least some excuse for the conduct of the young men in attacking the printing office. The passage is this : " The real cause of the step is well known to all ; it is not to be ascribed to any malice, political feeling, or private animosity; the *personal calumnies* of the latter *Advocates* point out sufficiently the true and only motive that prompted it, and I have now to offer to pay at once the full value of the damage occasioned to the press and type, to be determined by indifferent and competent judges selected for that purpose." *

This episode shows the extreme party spirit of the time, and the relation in which Mr. Mackenzie, the principal promoter of the rebellion, stood with the Government and its adherents. Mr. Mackenzie could not but profit by the occurrence which brought about the

* See Lindsey's Life of William Lyon Mackenzie, pp. 78-100.

trial, and put $2,500 of good money in his pocket. Without this assistance the *Advocate* would probably have been discontinued, and the officials relieved from its irritating remarks. After the trial, Mr. Mackenzie himself, according to his biographer, Mr. Charles Lindsey, referring to the result, said : That verdict re-established on a permanent footing *The Advocate* press, because it enabled me to perform my engagements, without disposing of my real property."

A series of accusations, recriminations, assaults, libels and other proceedings, legal and illegal, followed in the wake of the trial of the young men who destroyed Mr. Mackenzie's property. Mr. Mackenzie was not the only libeller of those days. At this time (1828), Mr. Frank Collins edited a paper in York, which, following in the footsteps of the *Advocate*, was very unsparing in its attacks on the officials of the Government.

In April, 1828, Mr. Robinson, afterwards Sir John Robinson and Chief Justice, felt it his duty to prosecute Collins criminally for four libels published in his paper, *The Freeman*. Mr. Collins, by way of retaliation on the Attorney General, determined to make it hot for the young men, whom Mackenzie had prosecuted for the attack on his office. These young men were friends and political supporters of the Attorney General, and so Collins would stab the Attorney General and the members of the House, his friends, named in the article, by instituting criminal proceedings. Seven were tried, and after a prolonged trial were found guilty. To the credit of Mr. Mackenzie, be it said, that he was no party to this prosecution. In giving his evidence at the trial, he disclaimed all connection with it, and expressed the wish that the rioters, if convicted, should be let off with but nominal damages, and this was the result.

Prosecutions for libel seem to have been the order of the day. Mr. Neilson, a publisher in Lower Canada, was at the same time undergoing the ordeal of trial for libel, keeping pace fairly with Mr. Collins and Mr. Mackenzie. One could almost have wished that Mr. Mackenzie, owing to his generous conduct in the Collins' trial, would have been excused for his next offence. His restless nature would not allow him to stop. It was not long before he gave an opportunity to the authorities for another prosecution for libel.

In an article in the *Advocate*, which dealt with a report of a select committee of the House of Assembly, on the complaint of one Forsyth of Niagara Falls, complaining of the conduct of the Crown officers, and of the defective and partial administration of justice, Mackenzie said: "The report speaks a language not to be misunderstood; and we trust that a perusal of it will serve to stir up the dormant energies of the wholesome part of the population, and induce them to exert themselves manfully to clear the House of Assembly next election of the Attorney General, Speaker Wilson, Jonas, David and Charles Jones, Messrs. Burnham, Coleman, McLean, Vankoughnet, and the whole of that ominous nest of unclean birds, which have so long lain close under the wings of a spendthrift executive and (politically to speak) actually preyed upon the very vitals of the country they ought to have loved, cherished and protected. No wonder is it that Parliament should find its energies all but paralyzed when such an accumulation of corrupt materials is left unswept with the besom of the people's wrath from out of these halls they have so long and so shamefully 'defiled with their abomination.'"

The incisiveness of the libelous matter was no doubt the cause of the prosecution which inevitably followed. The article was evidently intended as an "avant courier" in the race for the next Parliamentary election, an election which Mr. Mackenzie and his friends hoped would sweep every particle of Toryism out of the Assembly. The indictment was laid, but was never brought to trial before a jury, but seems to have been laid over for trial by the electors of the Province.

Before the time fixed for the next Parliamentary election, Mr. Mackenzie was given an opportunity to make friends in the constituencies of very many who had been supporters of the Government. The means to this end was afforded by the wretched condition of the Alien Law. As this law then stood, American citizens, even those who had taken up arms on the British side during the Colonial Revolutionary War, were denied the rights of British subjects in Canada, if born in the old Colonies before the Treaty of 1783, or if they had continued to reside in the United States for the period of one year after 3rd September, 1783, and a British subject who came to Canada, by way of the United States, was held to have become an alien. We have seen how, in 1825, the law was pressed in the case of Gourlay. This state of affairs was by virtue of Imperial legislation, and the treaty between Great Britain and the United States, under which the Americans secured their independence. By the joint operations of these measures, such persons were considered American citizens. Besides the class of old colonists of ante-revolutionary days, the latter-day Americans, that is to say, Americans born under the Stars and Stripes, who had no ideal but the Republican form of government, sought to get a foothold in Canada by taking up land, more for speculative purposes than otherwise.

The rights of such last named persons to hold lands in Canada was disputed by the old settlers. When the alien laws and the treaty came to be consulted, and a legal decision had on the subject, it was found that the old settlers were in no better condition in the matter of citizenship than the new. Mr. Mackenzie came to the rescue of the old settlers, and strongly denounced the alien laws, at the same time advocating legislation to place the old settlers on the same level as British subjects born within the boundaries of the British Isles. When it is considered that a great portion of the lands of these old settlers were in jeopardy, because of the alien law, and their being placed in the category of aliens, it will readily be seen what a powerful lever Mr. Mackenzie had to work with.

This lever he used for its full power. He roused the interested, got an agent sent to England to advocate repeal of the laws, and finally succeeded in getting the law placed on a footing that secured to the old Canadian settlers titles to their lands, thus gaining the confidence of many former opponents, and paving the way for a seat in the Legislature, which, at no distant day, would have to receive, if not to welcome him within its halls.

Mr. Mackenzie was not an admirer of the American Constitution. On the contrary, he preferred the British Constitution, and would have been satisfied with that Constitution enforced in its entirety, including responsibility of the Executive to the Elective House and so to the people, instead of its responsibility to the Crown, as it prevailed in Canada. When he succeeded in getting Mr. Randall appointed a delegate to England, to advocate a repeal of the alien laws, he addressed letters to Lord Dalhousie, Governor-General, in which, after making strong profession of loyalty, and referring to the American Federal Union and its then threatened disruption, he said: "And is this the Government, and are these the people whose alliance and intimacy we ought to court instead of those of England? No, my Lord, their constitutional theory is defective, and their practice necessarily inconsistent. Their Government wants consolidation. Let us take warning by their example." *

The Ninth Provincial Parliament, the last held under the administration of Sir Peregrine Maitland, was dissolved

* Lindsey, Vol. I, p. 128.

in July, 1828. **Mr. Mackenzie, always in advance of** the times, issued **his first** Parliamentary address **for** the election to **follow the** dissolution so early as the 17th December, **1827.** This address was to the Electors of the County of York. In his address to his constituency Mr. Mackenzie exhibited the same independent attitude and uncompromising opposition to the ruling power, as he had shown by his writings in the press. He said: "That corrupt, powerful and long endured influence, which has hitherto interfered with your rights and liberties, can only be overthrown by your unanimity and zeal. I have been a careful observer of the conduct of the people's representatives in the Colonial Assemblies. I have seen men, in whom was placed the utmost confidence, fall from their integrity and betray their sacred trust. But there are others who continue to maintain and uphold the interests of their country. . . . Among this latter class I am desirous of being numbered." *

An independent House of Assembly would be an inestimable boon for Upper Canada, and Mr. Mackenzie, to attain that end, desired to clear the House of all officeholders. Especially was it his desire to dispossess the existing Legislative Council, and if possible to have their places filled with men of advanced ideas, such as Marshall S. Bidwell, Peter Perry, Ketchum, Randal and others who had espoused the Mackenzie political faith.

There was one man in **the** Reform ranks **of that day, who, while strongly** impressed **with** reform **doctrines, was**

* Lindsey, Vol. I, p. 144.

12

of the more conservative class of Reformers, not disposed to be led, but rather wishing to lead Mr. Mackenzie and his friends. He was a man of excellent judgment, honest in his convictions and deservedly popular. That man was Dr. Baldwin. Dr. Baldwin was a Whig, Mr. Mackenzie was a Radical. In that lay the difference.

In seeking the suffrages of York, Mr. Mackenzie made a good choice. It was the county in which the capital of the Province was situated. There was his home, and there he had built up for himself a reputation; true, a bad reputation in the eyes of the reigning powers, but, in the eyes of those opposed to the prevailing system, he was looked upon as the man to force the citadel of Toryism, and to open the gates for the incoming of men who were to shake the fortress to its foundations, and plant upon the ramparts the banner of Reform, if not the flag of Revolution.

Mr. Mackenzie commenced the campaign for the election of 1828 by publishing a "Legislative Black List," in which he set down the names of members who had, as they believed, faithfully served their constituents in the Ninth Parliament, but who had not been able to see eye to eye with Mr. Mackenzie. Mr. James E. Small, of York, was a Reformer, but not of the advanced school of Mr. Mackenzie. Mr. Small had indeed been Mr. Mackenzie's attorney in his actions for damages against the type distributors, and, strange to say, it was Mr. Small who contested with Mr. Mackenzie the constituency, and was made to feel that Mackenzie the Radical was master of a power greater than that exercised by the moderate reformers of his own class. Mr. Mackenzie was elected over his political friend, but less advanced reformer, James E. Small.

Sir John Colborne succeeded Sir Peregrine Maitland as Governor, and opened the Tenth Provincial Parliament in January, 1829. Mr. Bidwell was elected Speaker, and from this circumstance the political complexion of the House may be gathered, as also from the address of the House, in reply to the Governor's speech at the opening. The House said: "Although we at present see your Excellency unhappily surrounded by the same advisers as have so deeply wounded the feelings and injured the best interests of the country, yet in the interval of any necessary change, we entertain an anxious belief that under the auspices of your Excellency, the administration will rise above suspicion."

"Unhappily surrounded by the same advisers,"—"Intervals of any necessary change." That was it. The House fondly hoped there would be a change in the personnel of the Government, in its policy, in its general administration. And so there would have been if there had existed in the Colony Responsible Government, as it exists at the present day. Unhappily that was not the system of Colonial Government in Canada, or in any other British Colony, at the time, the great difference being that then, the Colonial Government was responsible to the Colonial Office, now, the people's representatives have it in their power to change the Government, whenever, in their wisdom, they think it should be changed.

Mr. Mackenzie, as a member of the Assembly, showed the same unflagging energy, which he had shown in everything he had undertaken in life. In Committee, or in the House, he was the same prying, inquisitive, irritating Mackenzie. Everything, in his estimation, had gone wrong. He first attacked the Post Office Department, which was then under Imperial control. It was urged that the postage on letters and newspapers was unnecessarily high, that the Department was inefficiently managed, that it should be taken out of the control of the Imperial Government, and placed under local control. The principle he advocated was no doubt a good one, but in this, as in everything else, Mr. Mackenzie was in advance of his contemporaries, and of the times, and this, his biographer, Mr. Lindsey, has frankly admitted. Mr. Lindsey has had much experience in political matters, and no one is better qualified to give an opinion on such a subject.

Mr. Mackenzie, before the close of the first session of the Assembly, introduced to the House thirty-one Resolutions, enumerative of grievances, that, in his judgment, afflicted the Province, and required to be remedied.

The principal grievances of which he complained were:

The absence of local self-government—substantially Responsible Government

The institution of criminal prosecutions at the instance of the Crown for political libels.

The want of independence of the judges.

The power of the sheriffs, holding office during pleasure, in the selection of juries.

The patronage exercised by the Crown and the Lieutenant-Governor of the Province, uncontrolled by the Legislature.

The unpaid war losses (War of 1812), or their being charged to the Provincial, instead of the Imperial Government.

The absence of a protective system in the trade of the Province.

The budget of grievances was enlarged by other complaints, but they were of a minor kind or administrative character.

The resolutions were not pressed on the House for adoption, but were referred to a special committee, of which Mr. Mackenzie was chairman, called "The Committee on Grievances."

Mr. John Beverley Robinson was Attorney-General of the Province throughout the first session of the Tenth Parliament, in which Mr. Mackenzie had a seat. It fell to his lot to defend the Government against the assaults of the new member. There had never been in the House, up to this time, so fearless a denunciator of the ruling powers, and all connected with them, as Mackenzie. The nature of the Government was such, however, that he was powerless to alter the existing state of things. The Government had the patronage and control of the purse. They cared no more for hostile resolutions of the House of Assembly than they would have cared for as many blank cartridges, fired into their midst. Mr. Mackenzie had hoped, that with the incoming of Sir John Colborne as Governor, the Parliamentary majority would have had a voice in the regulation of the affairs of the Province. He soon found it was a very small voice, not louder than the utterance of the Assembly of Lower Canada, explained in a previous chapter, and for the same reason— the controlling power of the Legislative Council.

Mr. Mackenzie was comforted by one thing during the recess following the session of 1829. A vacancy in the representation of York having occurred through the elevation of Mr. John Beverley Robinson to the Bench, as Chief Justice of the Province, Mr. Mackenzie was enabled to welcome, as a member to fill his place, Mr. Robert Baldwin, who, if he did not share all Mr. Mackenzie's opinions, was more congenial to his tastes than the talented Attorney-General. Mr. Baldwin had been opposed in his candidature for a seat in the House by Mr. James E. Small, who, as we have seen, was the candidate in opposition to Mr. Mackenzie, when he was elected for York.

The second session of the Tenth Parliament was opened by Sir John Colborne, in January, 1830. The Legislative Assembly seized at once upon the opportunity to inform His Excellency that the advisers about His Excellency, in other words the Executive Council—"from the unhappy policy they had pursued in the late administration, had long deservedly lost the confidence of the country." This they did in reply to His Excellency's speech, at the opening of the House. Such a reply to the speech from the throne, in England, would inevitably have led to a change of the Monarch's advisers. Why should not the same result follow in the case of the Canadian Executive Council?

It must not be supposed that the British Government was not impressed with the incongruous position of the Executive and Legislative Councils in the Provinces. Sir George Murray, the Colonial Secretary, in 1829, had, in September of that year, written to Sir James Kempt, administrator in chief, who advised Sir John Colborne of the despatch : " The constitution of the Legislative and Executive Councils is another subject which has undergone considerable discussion, but upon which His Majesty's Government must suspend their opinion until I shall have received some authentic information from your Excellency. You will, therefore, have the goodness to report to me, whether it would be expedient to make any alteration in the general constitution of those bodies, and especially how far it would be desirable to introduce a larger proportion of members not holding offices at the pleasure of the Crown ; and if it should be considered desirable, how far it may be practicable to find a sufficient number of persons of respectability of this description."

The newspaper organs of the two recognized parties in the Province in 1830, the Tory and the Reform parties, were but a little less chary in their calumnies, charges and recriminations than were the newspapers in Lower Canada. The Reformers and their leaders being accused of disloyalty by the Tory press, Mr. Mackenzie, the champion of Reform, advocated their cause with all the energy he could master. He published a series of letters, addressed to Sir John Colborne, aimed at removing the stigma of disloyalty which the Tory party sought to fix upon them. In one of his letters he wrote: "The people of this Province neither desire to break up their ancient connection with Great Britain, nor are they anxious to become members of the North American Confederation; all they want is a cheap, frugal, domestic government, to be exercised for their benefit and controlled by their own fixed land marks; they seek a system by which to insure justice, protect property, establish domestic tranquillity, and afford a reasonable prospect that civil and religious liberty will be perpetuated, and the safety and happiness of society effected."

The death of King George IV, in 1830, caused a dissolution of the House, and a new election. Mr. Mackenzie again offered himself as a candidate for the County of York, and, with his colleague, Mr. Jesse Ketchum, was elected over his Tory opponents by a considerable majority. The general complexion of the House after this election, however, was different from that of the previous Assembly. Mr. Mackenzie secured his own election, but his party was not so successful as a whole. Many of the old members were defeated, and Mr. Baldwin's name does not appear among the names of those who were elected. The majority in the Assembly was decidedly Tory.

So far as Mr. Mackenzie was concerned, this House was an unfortunate one to deal with. He made attempts to carry Reform measures, but generally failed. He did however get a Committee on the Representation of the Province appointed, of which he was chairman. His object was to call attention to the weakness of the Assembly as a representative body, inasmuch as many members were office-holders under the Crown, and dependent on the Crown for their salaries. The same was the case with certain members of the Legislative Council.

Mr. Mackenzie magnified grievances as no one else could, and he was certain to make the most of this, as of other complaints. His prying disposition and succession of assaults, political of course, on the Government and its supporters, made him obnoxious to the House. It was determined that he should be got rid of in some way. It was first proposed to expel him from the House for having published the journals of the House without its consent. This project, however, was not carried out; but a libel on the House published by him was seized upon as a ground of expulsion. On the 10th December, 1831, a motion was carried in the House for the expulsion of the obnoxious Mackenzie. During the proceedings in the House, on the motion for his expulsion, he was called a "reptile" by the Attorney-General, and by the Solicitor-General a "spaniel dog." These certainly were unpleasant names to be given by one member of the House to another, but the character of Mr. Mackenzie's calumnies brought upon him the full force of the eloquence of the Crown officers, coupled with a good deal of abuse.

The expulsion of Mr. Mackenzie caused a great sensation at the time. His constituents, and those sympathizing with him, to the number of nearly a thousand, petitioned the Lieutenant-Governor against the proceedings of the House, commenting on the unfairness of visiting on Mr. Mackenzie the penalty of expulsion, when it was contended that Tory papers had been equally culpable and had not been prosecuted. The Governor dismissed the petition by merely acknowledging its receipt and making no further reply. This incensed the petitioners, and they determined to show the Government and the Assembly that they would stand by the expelled member. They proceeded to his house, took him under their protection, carried him through the streets of the town of York, and visited the Parliament House, when the procession halted and cheered the honorable member to the echo. On the same day that Mr. Mackenzie was expelled the House a writ was issued for a new election in the constituency. "The freedom of the press" became the watchword. On the 2nd January, 1832, the electors of York reversed the judgment of the House of Assembly, and returned Mr. Mackenzie as their member, his opponent receiving but one vote.

Mr. Mackenzie's constitutents, to the number of a thousand or more, escorted him to the House when he went to take his seat on his re-election, with great parade and loud acclamations. His triumph was complete, but did not last long, as he was again expelled in a few days after his triumphant entry to the Halls of Legislation, for another libel on the Assembly, published in his *Colonial Advocate* of the 5th January, 1832. On this occasion, the House, by its vote, not only expelled, but declared him disqualified to be a member of the House.

This second expulsion of Mr. Mackenzie from the House was the cause of great excitement in many parts of the Province. Public meetings were held, denouncing the whole proceedings as tyrannical and arbitrary. At the meeting at Hamilton, on the 19th March, 1832, the opposing parties nearly came to blows on the preliminary question as to who should be chairman of the meeting. At the meeting held in the town of York, on March 23rd, 1832, there was much violence. The turbulence rose to the dimensions of a riot, and Mr. Mackenzie's printing office was again robbed, a portion of the building destroyed, and some of the type scattered. At this meeting Mr. Mackenzie was burnt in effigy.

The Governor, hearing of the disturbance, ordered a company of soldiers to be in readiness to act, in case the civil authorities should prove that they were unable to put down the rioting or prevent its renewal.

Amidst all this excitement, Mr. Mackenzie found time to have petitions to the King and to the Imperial Parliament signed by a great number of persons, complaining of grievances, and he himself became bearer of the petitions to England.

In April, 1832, he sailed for England, where he met Mr. Viger, the agent of Lower Canada. They got a hearing at the Colonial Office, and Mr. Mackenzie was surprised to find that he was courteously received. It was something new to him to be received with consideration in Government circles. This had not been his experience in Canada.

When the petitions were laid before the House of Commons by Mr. Hume, whose interest and influence Mr. Mackenzie had gained, Mr. Hume said that he presented the petition, not only with the knowledge and consent of the Government, but: "he was happy to have the assurance of Viscount Goderich, Secretary of State for the Colonies, that his Lordship was busy inquiring into the grievances complained of with a view of affording relief." After an interview of three hours with the Colonial Secretary, on the 3rd August, accompanied by Messrs. Hume and Viger, Mr. Mackenzie wrote to his friends in Canada : "We left the Colonial Office, well satisfied that measures are about to be taken that will go a great way towards neutralizing the existing discontent."

The discontent referred to by Mr. Mackenzie had, in many cases, been aroused and promoted by himself. It was not the discontent of the people of Upper Canada as a whole, but of a faction led by Mr. Mackenzie; but whatever it may have been, the Governor was now instructed by the Colonial Office to apply remedies quite sufficient to cure, without the attempt to kill the patient, an attempt afterwards made by Mr. Mackenzie and his followers in the Province of Upper Canada.

CHAPTER IX.

The Real Rebellion in Lower Canada—Mr. Papineau and Despotism—Despatch of Mr. Stanley—The King Will Not Assent to Elective Legislative Council—In the Future Institutions of Canada May Be Modified—The Monarchical Form Must Be Maintained—Papineau's Ninety-two Resolutions—His Speech on Introducing to Assembly—The Resolutions—Resolutions Revolutionary—Mr. Morin Sent to England—No Supply Bill Passed by Assembly—Mr. Roebuck and the English House of Commons—Roebuck Champion of Lower Canada—Mr. Stanley Checkmates Roebuck—Resolutions Referred to Committee—O'Connell and Bulwer Members of Committee—Hume and "Baneful Domination of Mother Country"—Report of Committee on Ninety-two Resolutions—Mackenzie in London—Agent of Malcontents in Upper Canada—Report of Committee Censured by Mackenzie's Followers—Grievance-mongers—Roebuck and Hume Favour Mackenzie and Papineau and Their Principles—"Reform Committees and Constitutional Associations"—A French-Canadian Killed—His Blood Must Be Avenged—French Ascendancy in Lower Canada—Lower Canada Assembly of 1835—Papineau at the Pinnacle of his Power—Assembly Expunge Governor's Speech from Journals—Morin Moves Resolution to Consider State of Province of Lower Canada—Speeches of Papineau and Gugy thereon.

LET us now return to the narrative of still more important events in Lower Canada, which lead to the Rebellion, and which has been left in order to deal with Mr. Mackenzie and his group of friends in Upper Canada. For the really serious Rebellion had its seat in Lower Canada, the part or share in it which developed itself in

Upper Canada, bearing to it about the same proportion that the smallest stream in Canada bears to the mighty St. Lawrence,

In April, 1832, the Governor-in-Chief, Lord Aylmer, communicated to the House of Assembly a despatch from the Home Government, refusing sanction to a Colonial Act to incapacitate the judges from sitting or voting in the Executive Council, and giving the reasons for such refusal. The House of Assembly had now become convinced that the reforms asked by it would not be granted by the Imperial Government. Mr. Papineau set to work to prepare a stupendous series of Resolutions for submission to the House of Assembly, declaratory of the grievances of which the French party in Lower Canada complained, as affecting their political condition. These Resolutions were prepared as an offset to a despatch from the Colonial Office, then presided over by Mr. Stanley, in answer to an address from the House of Assembly to the King, which was laid before the Assembly in January, 1834.

Referring to the address of the Assembly, Mr. Stanley wrote, that: "The object of this address was to pray His Majesty to sanction a national convention of the people for the purpose of superseding the Legislative authorities and to ascertain whether in order to destroy the Constitution it was better to introduce the Elective principle to the Legislative Council, or abolish that body entirely. His Majesty was willing to put no harsher construction on such a proposal than that of extreme inconsiderateness; but he can never approve of such a measure, inconsistent as it would be with the very existence of monarchical institutions; yet His Majesty on the other hand was well-disposed to sanction every measure likely to secure the independence and raise the character of the Legislative Council." He said he was not prepared to advise the King to propose to Parliament a measure of such import as a repeal of the Act of 1791; but if events should constrain the British Legislature to interpose its supreme authority to compose the internal dissensions of the Colony, it would then, indeed, become his duty to submit for the consideration of Parliament some modifications of the charters of the Canadas, not, however, for introducing institutions inconsistent with monarchy, but to maintain and strengthen the connection with the Mother Country, adhering ever to the spirit of the British Constitution, confirming too, within their due limits, the rights and privileges of all classes of His Majesty's subjects.

An idea of the purport and intent of the Resolutions prepared by Mr. Papineau may be gathered from his speech in introducing these to the House.

"Long have we uttered our complaint," said he, "and we are all of one mind regarding our grievances; there is no doubt as to the parties who inflict them upon us; the only difficulty is, how to find a remedy: it is time now to set about obtaining it. There are persons among us, whose minds, preoccupied with the workings of European institutions, would have us to adopt their ideas in this matter. But it is not for us, imperfectly informed as we are of the nature of such institutions, to judge of their merits or demerits. Let us enquire rather into things that more nearly concern our own destiny, and strive to build up our liberties as socially and durably as possible. It is certain that before long the whole of America will be republicanized. If a change be necessary in our present constitution, is it to be undertaken in view of such a conjuncture as I have just mentioned? Would it be a crime were I to demand that it should? The members of this House are all answerable to their constituents for whatever decision they may come to in this regard, and even though the soldiery should slaughter them for it, they ought not to hesitate, for a moment, to pronounce for any change which they may consider beneficial to their country. It needs not that we enquire what is our present, what was our past situation in America. Britain herself has founded mighty Republics on this continent, wherein flourish liberty, morals, commerce and the arts. The French and Spanish-American colonies, with political institutions much less free, have been unfortunate, and had to struggle against the inherent vices of their constitutions. But British rule in the Colonies, what has been its nature? Has it been more aristocratic than democratic? It is therefore a great mistake on the part of Mr. Stanley to discourse to us of British Monarchical sway in this present year, eighteen hundred and thirty-four. In the days of the Stuarts, those who maintained that the monarchic principle was paramount in Britain lost their heads on the scaffold. Ever since that age Britain has had a government called mixed, and no other qualification can we apply to .t. Owing to this, its true quality, it is that Mr. Stanley has got into place and power, the entry to which would have been barred against him, if a vote of the House of Commons had not constrained Royalty to give up its own wishes. The King was told to yield, else he would be discrowned. And yet this man, despised as he is by the British people, now enlarges, for our edification, on the monarchic government of Britain. We, the while, well knowing that the British people, so great for their commerce, for their institutions, for their progress in civilization and the arts, and yet more for the liberty which they have borne to the ends of the earth, are free at any moment to upset the monarchy thus spoken of, whenever they list."

Following his speech, Mr. Papineau introduced his ninety-two Resolutions, which, in the published proceedings of the Assembly, are dated 21st February, 1834. In their printed form they take up forty-six pages of the proceedings.

The first five Resolutions are protestations of loyalty to the Empire on the part of the people of Lower Canada.

Resolutions 6 and 7 refer to a Petition, in the year 1827, of 87,000 persons of the Province to Imperial Parliament, complaining of grievances; that such grievances did then, and still exist; that a Committee of the House of Commons after investigation reported on 18th July, 1828:—

1st. That the embarrassments and discontents that had long prevailed in the Canadas, had arisen from serious defects in the system of laws and the constitutions established in those colonies.

2nd. That these embarrassments were in a great measure to be attributed to the manner in which the existing system had been administered.

3rd. That they had a complete conviction that neither the suggestions which they had made, nor any other improvements in the laws and constitutions of the Canadas will be attended with the desired effect, unless an impartial, conciliating and constitutional system of government were observed in these loyal and important colonies.

Resolution 8. Bad administration continued; recommendations of committee not carried out.

9 to 39. Condemn the Legislative Council, the mode of appointment thereto. Its partiality and abuse of power. Its antagonism to the Assembly and general unsuitableness for the Colony.

Resolution 40. Expresses a wish that: " the Imperial Legislature will comply with the wishes of the people and of this House, and will provide the most effectual remedy for all evils, present and future, either by rendering the Legislative Council elective in the manner mentioned in the Address of this House to His Most Gracious Majesty of 20th March, 1833, or by enabling the people to express still more directly their opinions as to the measures to be adopted in that behalf, and with regard to such other modifications of the Constitution as the wants of the people, and the interests of His Majesty's Government in this Province may require; and that this House perseveres in the said address."

Resolutions 41, 42, 43, 44, 45, 46. That the neighbouring United States have a form of government very fit to prevent abuses of power, and very effective in repressing them: that the reverse of this order of things has always prevailed in Canada under the present form of government. That there exists in the neighbouring States a stronger and more general attachment to the national institutions than in any other country, and that there exists also in those States a guarantee for the progressive advance of their political institutions towards perfection, in the revision of the same at short and determined intervals by conventions of the people, in order that they may without any shock or violence be adapted to the actual state of things.

Resolutions 47 to 52. Condemnatory of the despatch of Mr. Stanley, Colonial Secretary, to which allusion has been made. That such despatch was ill-timed and abusive, and that if it was meant to contain a threat to introduce into the Constitution any other modifications than such as are asked for by the majority of the people of the Province: "This House would esteem itself wanting in candour to the people of England if it hesitated to call their attention to the fact that in less than twenty years British America would be as populous as the old American Colonies when they threw off their allegiance."

Resolutions 52 to 54. That the majority of the inhabitants of this Province are in no wise disposed to repudiate any one of the advantages they derive from their origin, and from their descent from the French nation, which, in the progress it has made in science, letters and the arts has never been behind the British nation.

Resolutions 54 to 62. Principally concerning seigniorial tenure, and the opportunity that had been given the seigniors to obtain grants direct from the Crown, to the prejudice of the people's claim.

Resolutions 63 to 74. Condemn Executive Government. Repudiation of its claims, set up for many years, to the control and power of appropriating public revenues levied in the Province.

Resolutions 74 to 78. That the preponderance of the French over English population was very great, yet that all the best offices were given to English, or those of British descent. That judges were brought out from England, or lawyers of English birth not familiar with Canadian laws were made judges.

Resolutions 79, 80, 81. House of Assembly claims all the rights, immunities and privileges of the English House of Commons.

Resolutions 81 to end. General maladministration. Complain of composition of Executive Council, the members of which are judges of the Court of Appeal. Exorbitant fees exacted in public offices. Judges frequently called upon in Executive Council to give their opinions on cases they are subsequently called upon to try. Accumulation and plurality of offices. Members of the Legislative Council interfering in elections. Military force interfering in elections. Crown lands appropriated by officials and official favourites. Increase of the expenses of government without the authority of Legislature. Too frequent reservations of bills. Neglect of Colonial Office.

Although Mr. Papineau was the author of these Resolutions, and the acknowledged leader of the French party as a whole, there were, nevertheless, in that party some members of the Assembly who were of opinion that the Resolutions were more revolutionary than the condition of the Province called for. There was a Quebec party, as well as a Montreal party in the Province, the Montreal party being the more revolutionary of the two. Mr. Bedard was understood, *sub modo*, to lead the Quebec party, while at the same time he was a personal friend and supporter of Mr. Papineau. The members of his section of the party had nothing to gain, but much to lose by a revolution. The Garrison of Quebec was a source of revenue to the people of that town, and, not only the town, but the whole surrounding country profited greatly by the great lumber and ship-building trade, then carried on so largely at this seaport. This business was chiefly in the hands of British merchants. British interests had therefore more charm for the Quebecers, of whatever race or religion, than for the inhabitants of the district of Montreal, where French influences and interests were largely in the ascendant. It would be a politic move, therefore, on the part of Mr. Papineau, to secure the support of the Quebec party in favour of his Resolutions; not that the Resolutions might not have carried in the House, without the aid of that party; still, it would give greater prominence to his radical measure, if he could gain the confidence of the more conservative members of the party of the Quebec district. At the previous session of the Legislature, Mr. Bedard had showed symptoms of distrust in Mr. Papineau. It was therefore necessary that he, and with him the Quebec section of the French-Canadian party, should be captured and reconciled to the great leader Papineau and to all his works. Mr. Papineau, with characteristic shrewdness, entrusted the introduction of the ninety-two Resolutions in the House to Mr. Bedard, which office Mr. Bedard undertook, having secured certain modifications which freed the Resolutions of their more offensive assumptions. After the elimination of the more objectionable parts, enough was left to satisfy the discontented French-Canadian and his aspirations.

The Resolutions were debated for several days. Mr. Neilson, a Scotch member of the House, and a party supporter of Mr. Papineau, was not prepared to break with the British Government, and moved an amendment, which, if it had been adopted, might have saved the Province from turmoil and bloodshed. Mr. Neilson's amendment was as follows: "That as the despatch of the Colonial Minister of date July 9th, 1831, in reply to the address of the House of March 16th previous, contained a formal promise that the Colonial

Office would co-operate with the Assembly in redressing the chief grievances complained of, it now became the duty of the Chamber to labour in conformity with the spirit of the despatch for the improvement of the Colonial Government within the limits of the existing Constitution, and to endeavour to maintain the tranquillity of the country meanwhile. That as the despatch from the Colonial Office, dated 14th January last, confirmed the promise already adverted to, the House ought to undertake the duty of ameliorating the condition of the Province generally, and that especially it ought to regulate the occupancy of waste lands, amend the laws affecting property, secure judicial independence, improve judicial procedure, increase official responsibility, bring in order the public accounts and abolish every useless office."

Mr. Neilson in support of his amendment, having due regard to his liberal principles and party prejudices, wishing for reform but not revolution, thus spoke:—

"I cannot vote for these Resolutions as they now stand. In Britain and the United States alike, I would observe, the rather because the example of the latter has been just held up for our imitation, that defenders of popular interests laboured to effect changes, not from a mere craving for reforms, but because their rulers were ever endeavouring to violate constitutions already existing. The line of demarcation is quite distinct, therefore, between our position and theirs in time past. It is this, that whereas the American Revolutionists and the British Liberals combined for the maintenance of franchises already acquired, we oppositionists are reaching out our hands, over-eagerly extended, for freedom we never yet possessed. The result in our case must necessarily differ.

History is always the safest guide for our direction; it is a monitor which tells us that consequences are always conformable to principles."

Notwithstanding Mr. Neilson's able attempt to stem the tide of Revolution, seconded as he was by the more conservative members of the French party, notably by Messrs. Cuvillier, Quesnel, and a few others, Mr. Neilson's amendment was defeated, and in February, 1834, the ninety-two Resolutions of Mr. Papineau were carried by a vote of fifty-six members, while only twenty-six members recorded their votes for Mr. Neilson's amendment.

The Resolutions having been carried in the House, the next step was to present them to the Governor, Lord Aylmer, for transmission to the Imperial Government; and Mr. Morin, who lent his support to them in the Assembly, was despatched to England to convey the address of the House, consequent on the passage of the Resolutions, to Mr. Viger, the Lower Canadian agent in London, for presentation to the Lords and Commons of England. No Supply Bill was passed at the session in which the Resolutions were passed, and the Governor, for want of a quorum, on the 18th March, prorogued the House.

Mr. Roebuck, the champion of the Lower Canadians in the House of Commons, on the 15th April, moved for the appointment of a select committee of the House to enquire into the means of remedying the evils which existed in the form of government of the two

Provinces of Upper and Lower Canada. Mr. Stanley, the Colonial Secretary, feeling that if blame was to be attached to any Government, the Liberal Government of England, of 1828, should bear its fair share of the blame, moved in amendment for a select committee to enquire into and report to the House, how far the grievances complained of in the year 1828, on the part of certain inhabitants in Lower Canada, had been redressed, and whether the recommendation of the committee, which sat thereon, had been complied with.

This move, on the part of Mr. Stanley, disconcerted Mr. Roebuck and the other Liberals of the Commons, and he withdrew his motion, thus giving place to Mr. Stanley's amendment. To this committee, composed of members on both sides of the House, the ninety-two Resolutions were submitted. Bulwer, the celebrated novelist, and Daniel O'Connell, the Irish patriot, were members of this committee; and Mr. Hume, the special champion of the Lower Canadians, would have been on the committee had he not contrived to have his name withdrawn, suspecting that the report of the committee would not sustain him in the somewhat extreme position he had assumed on Canadian affairs, thereby indirectly censuring his past course in relation thereto.

Mr. Hume was that honourable member of the Commons who wrote a letter addressed to William Lyon Mackenzie, published in the English newspapers, in which the Canadians were called upon to resist the "baneful domination of the Mother Country," which rang through all Canada, and brought down upon him the censure of the greater part of the British in the two Provinces.

The report of the Committee of the House of Commons, to whom these Resolutions were submitted for investigation, stated, in effect, that the Home Government had been unremitting in their endeavours to carry out the suggestions of the select committee of 1828, and that any want of success on their part was entirely owing to the quarrels between the two branches of the Canadian Legislature, and between the House of Assembly and the Home Government. The report further stated that it would be inexpedient to lay before the House the evidence taken, or the documents which had been submitted to the committee, and that the interests of the Empire would be best subserved by leaving practical measures, for the future administration of Lower Canada, entirely in the hands of the Imperial Government.

Mr. William Lyon Mackenzie, impressed with the conviction that affairs were approaching a crisis, had got himself appointed agent of the malcontents of Upper Canada, and was at this time in London, pressing on the attention of the British Government and Parliament the grievances alleged to exist in Upper Canada. He had, by this time, gained the confidence of the Reform and Liberal party in Lower Canada, the Central Committee of which passed a resolution strongly eulogizing

Mr. Mackenzie and Mr. Bidwell for the active interest they had taken in promoting the reform of grievances in Upper Canada. Mr. Mackenzie's followers in Upper Canada, and the followers of Mr. Papineau in Lower Canada, were much incensed on learning the decision of the House of Commons Committee. Especially were they incensed at that part of the report which declares "that the interest of the Empire would be best subserved by leaving practical measures for the future administration of Lower Canada entirely in the hands of the Imperial Government."

Mr. Mackenzie and his friends contended that this was declaring, in effect, that the state of affairs was such, in Canada, that the seat of government should be removed from the Province to the Capital of the Empire. Here was a splendid opportunity for the grievance-monger to ply his trade. Imperial rule, Arbitrary despotism, Tyrannical oppression, were phrases common in the speeches of the discontented.

The people had been clamorous to obtain the control of affairs, and here was a Committee of the House of Commons declaring that the people of Canada were not able to govern themselves, but ought to be governed by the Imperial Government, in which they had no voice or representation. It was said that this was but a repetition of the means which brought about the Revolution of the American Colonies, in 1776. Meetings were called in different parts of Upper and Lower Canada to protest. Committees were appointed

to give voice to the opinions of the people, or rather
that part of the people that took the same stand as did
Mr. Mackenzie and Mr. Papineau. The Montreal Committee was in correspondence with Mr. Roebuck. He
wrote that committee that he had no hope of reform
in the affairs of Canada so long as Mr. Stanley was
in office, but he had better hope of Mr. Spring Rice,
who seemed more tractable. Mr. Rice had at this time
been appointed to the office of Colonial Secretary, in
a Liberal administration, succeeding Mr. Stanley, Colonial
Secretary in the Tory administration, which had gone
out, owing to differences among its members regarding
the affairs of Ireland. Mr. Roebuck recommended the
committee to allow time to Mr. Rice to show his
hand. He added, "It were better to fight for the
privilege of self-government than to yield one's natural
rights, but all other means ought assuredly to be tried
before having recourse to force of arms." Mr. Roebuck
was a strong advocate for the abolition of the Legislative Council; more than that, he advised that the
people should be stirred up to stand by the principles set
forth in the ninety-two resolutions, and the other
resolutions which attacked the existing form of government of Canada, and sought to set it up on a new
basis. Mr. Roebuck had much to answer for in
fanning the embers of the flame of Rebellion in the
Canadas. Mr. Hume was equally to blame. It was
all very well for these Honorable gentleman, while
sitting on the opposition benches in the House of

Commons to hurl their anathemas at the heads of politicians, both in Canada and England, who did not see through the same spectacles as themselves. The evil effect of their course was felt when a Liberal Government, responsible for the administration of Colonial affairs, had come into power. In August, 1834, on occasion of a motion made in the House of Commons by Mr. Hume, relative to the ninety-two resolutions, Mr. Spring Rice, then Colonial Secretary, referring to the letter of Mr. Hume, in which he had called on the Canadas to resist "the baneful domination of the Mother Country," said: "It does not befit a man sitting in security here among us, and so far removed from the scene of action, to promulgate counsels inciting others to do that which may call down so many ills on Britain and Canada as ever attended on civil war. If a recourse be had to arms ultimately, I hope that those who conspired to bring it on will be signalized for conspirators, if not denounced as rebels." The advent to power of a Liberal administration in England gave great encouragement to the followers of Papineau and Mr. Mackenzie in both the Canadas: committees already formed were urged to increased activity and new committees of a revolutionary character formed both in Upper and Lower Canada.

The Tory party in the Province, not to be behind their political adversaries, were up and doing also. "Constitutional Associations" were formed, members enrolled, and all necessary steps taken to cope with a rebellion, if unhappily the malcontents should go so far as to jeopardise their lives and liberties in an attempt at revolt. In Lower Canada, the British party, composed of the English, Irish and Scotch in that Province, felt that their Anglo-Saxon and Celtic origin demanded that the people of another race should, at all hazards, be prevented from having ascendancy in a British Province. Not that some of them did not feel that certain reforms would be beneficial to the Province, but that the French-Canadians, according to their catechism, were seeking to oust the British population from the Province, and, let us add, from its offices and emoluments.

In Upper Canada, the "Reform Association" placed itself in communication with all the standing committees in Lower Canada, and thus was established an *entente cordiale* between the opportunists of the two Provinces.

It was becoming more apparent every day that unless the British Government acted vigorously there would be civil war in the Province of Lower Canada, if not in both Provinces. There really was not at this time any great fear in the minds of the more conservative people of Upper Canada, that a rebellion would occur in that Province. There was not a race and religion question to contend with in Upper Canada, as there was in Lower Canada. The majority of the people of Upper Canada, Protestant and Catholic, were loyal to the British Crown. The Reform party in that Province

ELECTION RIOTS AT SOREL.

was not all Mackenzieites; indeed, the majority of that party were just as loyal to the Crown as were the members of the Tory party. It is true that they joined with Mr. Mackenzie in opposing the Tory Governments of the Province; they were with him in the taking of all steps leading to constitutional reform, but they were not with him in promoting rebellion.

The year 1834 was not to pass without some blood being shed, but it was not shed in armed rebellion, and was only one of the incidents of a severe political contest in the election for the House of Assembly in the latter part of the year. In Montreal, the relations between the British and French party were very strained. In that city, the violence of the political contestants was so great that the elections had to be suspended for a time. No blood was shed, but at Sorel a French-Canadian was shot during an election brawl. As may be imagined, the incident added fresh fuel to the flame already spreading with great heat over the whole horizon. The blood of the French-Canadian must be avenged; such was the cry of the Papineau party in the Province of Lower Canada.

The elections terminated in favour of the French-Canadians. Their majority in the Assembly was greater than ever. This was found to be the case when the Legislature met in February, 1835; it was found also that by the assistance of the French-Canadian electorate, several members of British or American origin, but of French-Canadian sentiment, had been returned members of the Assembly. These members were from the Eastern Townships, that part of the Province bordering on Vermont, one of the United States of America. Mr. Papineau was now at the pinnacle of his power and in the height of his glory. His compatriots had expressed their entire confidence in him and his principles, however radical his principles may have been, and, besides this, he had members of British origin who lent him their support.

The first proceeding of the new House was to expunge from the journals the report of the speech of the Governor, made at the last prorogation of the House. What would be thought of expunging the King's or Queen's speech from the journals of the House of Commons? It certainly would be regarded as tantamount to a declaration of war by the Commons against the Crown. And in like manner in Canada, the expunging of the Governor's speech from the journals was looked upon as a declaration of war against the Crown Representative.

The second proceeding of the Assembly was when Mr. Morin moved the House into a Committee of the Whole, for taking into consideration the state of the Province. Mr. Gugy, afterwards Colonel Gugy, had been returned a member to this House. He opposed Mr. Morin's motion, observing that he would prefer to have an administration composed of men born in the Province. This gave Mr. Papineau an opportunity to make a speech, in which he, with great force and eloquence, denounced exclusiveness, especially that exclusiveness which prevented his French-Canadian countrymen from sharing in the honours and responsibilities of government.

Mr. Papineau was essentially a French-Canadian. It galled him to the quick to see places in the Government given to men whose homes and hearts were in England. He demanded justice for his countrymen, but not preference. In reply to Mr. Gugy's statement, that he would prefer to have an administration composed of men born in the Province to any other, Mr. Papineau said: "I have no such preference; the Government that I long for is one composed of friends of legality, liberty and justice, a Government which would protect indiscriminately every proper interest, and accord to all ranks and to each race of the inhabitants equal rights and privileges. I love, I esteem all good men as men, not preferentially because they are of this or that descent, but I detest those haughty dominators who come among us and dispute our right to enjoy our own laws, customs and religion. If such be not content to intermix with us, let them remain in their own country. There is no lawful distinction between their status in the Province and ours, the same rights and a like just claim for protection are common to us both. Assuredly I should prefer a Government composed of such men as I have indicated, and as certain is it, too, that my own countrymen have given proofs of a capacity and the possession of such integrity as would enable them to become members of a most desirable Government. Those parties even who claim exclusive governing privileges disapprove of them in their hearts, and, if obtained, will themselves be victimized by them in the end. For supposing that the Exclusionists succeeded in making an Acadia of Canada, and could expel from it all its French derived people, they would soon fall out with each other. Did they find means to constitute rotten borough representation, it would quickly be turned against its creators. It is natural to the mind of man to abhor all exclusive privileges, but passion and party spirit pervert the judgment of too many. The call is made upon us, 'Let us all be as brothers.' I respond, so let us not be, if you, who thus adjure us, keep a selfish grasp of all place, power and emolument, and refuse to share these with us. That is unjust, and we cannot suffer such injustice. Briefly, we demand for ourselves such political institutions as are in accordance with those of the rest of the Empire and of the age we live in."

No one can read the sentiments of Mr. Papineau, as expressed in this address, but must feel that he was animated by a high feeling of love for his fellow-countrymen. The greatness of the man is evidenced by his love of liberty and justice. Those, however, who are not French-Canadian will perhaps take exception to that part of Mr. Papineau's speech wherein he strenuously claims the right of the French-Canadians to enjoy their laws, customs and religion, and implies that this right was denied them. Now there never has been a time when these rights were denied to the French-Canadians, so far as those laws, customs and exercise of religion were granted to them by the British Empire. It is only when they showed a disposition to place these laws and customs and their religion above the laws of the Empire, and beyond the rights and privileges secured under the Treaty of Paris and the Constitution of the country, that they came in conflict with the English. The disaffected French-Canadians of that time **made claims to** rights **as existing under** the **Treaty** which never did so exist. As against all such claims the British-Canadians set their face. Beyond that, they ought not to be subject to the reproach of endeavouring to hinder the patriotic French-Canadian from enjoying all the liberty he was entitled to, as a subject of the Empire and of his native Canada. Such grievances as he could justly complain of were common to **all** inhabitants of the Canadas, **and** were owing to the **want** of self-government; and, **as has been** seen, England very naturally hesitated to give absolute self-government to a people animated as they were with feelings inimical to the British race, **and** with no desire but the absolute supremacy of the French-Canadian, a supremacy **which it was justly feared** would operate most harshly **upon the British minority.**

CHAPTER X.

Mackenzie's Prophecy in 1832—Papineau and Mackenzie in Concert—Reform Central Committee and Montreal Committee in Correspondence—Petitions to Home Government For and Against a Change in the Constitution—Lord Aylmer Informs Lower Canada House that the British Government Were About to Adopt Coercive Measures to Allay Discontent—Papineau's Defiant Speech—House of Commons Appoint Special Committee to Report on Canadian Grievances—Gosford, Grey, and Gipps—Instructions to Commissioners—Lord Gosford's Address to Canadians—Montreal Constitutional Association Organizes—Concessions of Lord Gosford and British Government—British Party Dissatisfied—Colonial Secretary's Concessions to Mackenzie—Attorney-General Boulton—Mackenzie, Mayor of Toronto—Mackenzie Acquitted of Personal Resentment—House of 1835—Reform Majority—Mackenzie's Seventh Report on Grievances—Reform Party Loyal to the Crown—Lord Glenelg's Answer to Seventh Report on Grievances—Sir F. B. Head, Governor—Parliament of 1836—Governor's Speech and Assembly's Answer—Instructions of Home Government—Lord Gosford's Criticisms Thereon—Assembly's Answer—Papineau's Address to House—Shows Determination to Resist All Attempts at Conciliation—Dunn, Baldwin and Rolph Made Executive Councillors in Upper Canada.

IN a narrative of the Canadian Rebellion it is impossible to dissociate the names of Papineau and Mackenzie. They were joint leaders in the two Provinces of a movement which each must have seen, must, if persevered in, almost inevitably end in bloodshed. That this was apparent to Mackenzie is shown by what he afterwards termed a prophecy, made by him when in London in 1832, pressing the Government to take immediate steps to remedy the grievances which he complained of as existing in Canada. On this visit he had many interviews with the Colonial Secretary, and was permitted to place his views in writing before that official. This he did in many papers. In those papers he gave the Colonial Secretary to understand that unless the system of government in Upper Canada were ameliorated the result must be civil war. We have seen that a correspondence was carried on between the Central Reform Committee in Montreal, and the Upper Canada Committee formed for similar ends. It is therefore apparent that the two leaders must have been well acquainted with the designs which each had in pushing his demands to the utmost length.

The petitions which Mr. Mackenzie carried with him to England, craving redress of grievances, had attached to them upwards of twenty-five thousand signatures, but on the other hand Lord Goderich had before him petitions signed by upwards of twenty-six thousand persons, who, as Lord Goderich informed Mr. Mackenzie, "concurred in expressing their cordial satisfaction in those laws and institutions which the other set of petitioners had impugned." The Colonial Office was in fact deluged with petitions both from Upper and Lower Canada, presenting entirely different views as to the alleged grievances existing in Canada.

In the session of the Parliament of Lower Canada held in 1835, the Governor, Lord Aylmer, having become hopeless of reconciling Mr. Papineau and his party to the Government, opened the House by a speech, in which he informed the House of the change in the office of Colonial Secretary ; that he expected further instructions, which he would communicate ; that he had issued warrants for payment of the officials, in consequence of the last House having stopped the supplies, and that beyond this he had nothing in particular to communicate to Parliament. The Assembly took this to mean that Lord Aylmer felt himself bound in some measure to show his entire dissatisfaction with the proceedings of that body, and had taken this means to do so. The Governor, in the performance of his duty, on the 5th of March, communicated to the House a despatch from the Colonial Secretary, stating that the decision of the Committee of the House of Commons, to which their petitions of the previous session had been referred, was adverse, and that while the Government had not decided to introduce a bill suspending the powers of the Assembly, it might be necessary to introduce a bill of that character, although the new Secretary, Mr. Spring Rice, trusted that the necessity for any such measure might be averted. The Assembly voted an address to the British Parliament, reiterating former complaints, and demanding the recall of the Governor, to whose requests they paid no attention, and whose address, in closing the last session, they now formally ordered to be expunged.

A debate occurred on the address. The members of Mr. Papineau's party even were not unanimous in voting for this address. Some of the recalcitrants, especially Mr.

Bedard, declined to vote for it, as the address, in its terms, in a peremptory manner, contained a refusal to comply with the wishes of the Governor, complained of his "arbitrary and unbecoming conduct," and even went so far as to say that they considered his conduct, in neglecting the application of the corporation of Montreal for extended quarantine regulations, was one of the principal causes of the frightful ravages committed by the Asiatic cholera during the preceding summer. In speaking on the motion for the address in the Assembly, Mr. Papineau said: "It would be a libel on Britain to assume that she may possibly pass a coercive bill against us and send ten regiments over to enforce it. If such were the case, however, we ought to be prepared all the sooner to rid ourselves of so tyrannical a domination. If there is ground for apprehending such a struggle, we may say that the danger exists at this hour, and that we have already gone much further in bringing it on than the stride taken in this address." After such an inflammatory speech from the acknowledged leader of the French party in Lower Canada, the surprise is not that there was a rebellion in that Province, but rather that the insurrection did not take place at once, instead of being delayed for more than a year.

The address was carried in the House, and was sent to England, to be presented to the House of Commons by Mr. Roebuck, the champion of the French-Canadian interests in the Commons; but long before it reached England, and in fact before the address was passed, the Government of England had determined to make an exhaustive investigation of Canadian affairs, and to this end to send to the Colony commissioners, charged with the duty of examining into all alleged grievances, who should report the result to the Home Government. Lord Aylmer called Parliament to meet, and, on the 30th of May, communicated the intention of the Home Government to appoint this Commission Extraordinary, which should have the advantage of personal instructions from the Government and would know their views better than could be communicated by means of despatches.

Notwithstanding the fact that Lord Aberdeen, the Premier, had stated in the House of Lords that "if he could have prevailed on himself to recall Lord Aylmer, he should never have thought of sending out a commissioner," the Government decided upon his recall, which was announced in a despatch in the official *Quebec Gazette* of June 25th. We are told by Mr. Christie* that his recall created a very general feeling of regret among the British population of Lower Canada, who joined in presenting addresses to him, regretting what they termed his "untimely recall," and a farewell entertainment was given to him and Lady Aylmer by the principal citizens of Quebec on the eve of his departure, which took place on September 17th. Lord Aylmer seems to have been actuated in all his public acts by the highest motives. That he had no antipathy to the French is shown by the fact that he erected a marble slab to the memory of Montcalm in the Ursuline Convent at Quebec. Before

* Christie's Lower Canada, Vol. IV, p. 84.

leaving Canada he now erected, at his own expense, a monument on the Plains of Abraham, marking the spot where Wolfe fell, which, having been almost destroyed by memento seekers chipping off pieces, was, in 1849, superseded by the more ambitious shaft now there, erected by the officers of the British army serving in Canada.

The Commission, that was to settle the interminable complaints of the French-Canadians, was composed of three persons whose capacity and aptitude in political affairs were sufficiently acknowledged to enable them to undertake the important task laid before them. The Commissioners were the Earl of Gosford, Sir Charles Grey and Sir James Gipps. Lord Gosford was not only Commissioner Extraordinary, but was also appointed Governor-in-Chief, to succeed Lord Aylmer. The supposed advantage to be gained in having Commissioners was that people of all classes, creeds and parties could go before the Commission and be heard. The Commissioners were specially instructed to hear complaints from whatever quarter arising; that they were to put themselves in familiar relations with all manner of applicants, to note the acts and discourses passing and spoken at public meeting, to study social relations, to make inquests in different parts of the country, and generally to remark all that took place which might in any way assist them in forming an opinion as to the cause of the unsettled state of affairs in the Province.

Nothing goes further to show that the policy of the English Government at this time, as it had been the policy of all Governments since the Act of 1791, and even before that Act was passed, was to retain a legislative control, not only in Canada, but in all other colonies, than the restraint placed on this commission. Whatever else they might do they were not to lay their hands on the Legislative Council, the very institution which above all others caused contention in Canada.

The Commissioners arrived at Quebec in August, and Lord Gosford at once set about the duties he had undertaken. He was very gracious to all with whom he came in contact. The French party especially he moved with marks of evidence of his solicitude. He invited the leaders to his house. He visited their religious institutions, and sought in every way to gain their confidence. But just so much as he fondled and conciliated the French party he estranged the British residents. To do what he thought was necessary to satisfy the French-Canadians, he informed them that their social institutions would remain intact. In opening the session of Parliament, in October, 1835, he spoke both in the French and English languages, a delicate compliment to the nationality of the great majority of members of the House. Appealing to the Colonists, he said: "To the Canadians, both of French and British origin, I would say, consider the blessings you might enjoy, but for your dissensions. Offsprings, as you are, of the two most foremost nations of the earth, you hold a vast and beautiful country, having a fertile soil, with healthful climate; while the noblest river in the world makes seaports of your most remote havens."

The British party in the Province, from the tone of the French press, the speeches of members of the Assembly, and the general demeanor of the French party, were still suspicious of the loyalty of their fellow-subjects of French-Canadian origin. The Montreal Constitutional Association resolved to organize District Committees in each quarter of that city, in case union and force became needful. This organization believed in the adage "to be forewarned is to be forearmed." It raised a body of volunteer riflemen, with cries of "God save the King."

This determination of the Montreal Constitutional Association was incited, at the present time, by the feeling which prevailed among the British residents that their rights, which they had enjoyed as British subjects, were about to be surrendered to a French-Canadian domination. It was true that the language of the French press had not been as insulting as it had been before Lord Gosford's advent, but then they attributed this to the desire of the French party to gain concessions, and so their real aspirations were veiled. Lord Gosford's speech, in his address on opening the House, was too full of concessions to please the British party. He said, "Some of the grievances complained of could be redressed by the Executive alone, others by the aid of one or both branches of the Legislature, but some of their demands could only be complied with by the act of the Imperial Parliament." He declared himself prepared to act impartially in every respect. Plurality of offices should no longer exist, and French-Canadians of talent and standing would have the path of official preferment opened to them equally with their British fellow-citizens. In future every information with regard to public accounts and all other public matters should be rendered to the Assembly, and copies of the Blue Book, or general, annual, financial and statistical return, which he invited both Houses to make in future as complete as possible, would be presented to each branch of the legislature. Bills should not, unless on the gravest grounds, be reserved for the decision of the Crown, nor would any undue partiality be given to the English language over the French. Whatever abuses might exist in the law courts, the members of the Legislature were themselves invited to remedy, as well as to regulate by enactment the matter of the Clergy Reserves. He offered his warrant to both Houses without any condition attached. "The Home Government was prepared," he said, "to surrender the control of all public revenues arising from any Canadian source, on condition of a moderate provision being made for the civil list." As regarded the inhabitants of British descent he urged, "they had nothing to fear on the score of commerce, the main support of the Empire," while to those of French origin he repeated, "that there was no design to disturb the form of society under which they had so long been contented and prosperous."

To ordinary minds the action of the Government, in appointing the Commission, and this assuring speech of the Governor to Parliament, ought to have been sufficient to quench the fire of discontent in Lower

Canada. Not so, however, with Mr. Papineau. He had in fact become imbued with the idea that Canada should be a Republic, with perchance Louis Joseph Papineau at the head of it. In a speech which he made at the Assembly, he said: " The time has gone by when Europe could give monarchies to America. On the contrary, an epoch is now approaching when America will give Republics to Europe."

The House of Assembly, in answering the Address from the Throne, avoided all notice of the Commission, and an amendment being moved expressing satisfaction at the appointment and hoping for a satisfactory result to its labours, it was negatived by the House. Mr. Papineau declaimed at great length, as usual. He said that he considered the appointment of the Commission an insult to the House. The Commissioners, he contended, had no constitutional powers whatever. They might, it is true, report to the Home Government, and, if it coincided with the wishes of the House, well and good. But if they differed from the demands of the Assembly they might be assured that body would not recede one iota, but would force its claims to the utmost. Such was the attitude of the Lower Canadian French party.

The British Government at this time was prepared to make concessions, not only to Lower Canada, but to Upper Canada also. Mr. Mackenzie had gained considerable success in his mission and interviews with Lord Goderich, the Colonial Minister. Lord Goderich, after full consideration of the grievances urged by Mr. Mackenzie, determined to take action. In order to relieve the Canadian Government from the imputation of favouritism in the allotment of public lands, the King, on the advice of his Colonial Minister, forbade the gratuitous disposition of public lands, and directed that they should be made subject to public competition, with a view "to the utter exclusion of any such favouritism as is thus deprecated." In fact the Colonial Minister made so many concessions to Mr. Mackenzie that the Government party in the Upper Canadian House and in the country were disposed to treat Lord Goderich's despatch containing those concessions with a certain degree of contempt. The Legislative Council refused so much as to place it on their journals, and returned it to the Lieutenant-Governor. The view they took was that Mr. Mackenzie, an irresponsible agent, had gone to England, interviewed the Colonial Minister on grievances when they were not represented, gave a colouring to statements not borne out by facts, and had thus warped the mind of the Minister. Mr. Boulton, the then Attorney General of the Province, with more asperity than dignity, when the question came up in the Assembly, and the House was made acquainted with the representations, both verbal and written, which Mr. Mackenzie had made to the Colonial Secretary, said it ill became the Colonial Secretary to "sit down and answer all this ignoble trash," and that "it would much less become the House to interfere with it by giving it publicity." Mr. Mackenzie was not a man to be thwarted. Though, for the time being, while the Reform party was in the minority, the journals of the House were freed from the Colonial Secretary's despatch and the accompanying documents, Mr. Mackenzie, at a subsequent period, in a Reform House, caused the documents to be remembered in his celebrated "Seventh Report on Grievances."

It is a remarkable fact with reference to Mr. Mackenzie, that the more he was opposed by the Government and Government party, the more popular he became with a section of the people. Though five times expelled from the House, he was, in the year 1834, elected the first Mayor of Toronto. His election to the Mayor's chair was undoubtedly due to the sympathy felt for him by many in the capital of the Province who were not of his party. The combined suffrages of his party supporters and of the more moderate Tories placed him in the office of chief magistrate of the city. It has never been doubted that the choice then made was a good one. It is but fair to the memory of Mr. Mackenzie to say that, in all his political conduct and extravagances, he was not actuated by personal resentment. He was a determined advocate of reform, and in his political course made himself many enemies, but they were not personal but political enemies. His trenchant pen and carping style of criticism were his bane. The nature of the man was such that he could not mend his ways. Speaking of himself, he said, "I entered the lists of the opposition to the Executive, because I believed the system of government to be wretchedly bad, and was uninfluenced by any private feeling, or ill will, or anger towards any human being whatever." Mr. Mackenzie was a very different man from Papineau. The latter was cool, calculating, reflective; Mackenzie, on the other hand, was fiery, impulsive and of a most combative disposition.

In the House, which met in the month of July, 1835, Mr. Mackenzie found himself in a more congenial political atmosphere than had heretofore surrounded him in the Legislative Assembly of the Province. He had now around him such men as Mr. Marshall Bidwell, Mr. John Ham Perry and other Reformers, all bent on suppressing, if not destroying the Government that then subsisted. In the publications preceding the meeting of the House, and in the elective campaign which gave the Reformers a majority in the House, the party opposing the Government had been very fully taunted with disloyalty. Disloyal they were, but only to the Government of Canada, not to the Government of Great Britain. No man in Upper Canada had yet gone as far as Mr. Papineau in his declaration of hostility to monarchical rule, and favour to the introduction of Republican institutions into Canada. When the Legislature met, they felt the importance of declaring to the world that whatever else they might be accused of, they could not be justly charged with being disloyal to the Crown. In their addresses in answer to the Lieutenant-Governor's speech, at the opening of the session, they said: "His Majesty has received through your Excellency, from the people of this Province, fresh proofs of their devoted loyalty and of their sincere and earnest desire to maintain and perpetuate the connection with the great Empire of which they form so important a part, proofs which would serve to correct any misrepresentations intended to impress His Majesty with the belief that those who desire the reform of many public abuses in the Province are not well affected towards His Majesty's person and Government." The address concluded: "Should the government be administered agreeably to the intent, meaning and spirit of our glorious Constitution, the just wishes and constitutional rights of the people duly respected, the honours and patronage of His Majesty indiscriminately bestowed on persons of worth and talent who enjoy the confidence of the people, without regard to their political or religious opinions, and your Excellency's Councils filled with moderate, wise and discreet individuals, who are understood to respect and be influenced by the public voice, we have not the slighest apprehension but the connection between this Province and the parent state may long continue to exist and be a blessing mutually advantageous to both."

During this session Mr. Mackenzie made to the House a report of the committee of which he was chairman, which went by the name of "Mackenzie's Seventh

Report on Grievances." This report was practically an arraignment of the whole system of Colonial Government. It dwelt upon "the almost unlimited extent of the patronage of the Crown, or rather of the Colonial Minister for the time being." "Such," it added, "is the patronage of the Colonial Office, that the granting or the withholding of supplies is of no political importance, unless as an indication of the opinion of the country concerning the character of the Government."

The report entered at length into the objections which existed to the Legislative Council, showing that it was a body responsible to no one in Canada, and was appointed by and responsible only to the Crown. It recommended an independent Board of Audit of Public Accounts. In a political sense the most important passage in the report was that which said, "One great excellence of the English Constitution consists of the limits it imposes on the will of the King by requiring responsible men to give effect to it. In Upper Canada no such responsibility can exist. The Lieutenant-Governor and the British Ministry hold in their hands the whole patronage of the Province, they hold the sole dominion of the country, and leave the representative branch of the Legislature powerless and dependent. Finally the report wound up with a declaration that "the second branch of the Legislature had failed to answer the purpose of its institution, and could never be made to answer the end for which it was created," and that "the restoration of legislative harmony and good government requires its reconstruction on the elective principle."

The report is in itself a bulky volume. The statements made in regard to the Council, coupled with what has been said with regard to the Legislative Council in Lower Canada, which was a counterpart of that in Upper Canada, fairly express the grievances of Mr. Mackenzie and his Committee, so far as they were attributable to the Constitution, and most, if not all other grievances set forth in the report, flowed from the main source of the system of government and the constitution of the Province. It is but too evident that if the Legislative Council of the Province had been more liberal than they were, and had extended the Government patronage beyond the circle of their immediate friends and relatives, the seeds of rebellion, though planted, might not have taken root. The very first paragraph of the report goes a long way to prove this. The Reformers at this time saw themselves nominally in power, having a considerable majority at their back, and yet they were not allowed to enjoy what they considered were legitimate fruits of their success in the country. The advocacy of an Elective Legislative Council, as put forth in the report, was a radical proposal, absolutely differing from the Constitution as it existed, and it could not, therefore, receive countenance from the ruling powers in Great Britain, no matter what party, Whig or Tory, were in the ascendant in the parent State, unless that Constitution was amended. This neither party was prepared then to do. In Lower Canada the French-Canadians desired to get rid of the Legislative Council, that they might govern in place of the English. In Upper Canada there were no racial lines dividing the people; still we find the Legislative Council obnoxious to a considerable class in the community. Principally, no doubt, because owing to it the party of the people, as distinguished from the more aristocratic class which had the friendship of the Representative of the Crown, had no control of public affairs, or of the emoluments thereof. The Reform party sought for no more than was in force in England then, and in Canada soon after this time—Responsible Government. Possibly this boon was withheld from Upper Canada for fear of Lower Canada. It could hardly be granted to the one without the other, and if to the latter what would become of the English minority?

Lord Glenelg was Chief Colonial Secretary at the time the grievance report reached London and was brought to the notice of the Colonial Office. He did not give a mere perfunctory attention to this report, but examined it in every detail. After full investigation he, on the 5th December, 1835, sent a despatch to Sir Francis Bond Head, recently appointed Lieutenant-Governor of Upper Canada, in which he fully answered all the objections contained in the report. In reference to the subject of patronage of the Crown or of the Colonial Minister, which was the first grievance complained of in the report, Lord Glenelg said: "With respect to the patronage of the requisite offices, His Majesty's Government are not solicitous to retain more in their hands, or in those of the Governor, than is necessary for the general welfare of the people and the right conduct of public affairs. I confess myself, however, unable to perceive to whom the choice amongst candidates for public employment could with equal safety be confided. It requires but little foresight or experience to discover that such patronage, if exercised in any form of popular election, or if committed to any popular body, would be liable to be employed for purposes far less defensible, and in a manner less conducive to the general good. Chosen by irresponsible patrons, the public officers would themselves be virtually exempt from responsibility, and all the discipline and subordination which would connect together in one unbroken chain the King and his representatives in the Province, down to the lowest functionary to whom any portion of the powers of the State may be confided, would be immediately broken."

With respect to auditing the public accounts, and constituting by law a Board of Audit, Lord Glenelg said: "His Majesty will gladly concur in the enactment of any law which shall be properly framed for constituting such a board."

With reference to the Executive Government, Lord Glenelg said: "A very considerable part of the report is devoted to the statement and illustration of the fact that the Executive Government of Upper Canada is virtually irresponsible, and the conclusion drawn is that under the present system there can be no prospect of a good and faithful administration of public affairs. . . . Experience would seem to prove that the administration of public affairs in Upper Canada is by no means exempt from the control of a practical responsibility. To His Majesty and to Parliament, the Government of Upper Canada is at all times most fully responsible for its official acts. . . . This responsibility is not merely nominal. It is the duty of the Lieutenant-Governor to vindicate to the King and Parliament every act of his administration. This responsibility to His Majesty and to Parliament is second to none which can be imposed on a public man, and it is one which it is in the power of the House of Assembly at any time by addresses or petition to bring into active operation." Proceeding, Lord Glenelg said: "I next refer to two subjects of far more importance than any of those to which I have hitherto adverted. I refer to the demand made, partly in the report of the committee and partly in the address of the Assembly to His Majesty, for changes in the mode of appointing Legislative Councillors, and for the control of the Assembly of the territorial and casual revenues of the Crown. On these subjects I am, to a considerable extent, relieved from the necessity of any particular investigation, because claims precisely identical have been preferred by the Assembly of Lower Canada, and because in the instructions to the Commissioners of Inquiry, who have visited that Province, I have already had occasion to state the views which have received His Majesty's deliberate sanction. The principles of government in the two sister Provinces must, I am well aware, be in every material respect the same. I shall, therefore, annex for your information, as an appendix to this despatch, so much of the instructions to the Earl of Gosford and his colleagues as applies to these topics."

This despatch of Lord Glenelg was communicated by the Lieutenant-Governor to the Legislative Assembly, and thus gained publicity. The despatch accompanied, or was contained in the instructions given to Sir F. B. Head for his guidance, and it is doubtful if the Colonial Secretary intended that publicity should be given to it. However this may be, it got to the ears of the political leaders in Lower Canada, and was made the subject of comment by the press of that Province, both French and English.

Another circumstance of an untoward character occurred at this time, which gave an opportunity to the Reform leaders in both Provinces to clamour against the Government. Sir F. B. Head, who had just arrived in the Province of Upper Canada, on the 14th January, 1836, opened the session of the Upper Canada Legislature. The new Governor had had no political experience before coming to the Province. If it had been otherwise, perhaps he would not have so committed himself as to communicate to the Assembly his instructions, or a garbled statement of them, nor would he in his opening speech to the House have gone beyond the sphere of his duties by alluding to the affairs of Lower Canada, with which he had no concern. This, however, he did, and, in referring to the political conditions in Lower Canada, and to the labours of Lord Gosford and the other Royal Commissioners, gave the House fully to understand that come what might the Constitution of the Province would be maintained.

The answer of the House to the Governor's speech was both critical and remonstrative. The House said: "We deeply regret that Your Excellency has been advised to animadvert upon the affairs of the sister Province, which has been engaged in a long and arduous struggle for an indispensable amelioration in their institutions and the manner of their administration. We respectfully but firmly express our respect for their patriotic exertions, and we do acquit them of being the cause of any embarrassment and dissensions in the country."

The Quebec Gazette, a paper supposed to represent the opinions of the English and the more moderate of the French party in the Province of Lower Canada, dealing with Lord Glenelg's despatch, said: "The publication of the instructions has occasioned great regret and disappointed public expectations generally. Very certainly their tenor betrays dispositions and interests little suited to inspire confidence in ministerial liberality, or reliance on the soundness of official polity in respect to our interests. Lord Glenelg evidently plays a double part, that of a Reformer in London, of a Conservative in Quebec.

These instructions contain also, as did the opening speech, an untoward enunciation, which we have not dwelt upon as yet, namely, the mortifying mis-estimation of the oligarchic faction and the general population, for in speaking of each, the same weight and worth are assigned to the opinions and aspirations of both, with an equal claim to the consideration of the Imperial Government. This misapprehension arises, questionless, from the aristocratic training and usages in repute with denizens of the Old World. It is there believed that the oligarchy in the ascendant here fills the same place, with us, as the British nobles and gentry in the three kingdoms. This mistake and the prejudices attending it, if they be not corrected, and if more sound appreciations of Colonial circumstances and a better knowledge of Colonial society do not take their place, thence the loss of one of the brightest jewels in the British Crown may result at no distant date. It is only with ideas and principles of equality put in operation that Americans can now be governed. If British statesmen be not content to learn their duty through representations, they will be taught it ere long, in a rougher way, for things move on rapidly in this new world of ours. . . ."

This was pretty plain language for a Canadian journal. It shows two things: first, that the stilted uppishness of the oligarchy in the Province was distasteful to the independent people of Canada; second, that the spirit of democracy had got a fast hold on a considerable portion of the Crown's territory in the Province.

The instructions given to Lord Gosford and the Royal Commissioners were calculated to lead the people of Quebec to believe that reforms would be made in the system of government in the immediate future. The Quebec French-Canadian party, led by Mr. Bedard, was inclined to accept the assurances of Lord Gosford. Not so Mr. Papineau. The despatch of Lord Glenelg to Sir F. B. Head becoming known to him, and the Bedard party's seeming defection, spurred him on to further effort to enforce the principles of the Ninety-two Resolutions.

On a motion in the House of Assembly as to granting supplies Mr. Papineau spoke, and with his fiery eloquence and oratorical ability fairly carried the House by storm. Facing Mr. Bedard and those who followed him, he said : "We have yet to learn if there be any new circumstance in the political situation of the country which can justify those who now seem as if they would desert the cause of their country, or why they should now incline to separate themselves from the great majority of their compatriots, who adopted in spirit and sanctioned in act the votes deposited by their representatives in the electoral urn for sustaining the Ninety-two Resolutions passed by this House. . . . We are not struggling against any individual personally, but a system of vicious Colonial Government, which, as now explained by Lord Glenelg, contains in the essence of corruption the germ of manifold disorders. Our task is not light, indeed, for we are called on to defend the rights of all British Colonial dependencies, as well as that we inhabit. The same evil genius whose workings drove the provincials of the neighbouring States, in their own despite, into the paths of a righteous and glorious resistance, presides over our affairs also. That malign spirit it was which inspired the instructions given to the Commission now in our midst. . . . Briefly, these Commissioners' instructions comprise a formal refusal on the part of those who drew them up to listen heedfully to any representation of the many grievances which both Canadas have to complain of." This speech of Mr. Papineau, and the evident determination to resist all attempts at conciliation, prompted the Governor to immediately prorogue the House.

In Upper Canada Mr. Mackenzie, like Mr. Papineau, was provoking the House of Assembly to wage war with the Governor, the Government, and all who gave them countenance or support. He moved a series of resolutions in the House, aimed at discrediting the Government for not having carried out the Imperial wishes. This move of Mr. Mackenzie's had one good effect, it elicited from the Governor a communication to the House, which was then a Reform House, presided over by Mr. Bidwell, in which he asked from the House the consideration due to a stranger to the Province, unconnected with the differences of party, sent by his Sovereign with instructions "to correct, cautiously, yet effectually, all real grievances, while maintaining the Constitution inviolate." How this was to be done, and yet the Legislative Council maintained in its original shape, was a problem which would take a cleverer man than Sir F. B. Head to solve.

He, however, undertook a task in which he was sure to fail.

He commenced by calling three new members to the Executive Council. This office he performed on the 20th February, 1836. The new members so called were Messrs. John Henry Dunn, Robert Baldwin and Dr. John Rolph, all members of the Reform party. These gentlemen soon found, however, that the Governor's opinions were not their opinions. They wished to govern in accordance with the wishes of the House. He wished to govern in accordance with his own views. They acknowledged responsibility to the House. He would have it that they were only responsible to himself, the Governor. In discussing the matter with them, he said: "The Lieutenant-Governor maintains that responsibility to the people, who are already represented in the House of Assembly, is unconstitutional, that it is the duty of the Council to serve him, not them."

Not being able to come to an agreement with the Governor, as to their respective positions and responsibilities, the three newly appointed members to the Executive Council, on the 4th of March, resigned their offices.

The stand taken by the Governor brought down upon him the denunciation of the House and stoppage of the supplies. A report of a Committee of the House, to which was referred the duty of enquiring into the differences existing between the Governor and the Council, which report was adopted by the House, said that it was the

SIR F. B. HEAD DISSOLVES THE HOUSE.

duty of the House either "to abandon their privileges and honour, and to betray their duties and the rights of the people, or to withhold the supplies." The supplies were withheld, and thus a crisis brought about which bid fair to disrupt the Government and bring discredit on the Governor. To avoid this, Sir Francis, on the 14th March, appointed four new councillors, viz., Messrs. Robert B. Sullivan, William Allen, Augustus Baldwin and John Elmsley. Three days after these new appointments were made, the House, not to be baffled by the Governor, declared its "entire want of confidence" in the Council, and demanded their dismissal.

The Reform party, then in a majority in the House, which for some reason or other had laboured under the delusion that in Sir F. B. Head the Province had got a "Liberal Governor," were rudely awakened from their dream in finding their idol of a day was indeed a veritable autocrat. Sir Francis unreservedly threw himself into the arms of the "Family Compact," a name by which the ruling powers had come to be called, defied the House, and, on the 28th of May, 1836, dissolved Parliament.

CHAPTER XI.

Hon. Robert Baldwin—Conservative by Nature—Mackenzie Not the Reform Party—Reform Society of Upper Canada—Their Principles Announced—Address to Inhabitants of British North America—Governor Dissolves Upper Canada House, 20th May, 1836—Lower Canadians Distrust Royal Commission—Report of Royal Commissioners Disappoints the Hopes of Revolutionists—Mr. Morin's Comments Thereon—"Vive Papineau ; Vive la Liberté"—Death of William IV.—Ascension of Queen Victoria—Lord Gosford's Attempt to Reconcile Lower Canada—Excitement at High Pitch in Upper Canada—Upper Canada Elections of 1836—Riots and Disturbances—"Bread and Butter" Parliament—Question of Union of Upper Canada and Lower Canada Agitated—Confusion in the House—Declaration of Reformers to People of Upper Canada, June, 1837—Public Meetings—"Liberty or Death"—Plans for Revolt.

Mr. ROBERT BALDWIN, who was the son of that old Reformer Dr. William Warren Baldwin, was the most prominent Liberal of his day, but of a very different type from William Lyon Mackenzie. In everything but politics Mr. Baldwin was most conservative in all his ways. True it is, that he was associated with Mr. Mackenzie as a party man, but it can never be said that he was responsible for his actions. Mr. Mackenzie was "*sui generis*," and could not be restrained by anyone, not even by the most prominent of Reformers, from resorting to most extreme means to accomplish a purpose. The Reform party had within its ranks men of moderate and men of most advanced views. Mr. Mackenzie by no means represented the opinions of the whole party, but only those of a section.

The Reformers of those days, as a body, must be judged by their acts, as a body, and not by the individual acts of any one member. The Constitutional Reform Society of Upper Canada, formed on the 16th July, 1836, issued an address declaratory of their principles, which were:

1. The British Constitution in its purity.
2. Connection with the Parent State.
3. Encouragement of emigration from the Mother Country.

And it was said in the address, to secure and promote those objects for which they contended, they demanded:

1. Responsible advisers to the Governor.
2. Equal rights to all men, whether Protestant or Catholic, Churchman or Dissenter. The abolition of all the rectories established by Sir John Colborne, security being given that no dominant Church or Churches should be tolerated in Upper Canada.
3. The disposal of all revenues of the Province for the benefit of its inhabitants.
4. The reformation of the Legislative Council and the land granting department.
5. The redress of all known grievances.

The address concluded thus: "As Reformers they want no more; as British freemen they never will be satisfied with less." The address was signed by William Warren Baldwin, president of the society.

This address was issued on the eve of the election then approaching, necessitated by Sir F. B. Head's dissolution of the House. The abolition of the rectories, which had been established by Sir John Colborne, referred to in the address, was a new cause of grievance to the Reform party. Sir John Colborne, acting, as he held, within his province and the requirements of the Constitutional Act of 1791, had created fifty-seven rectories for the support of the Church of England clergy. As might be expected, this step of His Excellency was regarded by all other Churches than the Church of England as a great stretch of prerogative. The demand to abolish these rectories was now seized upon by the Reform party as a weapon with which to fight their opponents at the election. It was a good weapon, and with its aid the Reformers would doubtless have carried the elections, had not the Government party been spurred on to increased energy in the battle for power. The rectory question did not trouble the people of Lower Canada, but the dedication of lands for the support of a Protestant clergy was put forward, as a grievance in that Province, with as much force as in the Province of Upper Canada.

Leaving that particular subject for the present, and directing our attention to that which most concerned the Province of Lower Canada at this time, the beginning of 1836, viz., the proceedings and probable result of the inquiries of Lord Gosford and the Royal Commission, we find that both the British and French-Canadians were suspicious of the doings of this Commission. The French-Canadians, watching distrustfully the general conduct of the Commissioners, concluded that they were too gracious to be sincere, while the British-Canadians thought them too concessive to be trusted. The fact was they were trying to please both parties, and ended by pleasing neither. The enunciation which Lord Gosford had made at the opening of Parliament, and his evident desire to propitiate the French-Canadians, by offering to surrender to them privileges which the British party thought they ought not to enjoy, roused the Montreal Constitutional Association to action. The Association determined to appeal to all the people of British North America, in the hope of identifying all subjects in all the Provinces, Upper Canada, Nova Scotia, New Brunswick and Prince Edward Island, with the cause of their fellow-subjects in Lower Canada. To this end the Association, in the month of January, 1836, issued the following address: .

"ADDRESS FROM THE CONSTITUTIONAL ASSOCIATION OF MONTREAL TO THE INHABITANTS OF BRITISH NORTH AMERICA.

"When an industrious population, after years of suffering, are aroused to a sense of danger, by renewed attacks upon their rights and liberties, an appeal to those of kindred blood, animated by the same spirit, and allied by a communion of interests, can excite no surprise and requires no justification.

"Long and patiently have the population of British and Irish descent in Lower Canada endured evils of no ordinary description, relying on the interposition of the Imperial Government for relief. Deceived in their fondly cherished trust, they are impelled to seek from their own energies that protection which has been withheld by the power on whose justice they reposed.

"For half a century they have been subjected to the domination of a party whose policy has been to retain the distinguishing attributes of a foreign race, and to crush in others that spirit of enterprise which they are unwilling or unable to emulate. During that period, a population descended from the same stock with ourselves have covered a continent with the smiling monuments of their agricultural industry. Upper Canada and the United States bear ample testimony of the flood tide of prosperity, the result of unrestricted enterprise and of equitable laws, which has rewarded their efforts; Lower Canada, where another race predominates, presents a solitary exception to this general march of improvement. There, surrounded by forests inviting the industry of man, and opening a rich reward to his labour, an illiterate people opposed to improvements have compressed their growing members almost within the boundaries of the original settlements, and present in their laws, their mode of agriculture, a not unfaithful picture of France in the seventeenth century. There also may be witnessed the humiliating spectacle of a rural population not unfrequently necessitated to implore eleemosynary relief from the Legislature of the country.

"It were incredible to suppose that a minority, constituting nearly one-third of the entire population, imbued with the same ardour for improvements that honourably distinguishes their race throughout the North American continent, and possessing the undisputed control of all the great interests of the Colony, would resign themselves to the benumbing sway of a majority differing from themselves so essentially on all important points, whilst any mode of deliverance was open to the choice. Nor would supineness or indifference on their part produce a corresponding change in their opponents, or mitigate the relentless persecution with which they have been visited. The deep-rooted hostility excited by the French leaders against those of different origin which has led to the perpetration of outrages on persons and property and destroyed confidence in juries, who have been taught to regard us as their foes, has extended its pernicious influence beyond the limits of Lower Canada. Upper Canada, repulsed in her endeavours to open a direct channel of communication to the sea, has been driven to cultivate commercial relations with the United States, whose policy is more congenial with their own. Nova Scotia and New Brunswick will learn, with indignant surprise, that the destruction of their most important interests is countenanced and supported by the Assembly of this Province.

"A French majority in one Province has caused these accumulated evils. A British majority in the United Provinces will compel their removal.

"If it be the desire of the French-Canadians to isolate themselves from the other objects of the Empire by cherishing the language and customs of a country which stands to them in the relation of a foreign power, the effects of such a prejudice will chiefly be felt by themselves, and may be left for correction to the hand of time; but, when national feeling is exhibited in an active opposition to the general interests of the British American Provinces, when immigration is checked, the settlement of the country retarded, and the interests of commerce sacrificed to the visionary scheme of establishing a French power, it becomes the solemn duty of the entire British population to resist proceedings so pregnant with evil. Let it not be said that a million of freemen permitted their rights to be invaded, and their onward course impeded, by a faction which already recoils in alarm from the contest it has already provoked.

"Connected as are the Provinces of British America by a chain of rivers and lakes affording the means of creating an uninterrupted water communication between their extremities at a comparatively small expense, possessing within themselves the elements of an extensive trade by the interchange of those products which are peculiar to each, and forming parts of the same Empire, they have the undoubted right to require that these advantages shall not be sacrificed by the inertness or the mistaken policy of any one state, more especially when, as in the case of Lower Canada, that state, from geographical position, exercises a preponderating influence on the property of all.

"The facts which have been made public in two addresses emanating from this Association, conclusively establish the want of education among the French population, their subserviency to their political leaders, and the hostility of those leaders to the population of English and Irish descent. Many additional illustrations of their hostile policy might be adduced."

The address then gives several instances of such hostile policy, such as the encouragement of the Baltic timber trade instead of the Canadian, opposition to building the St. Lawrence Canal, opposition to the introduction of foreign capital, etc., etc., and then continues :

" It is to the great body of the people thus characterised, that His Excellency, the Earl of Gosford, the representative of a British King, and the head of the Commission deputed to enquire into our complaints, has declared that all future appointments to office shall be made acceptable. A Legislative Council constituted on such a principle would be but a counterpart of the Assembly ; it might, and no doubt would relieve the Executive from the odium of sanctioning the illegal appropriation of a part of the provincial revenues by the mere vote of the Assembly ; but it would not prevent the same misapplication of the public funds being effected by bill, which is now accomplished by an address to the head of the Administration. A Government thus conducted would forfeit all title to our confidence, would be regarded but as an instrument to secure the domination of a party, and the brief period of its duration would be marked by scenes of outrage and by difficulties of no ordinary description.

"The French leaders, if we are to credit their reiterated assertions, entertain an attachment so deep, so absorbing for elective institutions, that they would at once confer that important privilege to its fullest extent, without reference to previous habits, education or political dissensions. How much of this ardour may have been called forth by a desire to establish French ascendancy, and to depress British interests, may fairly be deduced from a review of the past proceedings. Without discussing the question of elective institutions, which it is obvious, cannot be introduced to the extent demanded by the Assembly, under the existing political relations of the Colony, which relations we are resolute to maintain, we distinctly aver, that we are not influenced by idle apprehensions of a government of the people and for the people, but it must be emphatically a government of 'the people,' truly represented, and not that of a French faction; the government of an educated and independent race, attached to the principles of civil and religious liberty, and not that of an uninformed population, strong for domination, and seeking to perpetuate in America the institutions of feudal Europe. To the people of the sister Colonies we appeal, earnestly recommending the adoption of measures for assembling at some central point a Congress of Deputies from all the Provinces of British North America. A British American Congress, possessing strength from Union and wisdom from Counsel, by the irresistible weight of its moral influence would supersede those other remedial measures which are the last recourse of an insulted and oppressed community. On it would devolve the solemn duty, calmly to deliberate on all matters affecting the common weal, and firmly to resist all attempts to invade the rights or impair the interests of the United Provinces.

"In submitting a brief recapitulation of the objects of the Constitutional Association, it may not be misplaced to offer a few observations explanatory of the position of parties in Lower Canada, and of the sentiments of the British population towards their fellow-subjects of French origin. The moral guilt of exciting national hostility undoubtedly rests with the French leaders, who alone benefit by the distracted state of the country, but the facility with which the French peasantry have received these impressions and the unanimity with which they support the aggressive policy of their leaders, render them, although less culpable, yet equally the determined opponents of our rights and of our liberties. Unhappily their want of education prevents a direct appeal being made through the press to their judgment, but those of their countrymen who are not blinded by the infatuation of party, who possess education to comprehend and opportunity to make known the sentiments of the British population, may be led to reflect upon the consequences that must result from their present delusion. Should the admonition be disregarded, on them let the responsibility rest.

"The Province of Lower Canada, whether regarded as a part of the British Empire or of the great North American family, is evidently destined to receive the impress of national character from those states by which she is surrounded. An obstinate rejection of all measures, having for their aim the gradual removal of those peculiarities which distinguish the population of French origin, may retard for a time an inevitable event that will certainly hasten the introduction of changes of a more abrupt and decisive character.

"A dispassionate examination of the changes required by the British population will satisfy all unprejudiced men that they are adapted to the general interests of society, are liberal and comprehensive in their character and unconnected with party objects.

"To relieve landed estate from the exactions and servitudes of feudal law.

"To introduce Registry Offices and put an end to the iniquitous frauds that grow out of the present system.

"To promote works of public improvement.

"To recognize an equality of rights among all classes.

"To resist the domination of sect or party, and to establish a general system of education, divested of sectarian tests.

"These are our objects and our demands. They are based on truth, are essential to national prosperity and to individual security; they admit of no compromise, and from them we will not recede.

"The threatening aspects of the time demand action; neutrality, the usual recourse of ordinary minds, will not be attended with an immunity from danger; it must remain with the population of French origin to decide whether, by continuing to support the leaders they have hitherto selected, they are to be regarded as hostile to our just claims, or by uniting with their fellow-subjects of British origin they will compel the introduction of salutary reforms, consign to their native insignificance the few individuals who alone profit by the present system of misrule, and by repudiating ancient prejudices and exclusive pretensions, place themselves in accordance with the spirit of the age.

"WILLIAM ROBERTSON,
"Chairman."

This address had a profound effect and influence in all the Provinces. In Nova Scotia and New Brunswick, resolutions which had been passed, condemning the Executive, were rescinded. In Upper Canada, the Lieutenant-Governor was encouraged thereby to dissolve the House of Assembly and appeal to the people. In Lower Canada it dissipated the hopes of the French-Canadians or such portion of them as thought that something advantageous to their interests might be obtained from the Royal Commission. They began now to consider a certainty that which they had surmised might be a possibility, namely, that the Royal Commissioners would be influenced to report to the Home Government adversely to the contentions of Mr. Papineau and his party.

In this supposition they were within the mark. One of Lord Gosford's associates embarked for England in November, 1835, and the other in the following February. They carried with them the report of the Commission, which was laid before the Imperial Parliament early in the next session. The report recommended:

1. Expenditure of the public income without the concurrence of the Assembly, and that coercion should be resorted to if the Assembly refused to submit.

2. It justified the Legislative Council for refusing to sanction supplies for six months only, and suggested that means be sought for to ensure a majority of the British party being returned through a recomposition of the electoral franchise.

3. It advised that the allowance of a fixed civil list of £19,000 a year, either for the sovereign's life or for a term of seven years at the least, should be insisted on.

4. That no Elective Council should be tolerated.

5. That Ministerial responsibility was inadmissible.

6. That the Commissioners considered a reunion of the two Canadas inadvisable.

The report was fully debated in the House of Commons in March, 1837, and its recommendations approved by a large and decisive majority.

Lord John Russell, who moved in the House of Commons the series of Resolutions on which the House acted, when discussing the report, said: "No other American dependency of Great Britain advances such pretensions as Lower Canada, and everything, therefore, forebodes a satisfactory arrangement between the other Colonies and ourselves. An Elective Council for legislation, and a responsible Executive Council combined with a representative Assembly, would be quite incompatible with the rightful inter-relationship of any Colony and the Mother Country." It is almost unnecessary to say that this doctrine laid down by Lord Russell is now exploded. Not a shred of it is left. No English statesman would promulgate such a doctrine at the present day.

Mr. Morin, one of the most prominent supporters of Mr. Papineau in Quebec, referring to Lord John Russell's resolutions and a Bill which had been introduced into the House of Commons founded thereon, under which it was proposed to administer the revenues of the Province without the consent of the Assembly, said: "This Ministerial measure is a violation of our most sacred rights and will cause the spoliation of our substance, it is an act of the greatest oppression and the most tyrannical character, it is a measure which the Canadians ought never to suffer being carried into operation, one which they ought to resist with every kind of power and by all means whatever. From what has just passed in Britain, it is clear that the people there have no sympathy with us, and that we must look for it elsewhere. We are despised, oppression is in store for us, and even annihilation. It is intended to put us under the yoke of degrading oppressiveness. No more liberty for us. Slavery is about to become our portion. But this state of things need endure no longer than while we are unable to redress it."

These words of this follower of Mr. Papineau did not fail to have great influence with the excitable French-Canadians. Meetings were held in different parts of the Province to denounce the report of the Royal Commissioners, Lord John Russell's Resolutions, the British House of Commons, and everything British coming within the sphere of the French-Canadian vision. These meetings were attended by Messrs. Papineau, Morin, Lafontaine, Girouard and others, but Papineau was the peer of them all. He was the man to whom the French-Canadians looked for guidance. Unfortunately for the Province he had gained an ascendancy which might in some degree be curbed, but not controlled. The minds of the people were kept in a constant state of agitation and unsettled, not by public meetings alone, but by writers in the press, who stimulated their action by representing that the oppression and tyranny of Britain could not long endure in the Colonies, that the United States Government would be obliged to intervene; that all must stand shoulder to shoulder, and keep up agitation; that trade must cease with Britain, and that these means being resorted to Britain might be brought to terms. In Montreal, the hotbed of Papineauism and rebellion, and in the districts around Montreal, the British residents were constantly compelled to hear the shouts of the Republican party—" Vive Papineau, vive la liberté, point de despotisme."

Lord Gosford summoned the House to meet on the 22nd of September, 1836. The House, in obedience to the summons, met at Quebec. The Governor did his best to conciliate the Assembly, but all to no purpose. The people's House rejected all his overtures, and, while expressing confidence in Lord Gosford personally, refused to pass a Supply Bill or transact any business till their demands were complied with. The Governor, finding his task hopeless, on the 4th of October, prorogued the House, with a clear intimation that, as the Assembly had abandoned its duties, other means would be resorted to for the government of the country.

Following upon the news of adoption of the report of the House of Commons, a continued succession of public meetings were held throughout the Province, Mr. Papineau being the chief speaker, escorted from parish to parish by processions on horseback and in calèches, the meetings being held principally at the church doors on Sundays. These proceedings, under a central committee of a revolutionary character, compelled Lord Gosford to take measures to stop them. On the 15th of June, 1836, Lord Gosford issued a proclamation exhorting all good subjects to eschew all meetings of a dangerous character, and calling on the magistrates and officers of the Militia to protect the laws of the Province. The meetings however continued, and such violent statements were made at some that the Governor felt compelled to call on Mr. Papineau, who held a commission as Major of the 3rd Battalion, Montreal Militia, for an explanation of his presence at one of the meetings. This he declined to give, stating that he treated the Governor's pretensions to interrogate him as an impertinence, which he repelled with contempt and silence. Mr. Papineau had apparently struck the stars with his exalted head. The Governor had no recourse but to dismiss him from the service, which he did in August, 1837.

In the meantime, King William the Fourth died on June 20th, the news of his death reaching Quebec on July 31st, 1837. He was succeeded by her Gracious Majesty, the beloved Victoria. The measures contemplated by the Home Government for governing Canada minus a Legislative Assembly, were for the time abandoned, and Lord Gosford instructed to call the House to meet again, which it did on August 18th. The members presented a singular appearance. Many of them were clad in homespun coats, striped blue and white trousers, straw hats, cow boots, and other home-made habiliments. This was according to general orders issued from their Central Committee to wear no goods of British manufacture. These advanced patriots were imitating the stalwarts of the American Revolution of 1776. The Governor addressed the House at length, informing it of the Resolutions of the House of Commons, and urging them to attend to the business of the Province. The House did nothing but consider this address and formulate an answer, delivered in eight days after meeting, in which they at great length repeated their protests, and stated they would not respect the unbridled and uncontrolled sway of the Colonial Minister. The House declining to fill their duties, the Governor dismissed the members with regret and assurances that he would continue to exercise his powers to the best of his judgment.

While these events were proceeding in Lower Canada, excitement was at a high pitch in the Upper Province; the general election for members of Parliament now being held under the auspices of Sir F. B. Head. There never was at any time so exciting an election throughout the Province of Upper Canada as that of

1836. The two rival parties, the Tories and Reformers, were arrayed against each other in hostile camps—two armies fighting for supremacy. The elections in these days lasted a whole week, and there was open voting. Riots occurred at many polling places; there was general confusion throughout the length and breadth of the land.

Mr. Mackenzie stood for the second riding of York. It was anticipated that violence would be resorted to at the nomination. Mr. Mackenzie made a speech which was calculated to inspire the violence his supporters professed to apprehend. The opposite party made a demonstration, but did not resort to violence. Bands of armed men paraded the streets of Streetsville, where the election was held, playing party tunes, but did no harm to Mr. Mackenzie or anyone else. Their object was to carry the election, and they succeeded, Mr. Mackenzie being beaten by his opponent, Edward Thompson, by one hundred votes. Bidwell, Perry and others of the party lost their elections, and the Reform party was generally defeated and put to a complete rout.

The writer remembers the election well. His father was Returning Officer for the County of Grenville, the election being held at Merrickville, in the rear part of the county. On the fourth or fifth day a party of men came in from the adjoining County of Leeds. They presented the appearance of a squad of Cavalry, being mounted. Taking advantage of the mid-day hour, when the poll was closed for dinner, they seized the poll books in the hands of the poll clerk as he was going from the polling booth to the Returning Officer's house for his dinner, tore it into a thousand pieces and left it littered on the village green. This caused a protest of the election. The Reform candidate, however, was ahead at the time the book was taken, and was returned as the successful candidate and took his seat in the House. The Returning Officer, of the Tory party himself, although deprived of the poll book, knew that the Reform candidate was ahead in the voting and gave him the benefit of his recollection of the state of the poll.

It has been said, and with a great deal of truth, that Sir F. B. Head not only took great interest in this election, but that he took active means to ensure the success of the Tory party. Lord Durham, who made an enquiry for the Home Government, speaking of it in his report, said : " In a number of instances, too, the elections were carried by the unscrupulous exercise of the influence of the Government, and by a display of violence on the part of the Tories, who were emboldened by the countenance afforded to them by the Government."

In referring to the Government, Lord Durham evidently meant the Governor, for Sir F. B. Head showed by his acts that he identified himself with his Council, not acting under their advice only, but as their master. He had thrown himself into the elections as if the success of the Government party were a matter of life or death to him.

In an address which the Governor issued to the electors of the Newcastle District, he said: "I consider that my character and your interests are embarked in one and the same boat. If by my administration I increase your wealth, I shall claim for myself credit, which will be totally out of your power to withhold from me; if I diminish your wealth, I feel it would be hopeless for anyone to shield me from blame. As we have therefore one object in view, the plain question for us to consider is, which of us has the greatest power to do good to Upper Canada, or in other words, can you do as much for yourselves as I can do for you? It is my opinion that you cannot. It is my opinion that if you choose to dispute with me, and live on bad terms with the Mother Country, you will, to use a homely phrase, only quarrel with your bread and butter." This was a direct appeal by the Governor to the electorate to support the Government. If a Governor at the present day were to attempt to control the electorate in this manner, he would soon be brought to account by the Home Government. But at that time more latitude was allowed to the Governors of outlying Provinces than at the present day, or at all events the Governor conceived he was justified in acting as he did. No Governor, however, before Sir Francis' time had gone so far as he in making so direct an appeal, even to the extent of appealing to their base material interests, to sustain the monarch's representative in his support of one party as against another. The excuse that has been offered for Sir F. B. Head is that he was deeply imbued with the idea that the Reform party, in which he had an utter want of confidence, was striving to destroy the system of British government in Upper Canada, with the purpose of raising on its ruins a Republic. It was unfortunate that he should have gone out of his way to influence the electors as he did. The use of an unhappy expression in the Newcastle address enabled the Reform party to apply to the Parliament, elected under his auspices, the name of "The Bread and Butter Parliament."

The session following the election, which was the first session of the Thirteenth Parliament, commenced on 8th of November, 1836, and ended on the 4th of March, 1837. An unprecedentedly long session. During this session complaints against Sir Francis Head were made by Dr. Duncombe, who had been a member of the Legislative Assembly, on account of his partisan conduct during the past elections. The complaint was transmitted to the Colonial Secretary, who in turn sent it to the Assembly, who referred it to a committee to deal with. The Committee, with praiseworthy thoroughness, not only fully exonerated the erring Governor, but declared that the country was greatly indebted to him for his patriotic conduct. Hardly any other report could be expected from the party whose election he had ensured by his addresses to the electors.

The question of a Union of Upper and Lower Canada was before the House during the session, and resolutions were passed condemning the project. Dr. Rolph, a member of the House, urged that the House should be dissolved, so that the **sense of the people might be** taken thereon, but before **his resolution could be** put the Governor **arrived** to prorogue the **House**. At the time of the Governor's arrival the House was in great confusion, a wild altercation going **on** between Dr. Rolph and Government supporters in the **House**, which, **but for** the intervention of the Speaker, might have **ended** in blows. The **Speaker** vainly tried **to** maintain order, while the more **moderate** members shouted for **respect** to the chair. **The** confusion would no doubt have **been prolonged** had not the opportune arrival of the Governor **allowed** the Speaker to announce that the time **had come** to wait on the Lieutenant-Governor. The Speaker's order was imperative, and the session was brought to a close with a parting salvo of wordy pyrotechnics, which to some gave indication that another session of the Legislature would not be held before this **war of** words would be succeeded by more **warlike** deeds.

At **this time, as if to** make the troubles of the country more unbearable, the additional calamity of a financial panic came to aggravate popular discontent. The banks of the United States suspended specie payment, and the banks in Montreal followed suit. With a malign determination to promote disorder, Mr. Mackenzie, in furtherance of his political schemes, now urged the farmers throughout the country to call on the bank of Upper Canada for their deposits, and for payment of their notes. He managed to create a run on the bank, but the bank,

17

which was in a perfectly solvent condition at the time, was able to delay payment by getting their friends to crowd the office, demanding payment, all day, and after the bank closed returning the money they had withdrawn. By this ingenious means the run was stopped and the bank saved.

The Bank of Upper Canada was the Government bank, and in order to help it over the difficulty and save its credit an extra session was called for the 19th of June. A Bill to protect its charter from forfeiture on account of possible suspension was passed, but very little other business was done, and the session only lasted a month.

On the 31st July, 1837, a meeting of Reformers took place at Doel's Brewery in Toronto, at which an address was passed which was afterward sent forth broadcast over the Province. The address was headed, "The Declaration of the Reformers of the City of Toronto to their fellow Reformers in Lower Canada," and was principally the work of Mr. Mackenzie and Dr. Rolph. It went forth to the country signed by T. D. Morrison, Chairman of the Committee, and John Elliot, Secretary. After reciting the many grievances that Reformers complained of, it declared, "We, therefore, the Reformers of the City of Toronto, sympathizing with our fellow-citizens here, and throughout the North American Colonies, who desire to obtain cheap, honest and responsible government, the want of which has been the source of all their past grievances, as its continuance would lead them to their utter ruin and desolation, are of opinion—

"1. That the warmest thanks and admiration are due from the Reformers of Upper Canada to the Honorable Louis Joseph Papineau, Speaker of the House of Assembly of Lower Canada, and his compatriots in and out of the Legislature, for their past uniform, manly and noble independence, in favour of civil and religious liberty; and for their present devoted, honourable and patriotic opposition to the attempt of the British Government to violate their Constitution without their consent, subvert the powers and privileges of their local Parliament, and overawe them by coercive measures into a disgraceful abandonment of their just and reasonable wishes.

"2. That the Reformers of Upper Canada are called upon by every tie of feeling, interest and duty, to make common cause with their fellow-citizens of Lower Canada, whose successful coercion would doubtless be in time visited upon us, and the redress of whose grievances would be the best guarantee for the redress of our own."

The address concluded with a recommendation that public meetings should be held throughout the Province. That a convention of delegates should be elected, and assembled at Toronto, to take into consideration the political condition of Upper Canada, with authority to its members to appoint Commissioners to meet others to be named on behalf of Lower Canada and any of the other Colonies, " armed with suitable powers as a congress to seek an effectual remedy for the grievances of the Colonists."

The meeting also passed resolutions appointing a Viligance Committee, to be composed of members who had prepared the draft Declaration, and that, "W. L. Mackenzie be invited to perform the important duties of agent and corresponding secretary."

The duties required of the agent and corresponding secretary were congenial to Mr. Mackenzie, and he entered upon them with alacrity. As many as two hundred meetings were held in different parts of the Province, at which the Declaration of the 31st of July was read and approved. Mr. Mackenzie attended very many of these meetings and was the moving spirit in their organization. One hundred and fifty vigilance committees were formed in connection with the Central Committee at Toronto. Disturbances of a most serious character took place at many of those meetings. Mr. Mackenzie got on very well with his meetings at such hotbeds of radicalism as Vaughan, Newmarket and Lloydtown, in which latter place a flag was displayed imprinted with a star surrounded with six minor stars, with a Death's Head in the centre, and the inscription "Liberty or Death"; but when he attempted to hold meetings in Albion, Caledon and Cooksville he met with a warm reception from the Orangemen, noted for their loyalty, and at some of the meetings his life was in danger.

While these meetings were being held there is no doubt Mr. Mackenzie had already laid his plans for a revolt, but only some of the members of the branch societies were actually trusted with the secret of the intended insurrection. Some of the active Reform leaders joined no association, either because they disapproved of extreme measures, or because they did not desire to be known in the movement. Like the French-Canadian clergy in Lower Canada, they were favourably inclined so long as reforms were advocated within the lines of prudence, but were not willing to commit themselves to revolutionary action. But Mackenzie had no mind for half measures. He was continually organizing men, enrolling members of his union and drilling them weekly, ready for service if he could arm them. Mr. Lindsey says that before November he had fifteen hundred men enrolled ready to bear arms.

It has been said of the Lower Canada French-Canadian clergy that they were silent spectators of the revolutionary movement in that Province, until such time as the movement got to such a head that they could not control it. It is at least the case that the clergy made no strong effort to stay the conflagration till the building was on fire. The clergy had a very difficult problem before them. If they set themselves against the people, they would incur their enmity. If they sided with them, they incurred the enmity of the State. So they preferred to disregard the frothy declarations of the agitators and to remain passive.

To all outward appearances the Roman Catholic clergy of the Province of Lower Canada have always been loyal to the Crown. The **Church**, which in that Province largely directs **public affairs, has** ever acknowledged its obligation **to the** British Government **for** the privileges it enjoys. There is **a** class of people who in their republican and revolutionary designs have no regard for Church or State. The means taken by the Church to **restrain** this class **in** the Rebellion of 1837, which, **if adopted** before the Rebellion was at its height, might have **stopped the** destruction of life and property, will be shown **as the** narrative proceeds.

CHAPTER XII.

Movement Towards Rebellion—Armed Men—French and English Organizations in Lower Canada—Revolutionary Meetings—Inflammatory Speeches—Papineau and Dr. Wolfred Nelson—Riot in Montreal—Incipient Rebellion—Warnings of the Church—Recommends Obedience to Authority—Fire of Rebellion Stronger than Ever—Birthplace of the Rebellion—St. Eustache, St. Charles, St. Denis—Battles and Defeat of Insurgents—"The Doric Club"—Death of Lieut. Weir—Papineau's Abandonment of Insurgents and Flight to United States.

THE condition of the Province of Lower Canada in the late summer and early autumn of 1837 was truly deplorable. Bands of armed men assembled, as was pretended to discuss political questions, but really to perfect themselves in drill to meet an armed foe. Mr. Papineau and other agitators prowling the country to incite the populace, by most violent speeches to resist the Government; clubs formed, bearing banners with inscriptions, such as "Papineau and the Elective System," "Liberty," "Independence," all tending to excite the people to throw off the yoke of what Mr. Hume had been pleased to call "the baneful domination of the Mother County." The British residents, not to be behind their neighbours, formed organizations to keep watch and ward over their opponents. In Montreal, district committees were formed in each quarter of the city. The Montreal Constitutional

Association raised a body of volunteer riflemen, who marched with cries of "God save the Queen." The "Doric Club" of Montreal, famed for its enthusiasm and loyalty, was at any time ready to meet the French-Canadian organization of the "Sons of Liberty" or any other French organization of whatever name or title. French and English passed each other on the streets with a frown. Suspicion was rife through the whole city. The clergy began to perceive that their silence had been encouragement to the rebel faction. How could it have been otherwise? Revolutionary meetings had been held after Mass on Sundays, under the eye and within hearing of the priests, and yet none protested. In the country parts the poor inhabitants, and in the city the bourgeoisie, were thus led to believe that the revolutionary movement had the sanction of the Church.

At St. Charles, within twenty miles of the city of Montreal, a meeting was held on the 23rd October, which was attended by two thousand people and by Messrs. Papineau, L. M. Viger, Lacoste, Coté, T. S. Brown and Girod, all of whom made inflammatory speeches to the assembled multitude. Armed militiamen, hostile to the Government, were present at the meeting, a kind of "Declaration of the rights of man" was subscribed, and resolutions passed insurrectionary in their character and import, no less than an appeal to arms. The resolutions were in fact worded so strongly that even Papineau disapproved. He had led the people to the brink of a precipice, but was himself afraid to make the plunge. Mr. Papineau, though a brilliant **orator** and Parliamentarian, was far from being a man of courage. He was **a** man of affairs, very well in the cabinet, but very inefficient in the **field**. Dr. Wolfred Nelson, **who** presided at the meeting at St. **Denis**, on the contrary, **was a man** of vigour and all **for war**. He was not for temporising, **and** strongly insisted that the Province must be **roused to** action. He carried his point, and the insurrectionary resolutions passed at the meeting were distributed all over the country.

M. Lartigue, the **Bishop of** Montreal, now began to take alarm, and **feared lest his** people should be caught in the meshes **of** an active and bloody rebellion. He issued a pastoral to his people to be on their guard against the evil counsels of Dr. Nelson, **and** reminded his flock that obedience **to the powers established was a** cardinal rule of the Romish **Church.**

M. Signaï, the Bishop of the See of Quebec, following the example of his brother Bishop of Montreal, issued a mandement, **which said :**

"For a long time back, dear brethren, **we hear of nothing but** agitation, yea even of revolt, and **this** in **a country** which has hitherto been distinguished by its loyalty, **its spirit** of peace, its love for the religion **of** our fathers. On every side we see brothers rise up against their brothers, friends against their friends, citizens against their fellow-citizens, **and** discord **from** one extremity of **this** diocese to the other seems to have burst asunder the bonds **of charity,** which united the members of the same body, the children of the same Church, the children of that catholicity, which is a religion of unity. It is not then our intention to give an opinion, as a citizen, on any political question between the different branches of government, which is in the right and which in the wrong. **This is one of** those things which

God has delivered to the consideration of seculars, but the moral question, namely, what is the duty of a Catholic towards the civil power established and constituted in each State? This religious question falling within our jurisdiction and competency it is undoubtedly the province of your Bishop to give you all necessary instruction on that subject, and your province is to listen to him. Should then any wish to engage you in a revolt against the established government, under a pretext that you form a part of the Sovereign people, suffer not yourselves to be seduced. The too famous National Convention of France, though obliged to admit the principle of the Sovereignty of the people, because it was to this principle that it owed its existence, took good care to condemn popular insurrections, by inserting in the Declaration of Rights, which heads the Constitution of 1795, that the sovereignty resides not in a part, nor even in the majority of the people, but in the entire body of the citizens. Now who will dare to say that, in this country, the totality of our citizens desire the overthrow of the Government?"

The address of the Bishop had a good effect and so had that of the Bishop of Montreal, but the fire of rebellion was too much ablaze to crown these efforts with success. The strong arm of the law was required to quell the incipient rebellion.

On the 16th of November, 1837, warrants were issued for the arrest of Papineau, T. S. Brown, O'Callaghan, editor of the defunct *Vindicator* (defunct by its destruction in the riots of the 6th and 7th November), Ovide Perrault and others. The four first named, having heard of the issue of the warrants, fled to the Richelieu District to join the rebels there, especially at St. Denis and St. Charles, then on the point of rising in insurrection. At this time there was a troop of Volunteer Cavalry in Montreal. This troop, under the command of Lieutenant Ermatinger, was despatched to St. John's, twenty-seven miles south-east of Montreal, to aid a constable to capture the postmaster there and a doctor charged with high treason. The arrests were made, and about three o'clock on the next morning, Ermatinger started on the return journey. A short distance from Longueil he was confronted by a body of some three hundred insurgents, armed with shot guns, muskets and other weapons, and securely posted behind a high fence. They at once opened fire on the Volunteers, who being armed only with sword and pistol could do little to protect themselves. In turning to retreat, the waggon in which were the constable and pursuers upset, and they had to be left behind by the Volunteers, who finally made their way across the fields into Longueil. Lieutenant Ermatinger and three others were severely wounded on this occasion.

The troop of Cavalry, under command of Lieutenant Ermatinger, was the first of the Volunteer corps in the Province to be engaged in active service. The rebellion brought into existence many other corps of Cavalry and Infantry in the Province. These Volunteer corps and the loyal Militia under the command of experienced officers did good service in aid of the regular troops. When it became necessary to strengthen the garrison of Montreal by drafts, some of the regulars, if not indeed the whole of the regulars then in Quebec, the Volunteers and Militia were left to guard the citadel in the old capital of the Province.

Sir John Colborne, who had surrendered the government of Upper Canada to Sir F. B. Head, and had arrived at New York on his way to England, had been summoned to Montreal to take command of the forces, and arrived in February, 1837, and the military operations were from that time under his direction.

The rebellion had its birthplace in the City of Montreal and in the parishes to the north-east of the city, and it may be said to have had its beginning in what took place in Montreal on the 6th and 7th of November, 1837.

Local historians, especially Messieurs Carrier, Globensky and David, have given very vivid descriptions of events in Montreal and surrounding districts. They differ so little from the account of the same events given by Capt. Lord Charles Beauclerk, an officer of the Royals, then stationed in Montreal and who was on active service, that I adopt his statement of the military operations connected with the rebellion, so far as they came under his notice.

The following is Captain Beauclerk's statement:—

"The Royals had scarcely fixed their quarters at Montreal, when visible indications of revolt occurred. In the outskirts of the city, the disaffected were to be seen at drill in hundreds, frequent meetings were held, and placards of a revolutionary character posted in different parts.

"The Constitutionalists were by no means idle witnesses of these proceedings.

"A meeting announced for the 6th of November by an anarchical body, calling themselves 'The Sons of Liberty,' at which Mr. Papineau was to preside, was looked upon by them with a jealous eye, and as a crisis of importance. Nor were they deceived, for in a yard belonging to a Mr. Bonacina, situated in front of the A. P. Church, G. St. James St., about 250 persons were assembled on that day, eventful as being the period of the first collision between British subjects of

English and French origin, in support of those political opinious which have so long estranged them from each other.

"After a short debate, it was resolved by 'The Sons of Liberty that a confederation of six counties should be formed at St. Charles on the Richilieu, and there raise the cap and plant the tree of liberty. An attack on the Royalists was the immediate consequence of this meeting, which with the assistance of a body of Constitutionalists styling themselves 'The Doric Club,' ended in the dispersion of the assailants, and the destruction of the office of the *Vindicator*, a paper of violent radical principles.

"In a house in Dorchester St., where the Patriots were in the habit of drilling, some firearms and a banner having inscribed on it 'En avant association des Fils de la Liberté,' were seized and handed over to the proper authorities. 'The Sons of Liberty' lost no time in carrying the resolution of the 6th into effect ; and as arms were supplied, the Priest of St. Charles, is said to have consecrated them.

"Summonses were immediately issued for the most active in committing this open breach of the law ; and a Constabulary force, aided by sixteen of the Montreal Volunteer Cavalry, under the command of Lieut. Ermatinger, received orders to serve them. Of eight that were arrested, two, Davignon and Demaray, whilst under the escort of the Montreal Cavalry from St. John's to Montreal, via Chambly and Longueil were rescued, about three miles from the latter place, by a large force of *habitants* well armed. The waggon conveying the prisoners was broken, the horses killed, and three of the little band of Cavalry wounded.

"The Canadians to a man had by this time vacated the city, the shops were closed, and a general insurrection commenced.

"Property was no longer held sacred, murders daily occurred, dwellings houses were fortified, breastworks thrown up, and the military openly defied. At L'Acadie in the neighbourhood of St. John's, and in several other parts of the confederated counties, a system of terror sanctioned by Papineau and Coté was adopted ; and against all those who refused to resign their commissions, whether as Justices of the Peace or as officers of Militia, a coercive crusade was commenced.

"OPERATIONS AGAINST ST. CHARLES AND ST. DENIS

"To dislodge the Rebels from their strongholds, St. Charles and St. Denis on the Richelieu, by different routes, making one combined movement, was the first step of Government.

"For this purpose two brigades were formed, the one consisting of the 24th, **32nd and** 66th detached companies with two pieces of artillery, under the command of the Hon. Col. Gore, the other under Col. Wetherall, of four companies of the Royals, two of the 66th, a party of artillery with two field-pieces, under Capt. Glasgow, and a detachment **of the** Montreal Cavalry, under Capt. David.

"The **Deputy Sheriff,** Mr. Duchesnay, and S. Bellingham and P. E. LeClere, Esq., **Magistrates,** accompanied them to authorize their movements.

"On the morning of the 18th Nov., the Brigades were in motion. Col. Wetherall marched for the Village of Chambly, formerly a strong depot of the French, distant about 18 miles, where there still remains a Fort, but at present almost in ruins. He arrived at sunset, and united to his force two companies of the 66th Regiment under Capt. Dames.

"With the exception of a partial destruction of the landing place on the eastern side of the St. Lawrence, where the Brigade disembarked, and of slight skirmishing, wherein seven prisoners were taken, no serious opposition presented itself. That armed parties of insurgents were seen is true, but on the slightest demonstration of attack they quickly dispersed. The broken waggon and dead horses lay near the spot, as we passed, where Davignon and Demary escaped, and tracks of blood marked the spot where the asssistance had been posted. The houses and barns by the road side were entirely deserted.

"Torrents of rain followed in quick succession during our stay at Chambly, and had not ceased on the evening of the 22nd, when in consequence of despatches brought by an officer of the 32nd Regiment **we** were, with the exception of the Grenadiers of the Royals, under Major Warde, and one Company **of the** 66th Regiment left in charge of the prisoners, in active motion, commencing a secret march for St. Charles one hour after sunset.

"The landing of the guns and horses on the east side of the Richelieu, crossed by Col. Wetherall in bateaux at the rapid of Chambly, caused, as might be expected, considerable delay. Four hours elapsed before the last section disembarked, and notwithstanding an incessant rain, which froze as it fell, each man took up his position on the road. During the landing, blue lights were seen, fired by the Rebels for the twofold object of ascertaining our numbers and signalising the march of the troops to their distant associates.

"The roads in Canada previously to the frost setting in, are of difficult passage, but so impracticable for artillery had the late rains rendered them, that in three hours we advanced but three miles, during the whole of which time the insurgents were skirting our line of march. After halting an hour at Pointe Olivier, we pushed forward for St. Hilaire de Rouville, our intended quarters, until further orders, where we arrived at ten in the morning. An agreeable reception awaited us here at the house of a Canadian gentleman, a Colonel of Militia, who entertained the officers; and in his outhouses and the adjoining villages, our men were quartered.

"From a neighbouring height, called the Beloeil mountain, the movements of the Brigade were closely watched by the insurgents, who had surrounded it on all sides, and more than once an attack was threatened, the fuse lighted and the troops placed under arms.

"Thus all communication with Montreal being cut off, the chances were very much against the safe arrival of despatches from Sir J. Colborne, now Lord Seaton, hourly expected; we also learned from report that Col. Gore's expedition against St. Denis had failed, with loss of a field piece and several killed and wounded.

"Col. Wetherall, with the aptitude and foresight of a veteran officer, most gallantly determined, notwithstanding the report of Col. Gore's defeat, to unite with his force the Grenadier Company of the Royals then at Chambly and march upon his own responsibility against St. Charles. To effect this union was no easy matter, for a considerable force of armed peasantry was collected between us and Chambly. As in such enterprises British soldiers delight, volunteers were not wanting to bear the necessary despatch; a selection from the Cavalry was, however, made, as being men well acquinted with the country.

The attention of the Rebels was so riveted to the camp movements, that Major Warde with his company by embarking on board bateaux and floating down the Richelieu, a movement the Rebels did not look for, joined the main body unmolested. At ten a.m. of the 25th Col. Wetherall commenced his march against St. Charles. All the bridges across the small streams, which contributed to the Richelieu, were destroyed, rendering it necessary to form temporary fords by throwing into them piles of rails from the fences. The last bridge near St. Charles was not only destroyed, but the pass fortified. Along a deep gully, at the base of a steep hill, a small stream takes its course, and crowning the height, where the road passes along, a breastwork was raised, which extended some yards on each side of the thoroughfare. Had the military attempted to pass by night, it was the intention of the Rebels to make this spot a place of active defence. To an able officer and man of courage, what a field of operations here presented itself. The Rebel leader at St. Charles, T. S. Brown, however, was not that man.

"In order that the troops might be harassed as little as possible, Col. Wetherall in his further progress to the fortified village, avoided the road by making a detour through the fields at the right. About a quarter of a mile from St. Charles the Light Company of the Royals, whilst skirmishing, and in advance of the main body, received a sharp fire from some houses and barns, which were loop-holed and occupied; these were the outposts of the Rebels, who, on delivering their fire, retreated on their position.

"The houses from which we received the fire were immediately in flames, and one prisoner taken, who, on our opening the view of St. Charles was sent to the town to demand a surrender. The summons was answered by a deafening cheer of contempt, the voice of hundreds. There being no alternative now left but to attack the place, Col. Wetherall deployed on his rear division, as the Brigade marched in close column, the Light Company being extended on each flank under Major Warde. In front of the deployment was a level space of ploughed fields, to the right well wooded land, and to the left the Richelieu, about 300 yards wide, taking a course parallel to the village, which was long and straggling.

" Col. Wetherall hoped that a display of his force would induce some defection among the infatuated people, but unfortunately for the sake of humanity, it was far otherwise. From the west side of the river the insurgents commenced a determined fire, that in spite of the distance did some execution, whilst from the woods an attack was made so desperate that the Grenadier Company of the Royals was sent to its support. The Artillery under Capt. Glasgow was now ordered to advance within 100 yards of the breastwork, and a severe cannonading of shrapnell, shell, round shot and canaster was commenced. The prudence of making a detour in the field was evinced from the fact that the Rebel guns were placed in embrasure to command the road, and thus prevented from doing execution, were, after firing a few guns, altogether silenced. From behind the breastwork a continual fire was directed against the centre of the line, ordered in consequence to lie down, notwithstanding which from the exposed position it materially suffered. This gave rise to an order for the three centre companies, headed by Col. Wetherall in person, to fix bayonets and charge the works ; seeing this the Rebels redoubled their efforts and a galling fire was the consequence, which raked the earth in every direction, yet, strange to say, some dwellings to the right of the breastwork were gained, with but the loss of one killed and a few wounded. Nevertheless, the place was far from being taken, the barns and outhouses which flanked each other, were so well fortified and so obstinately defended, that it took fully twenty minutes' sharp firing to reduce them. The defenders fought with great bravery, many maintaining their posts, until shot or put to the bayonet. By this time the guns had advanced a few paces, supported by a sub-division of the Royals, and poured in canaster shot upon the multitude of heads that appeared in front. At the same time, both on the right and left of the line, an active scene presented itself. To the left a constant discharge of musketry was directed against the breastwork, while to the right skirmishers were to be seen busily employed in cutting off the retreat of those who sought safety in the woods. The fire of the Artillery having in a great measure disorganized the Rebels at their strongholds, the breastworks were destroyed. The Rebels were mostly put to flight, but about fifty appeared on bended knees with arms reversed.

When the troops advanced to take their apparently willing prisoners, the traitors quickly assumed an attitude of attack, and in the discharge of their muskets killed a sergeant and wounded several men. This act of treachery caused, until restrained by the officers, a general massacre, which, whilst it lasted, was indeed dreadful, for many in their flight committed themselves to the Richelieu, choosing rather to meet a watery grave than to yield to the enraged soldiery. Poor creatures, it was but the struggle of the moment, for a severe frost having set in since morning, the icy stream at once paralysed their efforts, and they sank to rise no more. What an awful warning have we here to promoters and abettors of civil war. If one spark of humanity holds a space in the breasts of those who advocate the expediency of contending by force for a scheme of government of their own choosing, surely the fate of these poor deluded peasantry will arouse them to a sense of their wickedness.

"The no less brilliant and well judged attack led by our gallant Colonel, and the judicious and effective fire of Artillery under Capt. Glasgow, assisted by the handful of Cavalry under Capt. David, soon caused the total confusion and rout of the Rebels, and had our small force admitted of a reserve, a host of prisoners would have been taken.

"So deficient in courage was the Rebel leader that on the first appearance of the military, he left his dupes under pretence of procuring reinforcements, while Papineau and O'Callaghan preferred viewing the engagement from the house of a Mr. Drolet at St. Marc, on the opposite bank of the river. Not so the defenders of the village, who amounted to about 1,500. With a spirit worthy of a better leader and a better cause, they maintained their supposed rights, and the fact that Col. Wetherall's horse was shot under him, together with the loss in consequence of having been wounded of those of Major Warde, Capt. David and several others, tends to confirm it.

"The loss of the Royals consisted of one sergeant and one private killed, and fifteen rank and file wounded. Of the insurgents between fifty and sixty were taken prisoners, and about 150 lay stretched within their works, but the estimated loss was calculated at 300, many having perished by fire and water, while a few were carried away by their countrymen.

"The breastworks, composed of trunks of trees filled in with earth and supported at intervals by piles, extended to nearly nine acres round the dwelling of Mr. Debartzch, which was a large brick building, with a raised veranda. This house served as a commanding position for the insurgents and was completely riddled with shot-holes. The base of the breastwork was six feet in thickness, the height four feet, gradually narrowing to two and a half, while the exterior and interior slope equalled half the height.

"The cap of Liberty and pole were seized, 100 stand of arms taken and destroyed, and two French six-pounders, found mounted within the intrenchments, spiked and committed to the safe-keeping of the Richelieu. Attached to the Liberty pole was a tablet bearing this inscription, 'A Papineau par ses concitoyens reconnaissans.'

"Our guns having been placed to command the road in case of attack, both officers and men retired to rest, while the prisoners were placed under guard in the church. There I passed a sleepless night, it being requisite to keep a constant watch, as an attempt to rescue the prisoners was generally expected. The alarm was twice given and the windows manned, the lowermost panes having been broken out for the purpose of defence, by which means the temperature was reduced to that of the surrounding atmosphere, then much below zero. In the centre of the church a large fire blazed, where groups of soldiers were regaling themselves, along the gloomy aisles a single candle cast its dim light, by the altar lay the dead bodies of the soldiers, in the vestry room adjoining the church the prisoners were lodged, most of whom assumed a kneeling posture, engaged apparently in silent and solemn prayer. This scene made a deep impression on my mind not to be easily forgotten. The following day the dead of our own party as well as those of the Rebels were buried, and while preparing for the interment, a most repulsive sight presented itself. A drove of pigs were devouring the bodies, a scene so painful that to prevent its continuance, the voracious animals were ordered to be shot by a party brought out for the purpose.

"Amongst other matters of importance which occurred in the course of the day, was in the first place the seizure of a document containing a detailed account of the defeat of the troops at St. Denis and the murder of a British officer, no name given ; and secondly that which was more welcome, a report well authenticated, that of St Denis having been vacated immediately on their hearing of the fall of St. Charles. Their leader, Wolfred Nelson, or the 'Grand Loup,' as he was called, having tried in vain to muster his men, in anticipation of a second attack, forty only obeying him, he left them in disgust.

"The breastworks having been fired and thus converted into a watch-fire for the troops, we sat down about twenty in number at the invitation of some brother officers, who had been quartered in a substantial house with an abundant cellar and a well-stocked larder, to a banquet, far more sumptuous than any we had partaken of for some time, where much conviviality and good humour reigned in every face, and we soon forgot the disagreeable work we had to perform during the morning.

"The sun had set and the long-looked-for despatches had not yet arrived from Montreal, Col. Wetherall therefore determined to march for headquarters at dawn of day. The firm state of the ice afforded a shorter route than the outward march, but the Colonel having received information of a large body of insurgents collected for the purpose of disputing his return, determined upon humoring them. Accordingly on the morning of the 27th, Rouville was again the rendezvous, and after leaving the wounded with a detachment for protection, the march was resumed. Arrived within two miles of Point Olivier, the advance party gave information that the Rebel force was stationed upon a hill, which formed part of the road, when two companies of skirmishers were immediately thrown out, while the main body advanced in close column, but formed line during the advance. In front of the Rebels' position was an inclined plane, well wooded, having concealed among the trees a breastwork, against which our guns were directed ; the Rebels, however, soon retreated, with three field-pieces that had been planted to command the road, but left behind them several barrels of powder, and a few heaps of iron cut into squares, as a substitute for shot. The Cavalry pursued and came up with the guns at the river side, but the Rebels took to the ice and escaped, with the exception of their leader, who was killed, extraordinary it may appear, by a musket ball fired from a distance of at least 300 yards. In the hurry of retreat the Rebels abandoned their prisoners, most of whom had been entrusted with despatches to and from Sir John Colborne, but in every case the bearers had taken the precaution to destroy the papers, and in consequence underwent the severest ill treatment. It was not a matter of surprise, therefore, on crossing the Richelieu, that we should be welcomed as lost men by the 33rd Regiment there, by order of Sir John Colborne on their eve of commencing a march of research. We arrived at Montreal on the 30th, amid the enthusiastic cheering of hundreds, who had long since given us up for lost, and for the first time for fourteen days, enjoyed the luxury of a bed and a change of clothes.

"It was generally supposed, had the troops been defeated at St. Charles, that a large force would have crossed the lines to sympathize with the Rebels, and the sequel will render the supposition more than probable.

"The success of Col. Wetherall's gallant attack crushed rebellion while yet in its infancy, and thus formed the basis upon which the General Commander in Chief subsequently established a victorious career for Her Majesty's Troops and a land of peace for the Canadians.

"The citizens of Montreal were not insensible to Col. Weatherall's exertions, and expressed their gratitude in a most lasting manner by the presentation of a testimonial of value bearing an inscription of which the Colonel had just reason to be proud."

We now become acquainted with the particulars of the expedition against St. Denis, and the following is a brief description taken from notes furnished by an officer who was present:

"Col. Gore's brigade, consisting of two companies of the 24th Regiment under Lieut.-Col. Hughes, the Light Company of the 32nd, Capt. Markham, a detachment of Artillery under Lieut. Newcomen, with a few Volunteer Cavalry, left Montreal on the morning of the

22nd November by the St. George steamer for Sorel, where they arrived at 8 the same evening. Two companies of the 66th, already there, reinforced the Brigade, when Col. Gore pushed forward for St. Denis by the upper road via St. Ours, and notwithstanding a tempestuous state of weather and almost impassable roads, accomplished his march by 10 the following morning. Near the entrance of the village the advanced piquet of Cavalry made two prisoners, from whom it was ascertained that the Rebels, headed by Dr. W. Nelson, were posted in great force. Immediately afterwards the Light Company of the 32nd, under Capt. Markham, received, whilst skirmishing in advance, a sharp fire from several fortified houses. The guns maintained three distinct positions during the engagement, which lasted until 3 in the afternoon, about which time Capt. Markham, assisted by Lieut. Inglis and small party, in attempting to carry a building received a severe wound in his right leg and two in the left side of his neck that brought him to the ground. The Rebels had by this time gained considerable advantage. The Brigade was threatened in the rear by the seizure of the bridge and on all sides by the reinforcements of the Rebels, the larger field-piece, immovably fixed in a deep rut by the frost, could not be brought to bear; the ammunition nearly expended, and Capt. Markham's party driven back. Under these circumstances Col. Gore did not hesitate to make a retrograde movement to Sorel, leaving in the hands of the Rebels several killed and wounded and a howitzer. The gallant Capt. Markham was, moreover, on the point of being made a prisoner, when a sergeant nobly rushed forward in the face of the enemy, under a heavy fire, and bore him away in safety, but not until he had received a fourth wound, whilst in the arms of that brave soldier.

"The seizure of the bridge prevented Col. Gore from retracing his steps, but the lower road was yet open to him. Having reached Sorel in safety, or without further loss, a despatch was immediately sent to Sir J. Colborne.

"Leaving Col. Gore actively engaged in the defence of that place, I shall now return to headquarters.

"On the arrival of the troops from St. Charles, Sir John despatched a force to act under the Hon. Col. Gore, who had orders to follow up the advantage that had been gained and to subdue the whole line of disaffected country on the Richelieu. This force embarked on board two steamboats for Sorel, comprising the Light Company of the 24th, three companies of the 32nd, one of the 83rd, and two field-pieces. Reinforced there by one company of the 32nd and two of the 66th, Col. Gore, having passed through St. Ours, entered St. Denis on the 2nd of December, and St. Charles on the 3rd, without meeting with the least opposition.

"At St. Denis the howitzer and wounded were retaken, the fortified buildings of the Rebels reduced to ashes, and owing to information furnished by one of the prisoners, the mangled body of poor Lieut. Weir was found lying in a ditch by Lieut. Griffin. This unfortunate officer was the bearer of despatches by land to Sorel, the morning prior to the attack on St. Denis, and taking a wrong road, fell into the hands of the cowardly ruffians, and was basely murdered by a villain named Jalbert. His remains, mourned by the whole city, were buried on the 8th, at Montreal, with military honours."

Carrier in his book, "Les Evenements de 1837-1838," and other French-Canadian writers have, in an impartial manner, given details of the various events leading up to and directly connected with the rebellion which ought not to be overlooked. It will be seen from M. Carrier's statement that in the Montreal affair of the 6th and 7th of November the French-Canadian party were the assailants, the first to commence open hostilities. He says that on the 7th November the "Doric Club" and the Club of "The Sons of Liberty" met in the yard of a tavern, in Great St. James Street, the Dorics marching along the street, halting opposite the tavern, when the "Sons of Liberty" men sallied out of the yard and pelted the Dorics with stones and sticks. Some or one of the "Sons" fired a pistol, and the ball pierced the coat of a carpenter named Whitelaw. The

Dorics, of whom about a dozen members only were there, retired, and were followed by "The Sons of Liberty" along St. James Street, and were greeted with stones from all directions. "The Sons of Liberty" broke the windows of the house of Dr. Robertson and of many other houses. They descended St. Francis Street and entered Notre Dame Street, continuing to throw stones. They broke the windows and doors of Mr. Bradbury's shop and invaded the interior of the apartments. From Notre Dame the "Sons" re-entered St. James Street, where they were joined by others of their club; they there also unexpectedly met a body of the "Dorics," who hearing of the treatment their comrades had received, had hurried up to their rescue. At the sight of "The Dorics" the "Sons," now strengthened in numbers, fled by St. Lament Street. At the corner of Dorchester Street, club met club at close quarters and a fight took place, with the result that none were killed, but several were wounded. In Captain Beauclerk's account, he says that it was in a house on Dorchester Street that the rebels, or as they called themselves, patriots, met for drilling, and that here they had fire-arms stored and a flag said to have been consecrated by a priest of St. Charles. At one o'clock the riot act was read, the military called out, and through the excellent arrangements made by Col. Maitland of the Royals, the disturbed districts of Montreal were restored to a condition of comparative quiet.

M. Carrier in his account takes occasion to say that, "the violence of the journals and the commencement of hostilities compelled the Government to issue warrants of arrest against the most prominent of the Canadian party; notably MM. Papineau, Nelson, O'Callaghan, Morin, who evaded pursuit by concealing themselves in houses of sympathizers. Mr. Morin fled to the woods in rear of St. Michael, his native parish."

As regards the affair at St. Denis and St. Charles, there is one incident related by M. Carrier that deserves notice. This is connected with the death of Lieutenant Weir. Lieutenant Weir's regiment had been in Toronto before being removed to Montreal. It was a very popular regiment, and the Lieutenant a very popular officer, and his death roused a great feeling of sorrow in the Capital of Upper Canada, and in fact throughout the Province. Carrier, in describing the incident, says :—

"After the departure of the troops from Montreal for Sorel, Lieut. Weir of the 32nd Regiment was sent from Montreal by land to carry despatches to Col. Gore; arriving at Sorel, he found that the troops had already marched on; he hired a carriage to take him to join the Commandant, but the latter had avoided St. Ours by passing along the Pot-au-beurre road, and as Lieut. Weir had taken a shorter route, he did not meet the detachment and arrived at St. Denis at two o'clock in the morning. Here he was arrested by the rebel guard and taken before Dr. Nelson. When Lieut. Weir found himself in the presence of the Doctor and surrounded with rebels in considerable numbers, he asked in English, 'What they were going to do with him?' 'This is what we are going to do with you' said the Doctor, 'to treat you as a gentleman, as we would wish you to treat us under similar circumstances. You are going to remain our prisoner just on the eve of a battle, which is imminent, but we demand your word of honour that you will not attempt to escape from us; if you attempt to escape, I cannot answer for you, and more than that I will give orders to my soldiers to shoot you.' So that the Lieutenant should not take part in the combat, Dr. Nelson ordered that he should be conducted to the Rebel camp at St. Charles, under the guard of two men, but scarcely had they set out when he attempted to escape, near the convent of St. Denis. The Rebels did all in their power to stop him, but to no purpose, he leaped from the carriage and attempted to reach the troops ; as, however, he was bound by a rope it was not difficult to restrain him, as the guards did by striking him with their swords. They inflicted him with such wounds that he asked them as a favour to despatch him, which one of the guards did by firing a musket into his head."

Dr. Wolfred Nelson, into whose hands Lieutenant Weir fell, was acquainted with the proprieties and was a gentleman who was highly respected. He was the most prominent person in St. Denis, and owned considerable property there. He was born in Montreal, descended from a respectable English family by his father's side, while his mother was the daughter of a U. E. Loyalist. Shortly after the war of 1812 he settled at St. Denis, on the Richelieu River, became thoroughly identified with the French population, and as a medical man in large practice and the proprietor of an extensive brewery and distillery, acquired great influence with the *habitants*. Having represented the district in Parliament, he was brought into immediate contact with Papineau, whose republican principles he espoused. Hence we find him associating with Papineau in fomenting rebellion in Lower Canada. Taking Carrier's account of the capture of Lieutenant Weir and his subsequent escape and death to be the correct one, Lieutenant Weir must have known he took his life in his hands when he attempted to escape from his guards. He was a brave soldier and deserved a better fate than to meet an early death in a strange country, surrounded by men in rebellion against the Crown which he served. Even Dr. Nelson could not but lament his death, and the circumstances by which it was brought about. It will be observed that the Lieutenant when despatched was not in the immediate custody of Dr. Nelson, but of the two guards, who had set out with him from St. Denis, for the rebel camp at St. Charles. The English account differs entirely from that of M. Carrier. According to the English account, while pinioned and attempting to escape from his guards, in the scuffle he was mercilessly shot, sabred, hacked, and stabbed as though he had been a mad dog, and that he was, while seeking shelter from the cart from which he had escaped, foully murdered in the presence of a crowd of spectators. It is not possible to believe that Dr. Nelson personally had any hand in the murder, or whatever it may have been, for Dr. Nelson himself was a brave man, and worthy the blood from which he was descended. We have seen that at the revolutionary meeting held at St. Denis, on the 28th October, he differed from Mr. Papineau in the matter of calling the people to arms to redress their supposed grievances. Papineau, having started the flame, began to tremble for the result of his temerity, and would have, even at the last, temporized, while Dr. Nelson, who felt that the affair had gone too far to be halted, was for immediate action. T. S. Brown, who was in command of the rebel forces at St. Charles, was an American. He had been most violent in the affair of the 6th and 7th of November in Montreal, and was the recognized leader of "The Sons of Liberty" on that occasion. He had, in some way, impressed the too confiding French-Canadians with the idea that he was a leader of courage and ability, and thus was allowed to take command at St. Charles. His courage and ability, in fact, consisted in big words and small actions. He proved himself a coward when opposed to the "Doric Club" in Montreal, and was the first to take to his heels when the regular troops appeared at St. Charles. His conduct on that occasion ought to have proved a warning to the French-Canadians, that neither their lives nor their liberties were safe in the hands of the vaporing American. In truth it would have been better if they had trusted themselves entirely to the protection of their best friends, the British. There were many loyal French-Canadians who would have had it so, but the simple-minded peasants, led away by the gasconade and show of their self-appointed leaders, were easily entrapped. And so it happened that not only at St. Charles, but in subsequent affairs when they fell into the hands of sympathetic Americans, they learned to their cost that their new-made friends were but old deceivers, quite unworthy the confidence of the patriotic French-Canadian.

How different was the conduct of Dr. Nelson, who was in command of the rebel camp at St. Denis. Here we find a physician, not skilled in the art of war, nevertheless taking the precautionary steps of an experienced commander to protect his post. It was Nelson's good generalship that caused the bridges leading to the village to be destroyed, which retarded the advance of the troops led by Col. Gore. It was Nelson's genius that fortified St. Denis in a respectable manner, fit to oppose the advance of the regular troops. It was Nelson, in fact, who caused Col. Gore to retire, and for the time to abandon the attack on the village. The repulse of the corps under Col. Gore was, in fact, a victory for the rebels. It was not a lasting victory, but, nevertheless, one that gave the Canadians heart, and had they been well armed, which they were not, and better led than they were by such men as T. S. Brown, they might afterwards have shown considerable resistance to the British troops.

Papineau's physical courage was apparently not much greater than that of T. S. Brown. After his flight from Montreal, following the affair of the 6th and 7th of November, he was a guest of Dr. Nelson at St. Denis till the appearance of the troops under Col. Gore. Instead of joining his compatriots whom he had led into revolt and resistance of lawful authority, he abandoned them in the moment of danger and fled to Yamaska on the St. Hyacinthe River, whence he subsequently made his way, in company with his friend O'Callaghan, into the United States.

This ended Papineau as a rebel leader. He took no part in the following proceedings, but seems to have remained quietly, first in the United States and afterwards in France, until after the amnesty, when he came back to Canada, in 1845, and subsequently entered the House of Commons of the United Provinces of Upper and Lower Canada.

In considering Papineau's conduct one is met at the very threshold with the difficulty of explaining his action in leaving the rebels as he did. Was it fear, despair of success, or because he did not approve of the active rebellion then in progress? Papineau was a man of great personal magnetism. A man of culture and refinement, of education and talent, of commanding presence and speech. Ennobled with the divine gift of oratory, Papineau seems to have had absolute control of the French-Canadians. A man of undoubted Republican convictions, for which none can impute the slightest blame, and animated with the warmest love for his fellow-countrymen, his imagination seems to have been fired with the conception, grand in itself, of establishing a Canadian Republic. Here was where Papineau made his initial error. Had his people been oppressed, had their laws, their customs, their ancient religion been scorned, then indeed would he have merited a place in history with that great liberator, William the Silent, whose indomitable heroism and courage freed the Netherlands from the corrupt and cruel rule of the Spaniard. But such was not the case here. The rule of the English was honest, fair and impartial. The Colonial Office, as we have seen, had had the severe criticism in the House of Commons of such Radical leaders as Mr. Hume, and a Reform Ministry had made the most careful enquiry with a view to ruling these French-Canadians with the most impartial hand.

Papineau's theory of government was then purely ideal and imaginary, founded on his feelings and not on reason. Carried away by his own oratory perchance, he followed headlong on that career which led to the funeral of his hopes. Like the King of France he led his men up the hill and then—he faltered and fled. But why? Did his heart fail him? Was it want of courage, or was it, as we, to relieve the name of a leader most beloved of his fellows from the reproach of cowardice, in charity trust, that his eyes were at length opened—that he saw the men who had for years been trying to conciliate the French at last aroused—the lion awake and shaking free from the torpors of slumber and the steady march of men. The roll of that drum, whose tap encircles the world itself, awoke this dreamer, and he saw that he was only a petty leader in a really petty cause, leading his confiding countrymen to certain destruction, for nothing but an idea; no wrongs to be redressed, no injuries to be avenged, simply that he, Papineau the Canadian, might be ruler of his people. Little wonder is it that after, as Dr. Nelson says, penning a declaration of independence, the thought of his bleeding countrymen drove him to throw up all and become an exile.

Why did he not even then call them to halt? Was his pride greater than his love of his fellow men? Perhaps it was so, and that he preferred the rôle of defeated patriot, treating his opponents, to use his own language, with silence and scorn. Perhaps he felt that this struggle for his countrymen's claim to govern the country they inhabited was vain; but surely the reproach of cowardice laid at his door in after years by Dr. Nelson, and indignantly repelled by Papineau's friends, cannot be approved. Mr. Christie has devoted a great deal of trouble to collecting documents containing Nelson's attack on Papineau and the answer made by Papineau's friends. Dr. Nelson, it must be observed, did not attack Mr. Papineau until he (Nelson) had taken office under Mr. Lafontaine, Papineau's political opponent in the House. The whole controversy was not very edifying, but it may be fairly said to acquit him of the charge of cowardice.

CHAPTER XIII.

Revolutionary Clubs—Council of War—Mackenzie Unfolds his Plans—How to Take Toronto and Carry Off the Governor—Hon. R. Baldwin Disclaims Knowledge of Rebellion—Jack Cade's Rebellion—Mackenzie's Similar—Mackenzie's New Constitution—Publication in Mackenzie's Newspaper—Trip to the Country to Promulgate Constitution—Mackenzie as a Recruiting Sergeant—Appointment to Meet in Toronto on 7th December—Declaration of Independence—Arms and Ammunition—Samuel Lount—Dr. Rolph Alters the Day for Rising—Disconcerts Mackenzie—His Plans Upset—Tries to Retrieve—Sir F. B. Head Reluctant to Believe there Would be Rebellion—Col. FitzGibbon's Activity and Foresight—College Bell Rings Out Alarm—Mackenzie and Force at Montgomery's—Col. Moodie Shot—Threshold of Rebellion.

THE evidence is too clear to admit of doubt that the Rebellion in Upper Canada was started by its leaders with a regularly organized plan to overturn the Government of the Province, and to establish in its stead a Republic which should be entirely independent of England, if not directly attached to the United States. The vigilance committees throughout the Province, in correspondence with the central committee at Toronto, of which Mr. Mackenzie was agent and corresponding secretary, were nothing more nor less than revolutionary clubs, formed with the express purpose of carrying out their designs by unconstitutional means and a resort to arms. It cannot be said that all the members of even these vigilance committees were aware of their ulterior purpose, but that such was the design of Mr. Mackenzie, and those permitted to enjoy his entire confidence, does not admit of question.

Mr. Mackenzie had his own trusted agents, and Mr. Jesse Lloyd, of Lloydtown, thirty miles north of Toronto, was one of them. On the 9th October, 1837, Mr. Lloyd returned from Lower Canada with a message from the insurgent leaders there that the French-Canadians were about to make a brave strike for liberty, and asking Mr. Mackenzie to co-operate with them by raising the standard of revolt in Upper Canada.

Early in November a certain M. Dufort arrived in Toronto. He was a stranger to the city, but he came with a message from Mr. Papineau to Mr. Mackenzie and his associates in Toronto, the purport of his mission being an appeal to the Upper Canada Liberals to support their Lower Canada brethren, when a resort to arms should be made. Whether or not he made known to the Liberals of Toronto his further business is not known. It is however highly probable he did, as by this time a complete accord existed between Mr. Papineau and the revolutionary party in Upper Canada. It became known not long afterwards that Mr. Dufort's further business was a continuance of his journey to Detroit, in the State of Michigan, in the United States, to get up an expedition to assist the Canadians, in connection with Judge Butler, a prominent member of the House of Representatives of that State, to form (and they together in fact did form) a "Council of

War," embracing prominent and influential members of the House of Representatives, State officers and wealthy citizens.

About this time Mr. Mackenzie called upon fourteeen or fifteen persons with whom he had been acting in connection with the vigilance societies or committees throughout the Province, to meet him in the evening at the house of Mr. Doel, corner of Bay and Adelaide Streets, Toronto. They all attended, and Mr. Mackenzie proceeded to give his views of what ought to be the proper course to pursue in the then condition of affairs. Here is his own statement, which has been preserved.

"I remarked," he said, in substance, " that we had, in a declaration adopted in July, and signed approvingly by many thousands, affirmed that our wrongs and those of the old thirteen colonies were substantially the same ; that I knew of no complaint made by the heir of the house of Russell in 1685 against the Government of England, overturned three years thereafter, that could not be sustained against that of Canada ; that not only was redress from Britain hopeless, but that there was imminent danger that leading Reformers would be seized and sent to the dungeon ; that the House of Assembly had been packed through fraud—the clergy hired and paid by the State, the endowment of a hierarchy begun in defiance of the Royal pledge, the public credit abused and the Provincial funds squandered offices created and distributed to pay partisans, emigration arrested, discontent rendered universal, and government converted into a detestable tyranny ; while in Lower Canada chaos reigned, backed by the garrison troops ; and British resolutions to leave no check in the hands of the people, upon any abuse whatever, had passed the House of Commons. Law was a mere pretext to plunder people systematically with impunity—and education, the great remedy for the future, discouraged in Upper and unknown in Lower Canada—while defaulters, cheats, embezzlers of trust funds and of public revenue, were honoured and encouraged, and peculators sheltered from the indignation of the people they had robbed. I stated that when I saw how

Ireland, the condition of which was fully understood in London, had been ruled, I had no hope for Canada except in resistance, and affirmed that the time had come for a struggle, either for the rights of Englishmen in connection with England, or for independence. Canada, as governed, was an engine for the oppression of our countrymen at home.

"I spoke with great earnestness, and was only interrupted by some brief casual remarks.

"In adverting to the condition of society, I remarked that Head was abhorred for the conduct of those he had upheld and cringed to; that in the city all classes desired a change—credit was prostrate, trade languishing—and asked if the proper change could be obtained in any possible way short of revolution?

"Still there was no answer.

"I stated that there were two ways of effecting a revolution: one of them by organizing the farmers, who were quite prepared for resistance, and bringing them into Toronto, to unite with the Toronto people; and the other, by immediate action.

"Dr. Morrison made some deprecatory or dissenting remark, but I continued.

"I said that the troops had left; that those who had persuaded Head to place four thousand stand of arms in the midst of an unarmed people in the City Hall, seemed evidently not opposed to their being used; that Fort Henry was open and empty, and a steamer had only to sail down to the wharf and take possession; that I had sent two trusty persons, separately, to the garrison that day and it was also 'to let'; that the Lieutenant-Governor had just come in from his ride, and was now at home, guarded by one sentinel; and that my judgment was that we should instantly send for the Dutcher's foundry-men and Armstrong's axe-makers, all of whom could be depended on, and, with them, go promptly to the Government House, seize Sir Francis, carry him to the City Hall, a fortress in itself, seize the arms and ammunition there, and the artillery, etc., in the old garrison; rouse our innumerable friends in town and country, proclaim a Provisional Government, send off the steamer on that evening to secure Fort Henry, and either induce Sir Francis to give the country an Executive Council responsible to a new and fairly chosen Assembly to be forthwith elected, after packing off the usurpers in the 'Bread and Butter Parliament,' such new Assembly to be convened immediately;

or **if he** refused to comply, **go at once for** Independence, and take **the** proper steps to obtain and secure it.

"I also communicated, in the course of my remarks, important facts relative to Lower Canada, and the disposition of her leading men.

"Dr. **Morrison** manifested great astonishment and impatience toward the **close** of my discourse, and at length hastily rose and exclaimed that this was treason, **if** I was really serious, and that if I thought I could entrap him into any such mad scheme, I would find that he was not my man. I tried to argue with him, but finding that he was resolute and determined, soon desisted.

"That the proposition I made could have been easily and throughly carried into effect, I have never for a moment doubted; and I would have gone about it promptly, in preference to the course afterwards agreed upon, but for the indecision or hesitancy of those who longed for a change, but disliked risking anything on such issues. I made no request to anyone about secrecy, believing that the gentlemen I had addressed were honestly desirous to aid in removing an intolerable burthen, but that much difference might exist as to the best means of doing so; and that **the** Government would be kept inactive, even if it knew **all, its pretended** friends, headed by a fool, pulling one way, and its **enemies another."**

This rhodomontade did not have immediate weight with those who heard Mr. Mackenzie's appeal. Dr. Morrison, who was chairman of the meeting held in July, did not approve the seizing of public property, in the way proposed by Mr. Mackenzie. This he said was treason. No doubt he was startled **at** the sudden proposal for immediate action, which **was** doubtless premature. Mr. Mackenzie was rather **disappointed** at the stand taken by Dr. Morrison **and reasoned with him** afterwards. Whether or not he **gave him to understand he would** forego a part **of his enterprise is not known, but that** he afterwards **secured his co-operation is matter of history.** None of the **prominent leaders of the Reform party, as** for instance the

Baldwins or Bidwell, were present at this meeting. The Baldwins were too highminded to be engaged in such projects. Mr. Robert Baldwin, afterwards Attorney-General, in his statement made to the Commission in January, 1838, said : " With respect to the insurrection itself, I had no personal knowledge whatever of either the conspiracy itself, the intention to rise, the attack on the city, or the persons said to be implicated in it, and since my return from England, in February last, I have been wholly unconnected with the parties or politics of the Province."

It might almost be termed amusing, if the consequences had not been so serious, to follow the various steps taken by Mr. Mackenzie to redeem the Province of Upper Canada from the evils to which he asserted she was subject. It recalls the attempt to capture London, the capital of the Empire, in 1450. If we forget the disproportion of size, as between great London and small Toronto, we have history repeating itself in the resemblance that Mr. Mackenzie and his followers bore to those of Jack Cade and his army of yokels.

History tells us that Jack Cade was the leader of an insurrection, which broke out in Kent, June 1450, that Jack was an Irishman, an illegitimate relation to the Duke of York, and called himself Mortimer. With fifteen or twenty thousand men this son of Erin marched on London, and encamped at Black Heath, where he kept up a correspondence with the citizens, many of whom were favourable to his enterprise. The Court sent to inquire why the good men of Kent had left their homes. Jack, in a paper entitled "The Complaint of the Commons of Kent," replied that the people were robbed of their goods for the King's use; that mean and corrupt persons, who plundered and oppressed the Commons filled the high offices at Court, and explained further grievances. In another paper, called "The Requests of the Captain of the Great Assembly in Kent," Cade demanded that the King should resume the grants of the Crown, which he complained the preachers about the Royal person fattened on.

Cade, with better success than his antitype, succeeded so far as to get a lodgement in the city for two days, but making an attack on London bridge, was defeated. A promise of pardon sowing dissension among his followers, they dispersed, and a price being set upon Cade's head he fled, but was followed by an Esquire, who fought and killed him. Mackenzie's fate, as we will see, was less hard.

Mr. Mackenzie, in order to convince his followers that he did not intend to stop short in his advance on the enemies' bulwarks, with admirable forethought, prepared a draft constitution for the new state or province, which was to have been established under his regime. To avoid the reproach of being a usurper even in thought, he said he intended to submit his proposal to a convention of the people as soon as a provisional government should have been formed. This constitution was published in Mr. Mackenzie's newspaper, *The Constitution,* on the 15th of November, 1837. Within ten days after this publication he set out on a mission to the northern townships of the County of York, taking with him a printer and a small press for the purpose of striking off copies of this document. Mr. Mackenzie's Constitution for Upper Canada was as follows :—

"WHEREAS the solemn covenant made with the people of Upper and Lower Canada, and recorded in the Statute Book of the United Kingdom of Great Britain and Ireland as the thirty-first chapter of the Acts passed in the thirty-first year of the reign of King George III, hath been continually violated by the British Government, and our rights usurped; AND WHEREAS our humble petitions, addresses, protests and remonstrances against this injurious interference having been in vain; WE, the people of the State of Upper Canada, acknowledging with gratitude the grace and beneficence of God, in permitting us to make choice of our form of government, and in order to establish justice, ensure domestic tranquillity, provide for the common defence, promote the general welfare, and secure the blessings of civil and religious liberty to ourselves and our posterity, do establish this Constitution:

"1. Matters of religion and the ways of God's worship are not at all intrusted by the people of this State to any human power, because therein they cannot remit or exceed a tittle of what their consciences dictate to be the mind of God, without wilful sin. Therefore the Legislature shall make no law respecting the establishment of religion, or for the encouragement or the prohibition of any religious denomination.

"2. It is ordained and declared that the free exercise and enjoyment of religious profession and worship, without discrimination or preference, shall forever hereafter be allowed within this State to all mankind.

"3. The whole of the public lands within the limits of this State, including the lands attempted, by a pretended sale, to be vested in certain adventurers called the Canada Company (except so much of them as may have been disposed of to actual settlers now resident in the State), and all the land called Crown Reserves, Clergy Reserves, and Rectories, and also the school lands, and the lands pretended to be appropriated to the uses of the University of King's College, are declared to be the property of the State, and at the disposal of the Legislature, for the public service thereof. The proceeds of one millions of acres of the most valuable public lands shall be specially appropriated to the support of Common or Township Schools.

"4. No minister of the Gospel, clergyman, ecclesiastic, bishop or priest of any religious denomination whatsoever, shall, at any time hereafter, under any pretence or description whatever, be eligible to or capable of holding a seat in the State Senate or House of Assembly, or any civil or military office within this State.

"5. In all laws made, or to be made, every person shall be bound alike, neither shall any tenure, estate, charter, degree, birth, or place, confer any exemption from the ordinary course of legal proceedings and responsibilities whereunto others are subjected.

"6. No hereditary emoluments, privileges, or honours **shall** ever be granted by the people of this State.

"7. There shall neither be slavery or involuntary servitude in this State, otherwise than for the punishment of crimes whereof the party shall have been duly convicted. People of colour, who have come into this State, with the design of becoming permanent inhabitants thereof, and are now resident therein, shall be entitled to all the rights of native Canadians, upon taking an oath or affirmation to support the constitution.

"8. The people have a right to bear arms for the defence of themselves and the State.

"9. No man shall be impressed or forcibly constrained to serve in time of war; because money, the sinews of war, being always at the disposal of the Legislature, they can never want numbers of men apt enough to engage in any just cause.

"10. The military shall be kept under strict subordination to the civil power. No soldier shall, in time of peace, be quartered in any house without the consent of the owner, nor in time of war but in a manner to be prescribed by law.

"11. The Governor, with the advice and consent of the Senate, shall choose all militia officers above the rank of Captain. The people shall elect their own officers of the rank of Captain, and under it.

"12. The people have a right to assemble together in a peaceful manner, to consult for their common good, to instruct their representatives in the Legislature, and to apply to the Legislature for redress of grievances.

"13. The printing presses shall be open and free to those who may wish to examine the proceedings of any branch of the government, or the conduct of any public officer; and no law shall ever restrain the right thereof.

"14. The trial by jury shall remain forever inviolate.

"15. Treason against this State shall consist only in levying war against it, or adhering to its enemies, giving them aid and comfort. No person shall be convicted of treason unless on the testimony of two witnesses to the same overt act, or on confession in open court.

"15a. No ex post facto law, nor any law impairing the validity of legal compacts, grants, or contracts, shall ever be made; and no conviction shall work corruption of blood or forfeiture of estate.

"16. The real estate of persons dying without making a will shall not descend to the eldest son to the exclusion of his brethren, but be equally divided among the children, male and female.

"17. The laws cf entail shall be forever abrogated.

"17a. There shall be no lotteries in this State. Lottery tickets shall not be sold therein, whether foreign or domestic.

"18. No power of suspending the operation of the laws shall be exercised except by the authority of the Legislature.

"19. The people shall be secure in their persons, papers and possessions, from all unwarrantable searches and seizures; general warrants, whereby an officer may be commanded to search suspected places, without probable evidence of the fact committed, or to seize any person or persons not named, whose offences are not particularly described, and without oath or affirmation, are dangerous to liberty, and shall not be granted.

"20. Private property ought, and will ever be held inviolate, but always subservient to the public welfare, provided a compensation in money be first made to the owner. Such compensation shall never be less in amount than the actual value of the property.

"21. AND WHEREAS frauds have been often practised towards the Indians within the limits of this State, it is hereby ordained that no purchases or contracts for the sale of lands made since the   day of   in the year   , or which may hereafter be made with the Indians within the limits of this State, shall be binding on the Indians and valid, unless made under the authority of the Legislature.

"22. The legislative authority of this State shall be vested in a General Assembly, which shall consist of a Senate and House of Assembly, both to be elected by the people.

"23. The legislative year shall begin on the   day of   , and the Legislature shall every year assemble on the second Tuesday in January, unless a different day be appointed by law.

"24. The Senate shall consist of twenty-four members. The Senators shall be freeholders and be chosen for four years. The House of Assembly shall consist of seventy-two members, who shall be elected for two years.

"25. The Senate shall be divided into six Senate districts, each of which shall choose four Senators.

"The first district shall consist of, etc.

"The second district shall, etc., (and so on, as a convention may decide).

"26. An enumeration of the inhabitants of the State shall be taken, under the direction of the Legislature, within one year after the first meeting of the General Assembly, and at the end of every four years thereafter; and the Senate districts shall be so altered by the Legislature after the return of every convention, that each Senate district shall contain, as nearly as may be, an equal number of inhabitants, and at all times consist of contiguous territory; and no county shall be divided in the formation of a Senate district.

"27. The members of the House of Assembly shall be chosen by counties, and be apportioned among the several counties of the State, as nearly as may be, according to the numbers of their respective inhabitants. An apportionment of the members of Assembly shall be made by the Legislature, at its first session after the return of every enumeration.

"28. In all elections of Senators and members of the House of Assembly, the person or persons having the highest number of votes shall be elected. In cases in which two or more persons have an equal number of votes, where only one is required to be elected, there shall be a new election.

"29. All elections shall be held at those places which may be considered by the electors to be the most central and convenient for them to assemble at. No county, district, or township election shall continue for a longer period than two days.

"30. In order to promote the freedom, peace and quiet of elections, and to secure, in the most ample manner possible, the independence of the poorer classes of the electors, it is declared that all elections by the people, which shall take place after the first session of the Legislature of this State, shall be by ballot, except for such town officers as may by law be directed to be otherwise chosen.

"31. Electors shall in all cases, except treason, felony, or breach of the peace, be privileged from arrest during their attendance at elections, and in going to and returning from them.

"32. The next election for Governor, Senators and Members of Assembly, shall commence on the first Monday of   next ; and all subsequent elections shall be held at such time in the month of   or   , as the Legislature shall by law provide.

"33. The Governor, Senators and Members of Assembly shall enter on the duties of their respective offices on the first day of   next.

"34. And as soon as the Senate shall meet, after the first election to be held in puruance of the Constitution, they shall cause the Senators to be divided by lot, into four classes, of six in each, so that every district shall have one Senator of each class ; the classes to be numbered 1, 2, 3 and 4. And the seats of the first class shall be vacated at the end of the first year ; of the second class, at the end of the second year ; of the third class, at the end of the third year ; of the fourth class, at the end of the fourth year ; in order that one Senator may be annually elected in each Senate district.

"35. A majority of each House shall constitute a quorum to do business, but a smaller number may adjourn from day to day and compel the attendance of absent members. Neither House shall, without the consent of the other, adjourn for more than two days.

"36. Each House shall choose its Speaker, Clerk and other officers.

"37. In each House the votes shall, in all cases when taken, be taken openly, and not by ballot, so that the electors may be enabled to judge of the conduct of their representatives.

"38. Each House shall keep a Journal of its proceedings, and publish the same except such parts as may require secrecy.

"39. Each House may determine the rules of its own proceedings, judge of the qualifications of its members, punish its members for disorderly behaviour, and with the concurrence of two-thirds expel a member, but not a second time for the same cause.

'40. Any bill may originate in either House of the Legislature ; and all bills passed by one House may be amended or rejected by the other.

"41. Every bill shall be read on three different days in each House, unless, in case of urgency, three-fourths of the whole members of the House where such bill is so depending, shall deem it expedient to dispense with this rule ; in which case the names of the majority of members present and consenting to dispense with this rule shall be entered on the Journals.

"42. Every bill, which shall have passed the Senate and Assembly, shall, before it becomes law, be presented to the Governor. If he approve, he shall sign it ; but if not, he should return it with his objections to that House in which it shall have originated, which shall enter the objections on its Journal, and proceed to reconsider it. If, after such reconsideration, two-thirds of the members present shall agree to pass the bill, it shall be sent, together with the objections, to the other House, by which it shall likewise be reconsidered ; and if approved by two-thirds of the members present it shall become law. In all such cases, the votes of both Houses shall be determined by yeas and nays, and the names of the persons voting for and against the bill shall be entered on the Journals of each House respectively. If any bill shall not be returned by the Governor within ten days (Sundays excepted) after it shall have been presented to him the same shall be a law, in like manner as if he had signed it, unless the Legislature shall, by its adjournment, prevent its return, in which case it shall not be a law.

"43. No member of the Legislature who has taken his seat as such, shall receive any civil appointment from the Governor and Senate, or from the Legislature, during the term for which he shall have been elected.

"44. The assent of the Governor and of three-fourths of the members elected to each branch of the Legislature, shall be requisite to authorize the passage of every bill appropriating the public moneys or property for local or private purposes, or for creating, continuing, altering, or renewing any body, politic or corporate ; and the yeas and nays shall be entered on the Journals at the time of taking the vote on the final passage of any such bill.

"45. The members of the Legislature shall receive for their services a compensation to be ascertained by law and paid out of the public treasury.

"46. Members of the General Assembly shall, in all cases, except treason, felony, and breach of the peace, be privileged from arrest during their continuance as such members; and for any speech or debate in either House, they shall not be questioned in any other place.

"46a. No person shall be a Senator or member of the House of Assembly who shall not have attained the age of   years, and been   years a citizen of the State, and who shall not, when elected, be an inhabitant of the State.

"47. No Judge of any Court of Law or Equity, Secretary of State, Attorney General, Register of Deeds, Clerk of any Court of Record, Collector of Customs or Excise Revenue, Postmaster or Sheriff, shall be eligible as a candidate for, or have a seat in, the General Assembly.

"48. No person who hereafter may be a collector or holder of the public moneys shall have a seat in the General Assembly, until such person shall have accounted for and paid into the treasury all sums for which he may be accountable or liable.

"49. All officers holding their offices during good behaviour, or for a term of years, may be removed by joint resolution of the two Houses of the Legislature, if two-thirds of all the members elected to the Assembly, and a majority of all the members elected to the Senate, concur therein.

"50. The House of Assembly shall have the sole power of impeaching, but a majority of all its members must concur in an impeachment.

"51. All impeachments shall be tried by the Senate, and when sitting for that purpose, its members shall be on oath or affirmation to do justice according to law or evidence; no person shall be convicted without the concurrence of two-thirds of all the Senators.

"51a. The Legislature shall have power to pass laws for the peace, welfare, and good government of this State, not inconsistent with the spirit of this Constitution. To coin money, regulate the value thereof, and provide for the punishment of those who may counterfeit the securities and coin of this State.

    I. To fix the standard of weights and measures.
    II. To establish a uniform rule of naturalization.
    III. To establish uniform laws on the subject of bankruptcies.
    IV. To regulate commerce.
    V. To lay and collect taxes.
    VI. To borrow money on the credit of the State, not, however, without providing at the same time the means, by additional taxation or otherwise, of paying the interest, and of liquidating the principal within twenty years.
    VII. To establish post offices and post roads.

"52. Gold and silver **shall be the only lawful** tender in payment of debts.

"53. No new county shall be established by the General Assembly which shall reduce the county or counties, or either of them, from which it shall be taken, to less contents than four hundred square miles, nor shall any county be laid off of less contents.

"54. There shall be no sinecure offices. Pensions shall be granted only by the authority of the Legislature.

"55. The whole public revenue of this State, **that is, all** money received from the public, shall be paid into the treasury, without any deduction whatever, and be accounted for without deduction to the Legislature, whose authority shall be necessary for the appropriation of the whole. A regular statement and account of the receipts and expenditures of all public money shall be published once a **year or** oftener. No fees of office shall be received in any department which are not sanctioned by legislative authority.

"56. There shall never be created within this State any incorporated trading companies, or incorporated companies with banking powers. Labour is the only means of creating wealth.

"57. Bank notes of a lesser nominal value than   shall not be allowed to circulate as money, or in lieu thereof.

"58. The Executive power shall be vested in a Governor. He shall hold his office for three years. No person shall be eligible to that office who shall not have attained the age of thirty years.

"59. The Governor shall be elected by the people at the times and places of choosing members of the Legislature. The person having the highest number of votes shall be elected ; but in case two or more persons shall have an equal, and the highest number of votes, the two Houses of the Legislature shall, by joint vote (not by ballot), choose one of the said persons for Governor.

"60. The Governor shall have power to convene the Legislature, or the Senate only, on extraordinary occasions. He shall communicate by message to the Legislature, at every session, the condition of the State, and recommend such matters to them as he shall judge expedient. He shall transact all necessary business with the officers of Government; expedite all such measures as may be resolved upon by the Legislature ; and take care that the laws are faithfully executed. He **shall, at** stated times, receive a **compensation for** his services, which shall neither be increased **nor diminished during** the term for which he shall **have been** elected.

"61. The Governor shall have power to grant reprieves and pardon, after conviction, for all offences, except in cases of impeachment. A notice of all such pardons or reprieves shall be published, at the time, in some newspaper published at the seat of government.

"62. The Governor shall nominate by message, in writing, and with the consent of the Senate, shall appoint the Secretary of State, Comptroller, Receiver-General, Auditor-General, Attorney-General, Surveyor-General, Postmaster-General, and also all Judicial Officers, except Justices of the Peace and Commissioners of the Courts of Request, or Local Courts.

"63. In case of the death, impeachment, resignation, or removal of the Governor from office, the Speaker of the Senate shall perform all the duties of Governor, until another Governor shall be elected and qualified, or until the Governor so impeached shall be acquitted, as the case may be.

"64. The Executive authority shall issue Writs of election to fill up vacancies in the representation of any part of the Province in the General Assembly.

"65. The judicial power of the State, both as to matters of law and equity, shall be vested in a Supreme Court, the members of which shall hold office during good behaviour, in District or County Courts, in Justices of the Peace, in Courts of Request, and in such other courts as the Legislature may from time to time establish.

"66. A competent number of Justices of the Peace and Commissioners of the Courts of Request shall be elected by the people, for a period of three years, within their respective cities and townships.

"67. All Courts shall be open, and every person for any injury done him in his lands, goods, person or reputation, shall have remedy by the due course of law; and right and justice shall be administered without delay or denial.

"68. Excessive bail shall not be required; excessive fines shall not be imposed; nor cruel and unusual punishments inflicted.

"69. All persons shall be bailable by sufficient sureties, unless for capital offences, where the proof is evident or the presumption great; and the privilege of the Writ of Habeas Corpus shall not be suspended by any act of the Legislature, unless, when in cases of actual rebellion or invasion, the public safety may require it.

"70. In all criminal prosecution, the accused hath a right to be heard by himself and his Counsel, to demand the nature and cause of the accusation against him, and to have a copy thereof ; to meet the witnesses face to face, to have compulsory process for obtaining witnesses in his favour, and in prosecutions by indictment or presentment a speedy public trial, by an impartial and fairly selected jury of the County, District or Division in which the offence shall be stated to have been committed ; and shall not be compelled to give evidence against himself, nor shall he be twice put in jeopardy for the same offence.

"71. In prosecutions for any publication respecting the official conduct of men in a public capacity, or when the matter published is proper for public information, the truth thereof may always be given in evidence, and in all indictments for libel the jury shall have a right to determine the law and the fact.

"72. No person arrested or confined in jail shall be treated with unnecessary rigour, or be put to answer any criminal charge except by presentment, indictment or impeachment.

"73. It shall be the duty of the Legislature so to regulate the proceedings of Courts of Civil Jurisdiction, that unnecessary delays and extravagant costs in legal proceedings may not be a cause of complaint.

"74. Sheriffs, Coroners, Clerks of Peace, and Registers of Counties or Districts, shall be chosen by the electors of the respective Counties or Districts once in four years, and as often as vacancies happen. Sheriffs shall hold no other office and be ineligible for the office of Sheriff for the next two years after the termination of their offices.

"75. The Governor and all other Civil Officers under this State shall be liable to impeachment for any misdemeanor in office ; but judgment in such cases shall not extend farther than removal from office, and disqualification to hold any office of honour, profit or trust, under this State. The party, whether convicted or acquitted, shall, nevertheless, be liable to indictment, trial, judgment, and punishment according to law.

"76. After this Constitution shall have gone into effect, no person shall be questioned for anything said or done in reference to the public differences which have prevailed for some time past, it being for the public welfare and the happiness and peace of families and individuals that no door should be left open for a continued visitation of the effects of past years of misgovernment after the causes shall have passed away.

"76a. For the encouragement of emigration, the Legislature may enable aliens to hold and convey real estate, under such regulations as may be found advantageous to the people of this State.

"77. The River St. Lawrence of right ought to be a free and common highway to and from the ocean; to be so used, on equal terms, by all the nations of the earth, and not monopolized to serve the interest of any one nation, to the injury of others.

"78. All powers not delegated by this Constitution remain with the people.

"79. Such parts of the common law, and of the acts of the Legislature of the Colony of Upper Canada, as together did form the law of the said colony on the   day of   , shall be and continue the law of this State, subject to such alterations as the Legislature shall make concerning the same. But all laws, or parts of laws, repugnant to this Constitution are hereby abrogated.

"80. The Senators and members of the House of Assembly before mentioned, and all Executive and Judicial Officers within this State, shall, before entering upon the duties of their respective offices or functions, be bound, by an oath or solemn affirmation, to support the Constitution; but no religious test shall ever be required as a qualification to any office or public trust under this State.

"81. This Constitution, and the laws of this State, which shall be made in pursuance thereof, and all treaties made, or which shall be made under the authority of this State, shall be the supreme law of the land, and the judges shall be bound thereby.

"Several clauses for the carrying a Constitution like the above into practice are omitted, the whole being only given in illustration of, and for the benefit of a comparison in detail, with other systems.

"We have not entered upon the questions, whether any, and if so, what restrictions ought to be laid upon the right of voting, or as to residence in the State, taxation, performance of militia duty, etc. These matters, however, might be advantageously discussed by the public press.

"Committee Room, Nov. 13, 1837."

Truly Mr. Mackenzie believed in taking time by the forelock. It will be noticed, however, that even he could not make a republic in his own printing office, and that some matters were left unsettled, perhaps with a view to letting the people have some voice in the matter, as he suggests discussion in the public press. As for this builder of imaginary republics himself, he was not only busy in Constitution making, but active in enlisting troops in his service. He was a regular recruiting sergeant in this particular. On the 24th of November he left Dr. Rolph's house to rouse the disaffected in Stouffville, Lloydtown, Newmarket and other hotbeds of revolution in the County of York, to strike for liberty and independence. He carried with him a summons to his followers to join him with arms in their hands on the 7th of December, when they would see the downfall, not only of the Tory party but of monarchical government and everything connected with it. Not a vestige was to remain.

It is the custom of all great generals when they go forth to conquer or die, to strengthen the hearts of their followers with flowing words, and further to show them how much they will be benefited by striking down their enemy. This is what General Hull did when he came to take Canada in 1812. Mr. Mackenzie, not to be outdone by General Hull in generous offers to his followers, promised every volunteer several hundred acres of land. It will be doing injustice, however, to Mr. Mackenzie's war-like spirit and his literary talent unless the whole of the proclamation which he distributed among the inhabitants of North York, with no respect for persons, Tory or Liberal, be given :—

"INDEPENDENCE.

"There have been nineteen strikes for independence from European tyranny on the continent of America. They were all successful. The Tories therefore by helping us will help themselves.

"'The nations are fallen and thou still art young,
The sun is but rising, when others have set;
And though heavy clouds o'er thy morning hath hung,
The full tide of Freedom shall beam round you yet.'

"Brave Canadians! God has put into the bold and honest hearts of our brethren in Lower Canada to revolt—not against 'lawful,' but 'unlawful authority.' The law says we shall not be taxed without our consent by the voices of the men of our choice, but a wicked and tyrannical government has trampled upon that law, robbed the exchequer, divided the plunder, and declared that, regardless of justice, they will continue to roll their splendid carriages, and riot in their palaces, at our expense; that we are poor, spiritless, ignorant peasants, who were born to toil for our betters. But the peasants are beginning to open their eyes and to feel their strength; too long have they been hoodwinked by Baal's priests—by hired and tampered-with preachers, wolves in sheep's clothing, who take the wages of sin, and do the work of iniquity, 'each one looking to his gain in his quarter.'

"Canadians! Do you love freedom? I know you do. Do you hate oppression? Who dare deny it? Do you wish perpetual peace, and a government founded upon the eternal heaven-born principle of the Lord Jesus Christ—a government bound to enforce the law to do to each other as you wish to be done by? Then buckle on your armour, and put down the villains who oppress and enslave our country; put them down in the name of that God who goes forth with the armies of His people, and whose Bible shows that it is by the same human means whereby you put to death thieves and murderers, and imprison and banish wicked individuals, that you must put down, in the strength of the Almighty, those governments which, like these bad individuals, trample on the law and destroy its usefulness. You give a bounty for wolves' scalps. Why? Because wolves harass you. The bounty you must pay for freedom (blessed word!) is to give the strength of your arms to put down tyranny at Toronto. One short hour will deliver our country from the oppressor; and freedom in religion, peace and tranquillity, equal laws, and an improved country will be the prize. We contend that in all laws made, or to be made, every person shall **be** bound alike, neither should **any** tenure, estate, charter, degree, birth, or place, confer an exemption from the ordinary course of legal proceedings and responsibilities whereunto others are subjected.

"Canadians! God has shown that He is with our brethren, for He has given **them** the encouragement of success. Captains, colonels, volunteers, artillerymen, privates, the base, the vile hirelings of our unlawful oppressors, have already bit the dust in hundreds in Lower Canada: and although the Roman Catholic and Episcopal Bishops and Archdeacons are bribed by large sums of money to instruct their flocks that they should be obedient to a government which defies the law, and is therefore unlawful and ought to be put down; yet **God** has opened the eyes of the people to the wickedness of **these** reverend sinners, so that they hold them in derision, just as God's prophet Elijah did the priests of Baal of old and their sacrifices. Is there anyone afraid to go to fight for freedom, let him remember that

"'God sees with equal eye, as Lord of all,
A hero perish, or a sparrow fall.'

"That the power that protected ourselves and our forefathers in the deserts of Canada, that preserved from the cholera those whom He would, that brought us safely to this continent through the dangers of the Atlantic waves, aye, and who has watched over us from infancy to manhood, will be in the midst of us in the day of our struggle for our liberties, and for governors of our free choice, who would not dare to trample on the laws they had sworn to maintain. In the present struggle we may be **sure** that if we do not rise and put down Head and his lawless myrmidons, they will gather all the rogues and villains in the country together, arm them, and then deliver our farms, our families, and our country to their brutality. To that it has come, we must put them down, or they will utterly destroy this country. If we move now, as one man, to crush the tyrant's power, to establish free institutions founded on God's law, we will prosper, for He who commands the winds and waves will be with us; but if we are cowardly and mean-spirited, a woeful and **a** dark day is surely before us.

"Canadians! The struggle **will be of** short duration in Lower Canada, for the people are united **as one** man. Out of Montreal and

Quebec, they are as one hundred to one, here we Reformers are as ten to one ; and if we rise with **one** consent to overthrow despotism, we will make quick work of it.

"Mark all those who **join our enemies,** act as **spies for** them, fight for them, or aid them ; **these men's** properties shall pay the expense of the struggle ; they are **traitors** to Canadian freedom, and as such **we** will deal with them.

"Canadians ! It is the design of the friends of liberty to give several hundred **acres** to every volunteer, to root up the unlawful **Canada Company,** and give free deeds to all settlers who live on their lands ; **to give free** gifts of the Clergy Reserve lots to good citizens who have settled **on** them ; and the like to settlers on Church of England Glebe **lots, so that** the yeomanry may feel independent, and be able to improve **the** country, instead of sending the fruit of their labour to foreign lands. The fifty-seven Rectories will be at once given to the people, and all public lands used for education, internal improvements, and the public good ; £100,000 drawn from us in payment of the salaries of bad men in office, will be reduced to one-quarter, or much less, and the remainder will go to improve bad roads and to 'make crooked paths straight ;' law will be ten times more cheap and easy, the bickerings of priests will cease with the funds that keep them up, and men of wealth and property from other lands will soon raise our farms to four times their present value. We have given Head and his employers a trial of forty-five years, five years longer than the Israelites were detained in the wilderness. The promised land is now before us—up then and take it—but set not the torch to one house in Toronto, unless we are fired at from the houses, in which case self-preservation will teach us to put down those who would murder us when up in the defence of the laws. There are some rich men now, as there were in Christ's time, who would go with us in prosperity, but who will skulk in the rear, because of their large possessions—mark them ! They are those who in after years will seek to corrupt our people, and change free institutions into an aristocracy of wealth, to grind the poor, and make laws to fetter their energies.

"MARK MY WORDS, CANADIANS ! The struggle is begun, **it** might end in freedom ; but timidity, cowardice, or tampering on our part, will only delay its close. We cannot be reconciled to Britain, we **have** humbled ourselves to the Pharaoh of England, **to the** ministers and great people, and they will neither rule us justly nor let us go; we are determined never to rest until independence is ours. The prize is a splendid one. A country larger than France or England, natural resources equal to our most boundless wishes, a government of equal laws, religion pure and undefiled, perpetual peace, education to all, millions of acres of lands for revenue, freedom from British tribute, free trade with all the world—but stop—I never could enumerate all the blessings attendant on independence.

"Up then, brave Canadians. Get ready your rifles, and make short work of it; a connection with England would involve us in all her wars, undertaken for her own advantage, never for ours; with governors from England, we will have bribery at elections, corruption, villainy, and perpetual discord in every township, but independence would give us the means of enjoying many blessings. Our enemies in Toronto are in terror and dismay; they know their wickedness and dread our vengeance. Fourteen armed men were sent out at the dead hour of night, by the traitor Gurnett, to drag to a felon's cell the sons of our worthy and noble-minded brother departed, Joseph Sheppard, on a simple and frivolous charge of trespass, brought by a Tory fool; and though it ended in smoke, it showed too evidently Head's feelings. Is there to be an end of these things? Aye, and now's the day and the hour. Woe be to those who oppose us, for 'in God is our trust.'"

The appeal had its effect. The men engaged in the cause furbished up their arms. Pike-heads, forged in a blacksmith's shop of Samuel Lount, near Holland Landing, were got ready, and ammunition was provided. It was now necessary to secure a competent commander to lead the army of rebellion into action. Mr. Mackenzie, with his accustomed energy, had managed this. There lived in the County of Bruce a Liberal of advanced ideas, known to Mr. Mackenzie—a man who had been a colonel under Napoleon Bonaparte. His name was Van Egmond. To him Mr. Mackenzie wrote, desiring him to assume command of his army, which was to be marshalled at Montgomery's tavern, four miles north of Toronto, on Thursday, the 7th day of December. This was the day set for the rising by Mackenzie in concert with Dr. Rolph and the executive. But "the best laid plans of mice and men gang aft aglee." Dr. Rolph, during Mr. Mackenzie's absence in the country, owing to a fear he had that the loyal militia might be called out for service before the 7th of December, took upon himself, without consulting Mr. Mackenzie, to alter the day for the rising to Monday, the 4th of December, thus disconcerting all Mr. Mackenzie's plans. Mr. Mackenzie did not hear of the change till he arrived at Mr. Gibson's house, not far from Montgomery's. If Mr. Mackenzie's original plan had been carried out, Van Egmond would have had under his command as many as two thousand men for an attack on Toronto, which, in all human probability, would have been captured, as it would have been found wholly undefended. Sir Francis Head, either because he did not realize the importance of the rebellious movement that had been going on in different parts of the Province, especially in the Home District, for some time, or because he desired to earn glory for himself at the expense of the loyalists of the Province, had not taken any means to ward off the rebellion. The Governor had time and again been warned that the disaffected in various parts were drilling and accustoming themselves to bear firearms, and that meetings of rebels were being held for the purpose of concerted action. Miss Mary Agnes FitzGibbon, in her book "A Veteran of 1812," in a note referring to a conversation which the Reverend Egerton Ryerson had with his brother

William, regarding the efforts he had made to induce Sir
George Arthur to commute the sentence of death afterwards
enforced on Lount and Matthews for their conduct in the
affair, says that Rev. Egerton Ryerson said, " I also mentioned to the Governor that you [the Rev. William Ryerson]
and the Rev. I. Stinson had waited on Sir Francis about
four weeks previous to the insurrection, that you informed
him of insurrectionary movements about Lloydtown and
other places that you had learned from me, that you had
strongly urged Sir Francis to raise volunteers and put the
city and other places in a state of defence, that you and
I waited on the Attorney-General next day, and that we
had urged these things on him in a similar manner, but
that these statements and advice had been disregarded, if
not disbelieved." So deaf was Sir Francis to the representations made to him by the Rev. Egerton Ryerson
and others, that he had sent out of the Province to Lower
Canada all of the regular troops that had been quartered
at Toronto. Had these regular troops been retained there
would have been no rebellion. The Governor and his
Council, down to the very last, were blind to the rebellious
proceedings being enacted in their very midst. On the 2nd
of December, Saturday, but two days before the actual
breaking out of the rebellion, a Freemason, in the confidence
of brotherhood, informed Col. FitzGibbon, an officer who
had won much distinction in the war of 1812, that bags of
pike-heads and pike-handles had been collected, and that
he had observed all the signs of a rapidly ripening revolt.
Mr. Lindsey, in his " Life and Times of W. L. Mackenzie,"

says, " FitzGibbon sought out Judge Jones, to whom he repeated what he had heard from the Freemason. They went before the Executive Council together, where the statement was once more repeated. Mr. Justice Jones exclaimed, ' You do not mean to say that those people are going to rebel ?' FitzGibbon replied that undoubtedly they were, when Mr. Jones, turning to the Lieutenant-Governor, contemptuously exclaimed ' Pugh, pugh.' "

Col. FitzGibbon, with a better appreciation of the danger that threatened the city, on this same Saturday made an appeal to Sir Francis to permit him to warn some one hundred and twenty-six men whom he knew to be loyal, to be ready to repel an attack on the city should it be made. This he meant to do by ringing the Upper Canada College bell as a summons to the men west of Yonge Street, and St. James Cathedral bell as a summons to the men east of Yonge Street. So satisfied was the Colonel that the danger was imminent, that he told His Excellency that whether he gave his sanction or not, he, Col. Fitz-Gibbon, had determined to act, and if the Governor refused he should act on his own responsibility. It is doubtful if there was another man in Toronto at the time who would have had the courage thus to approach His Excellency. It is certain that no one in Toronto had so clear an appreciation of the danger and the necessity for immediate action as Col. FitzGibbon. Sir Francis reluctantly gave his consent to the Colonel's demand. Col. FitzGibbon went immediately to work, and had to order the alarm by the

College bell before he had time to warn more than fifty of the one hundred and twenty-six men he had on his list.

The truth is that Sir Francis did not believe there would be a rebellion, and had so impressed his Council and those around him with his own ideas that Col. FitzGibbon was set down as a mad man for daring to have a contrary opinion. By Saturday, the 2nd of December, FitzGibbon had become thoroughly alarmed, owing to recent information he had received, and laid the matter before the Governor and Council, who discussed the matter at great length—FitzGibbon urging preparation, and the Governor and Council holding to their opinion that there was no danger. The Honorable William Allan alone of the Council was more inclined to share in Col. FitzGibbon's apprehensions, and so informed the Governor.

On Monday morning, the 4th of December, Sir Francis Head, being at last aroused to action, sent for Col. FitzGibbon and read to him a militia general order appointing him Adjutant-General, which the Colonel was disposed to decline, as Col. Coffin was then Adjutant-General, and the law only allowed one of that rank. Col. FitzGibbon, with that high sense of honour that was a characteristic of his life, did not wish to interfere with the duty of Col. Coffin, but, yielding to the urgent demand made upon him, he accepted the position with the condition attached that he should be nominated Acting Adjutant-General. A Militia General Order was at once issued appealing to the officers commanding regiments and corps in the Province, and conveying instructions for their guidance in the event of a possible outbreak of rebellion. It was rather late in the day, but the first obvious duty had to be performed, even though the Governor and his Council could not be persuaded to see that the inevitable conflict was so near at hand.

There were no regular troops then in Toronto. There were six thousand stand of arms and some ammunition in the City Hall, which had been sent up from Kingston guarded by two constables; but of what use would these arms have been with only fifty men to use them against the hundreds of men that Mackenzie was assembling on the outskirts of the city? At ten o'clock of the night of the 4th of December, FitzGibbon got information which left no doubt in his mind that the rebels were at the very doors of the city. He lost no time in going to Government House, rousing the Governor, who had retired for the night, and warning him of the danger. An hour later the Colonel learned that the rebels were approaching from the north, by way of Yonge Street. Having given instructions for the ringing of the alarm bells he mounted and rode about the city, calling at the houses of the citizens and directing them to arm and gather at the Parliament buildings to be ready to meet the enemy. There was other work for him to do, and old campaigner that he was, he knew it. It was a busy night, not only for him, but for many another man in Toronto, that night of December, 1837. The Colonel had first to see that the cases containing the arms at the City Hall were opened and the arms distributed to the few who on such short notice could be got together. The ammunition had to be examined and everything got ready for an attack. The Colonel then, accompanied by two law students, Messrs. George Brock, a nephew of the lamented General Brock, and Bellingham, mounted on horses, proceeded up Yonge Street to reconnoitre the rebel position. Having gone as far north as Severn's Brewery in Yorkville, and not meeting with any organized body of rebels, the Colonel returned to the city, first taking the precaution to have a picket placed on Yonge Street between the city and Yorkville, to check any advance of rebels that might be made. Messrs. Brock and Bellingham continued their journey north, and had not gone far when they fell into the hands of the rebels and were made prisoners.

On his return journey to the city the Colonel met Alderman John Powell and a Mr. McDonald, also riding north to ascertain what truth there was in the rumours of the rebels mustering at Montgomery's.

When Col. FitzGibbon arrived at Government House he found that Mr. Powell had arrived there before him. He then learned that his young student friends had been made prisoners by the rebels and that Powell had also been made prisoner, but had escaped and had hurried back to Government House to give intelligence of what he had seen and heard. His report was that between Yorkville and Montgomery's he and McDonald had met Mackenzie and three others of the rebel force, and had been made prisoners; that they had resorted to stratagem and had made their escape. The fact was that Powell on being questioned as to whether he was armed or not, denied that he had arms. He, nevertheless, had a pistol on him, which he drew on Captain Anderson, one of the rebel guard, and shot him dead. This was a great loss to Mackenzie, as Captain Anderson was looked upon as the military leader of the party of rebels at Montgomery's hotel.

When Capt. Anderson was shot, Mackenzie returned to the hotel, and there found that Col. Moodie, a loyalist and retired officer of the regular army, had met the rebels when he was proceeding from his home to the north of Montgomery's, had turned to go back to town to give the alarm, and, in attempting to pass Mackenzie's guard at the hotel, had been shot dead by one of the rebel force from the platform of the hotel. Thus were two lives lost at the very threshold of the rebellion.

If the Mackenzie body of men, although but indifferently armed, had marched on the city that night, it might well have fallen, considering the very limited means of defence and the panic that often follows in a night attack. Mackenzie himself wished to make the advance, even though Capt. Anderson had fallen, but was overruled by his party. Not being a military man himself, and a determined advocate of popular rights, he had to submit or pronounce against one of his first principles of action. His attachment to popular government proved his ruin. His followers had their way, and their delay lost their promised reward.

CHAPTER XIV.

Sir F. B. Head Made to Realize the Situation—Leaves Government House at Night—Makes City Hall the Headquarters, Tuesday, 5th December—Preparing for Defence of City—Picket Placed at McGill Street—Attack on Picket—Rebels Retire—Governor Sends Messenger to Mackenzie Under Flag of Truce—Result—Rolph and Baldwin—Wednesday, 6th December—Arms Removed to Parliament Buildings—"The Men of Gore"—Rebels' Threat to Burn Toronto—Mackenzie Urges Attack on City on Wednesday, 6th December—His Men Refuse to Move—Dr. Rolph Flees for Safety—Rebels at Yorkville—Fire Dr. Horne's House—Lount and Mackenzie Intercept Mail—Van Egmond—His Arrival in Rebel Camp—Plan to Attack City—Loyalists Forestall Rebels—Attack Rebels at Montgomery's—Dispersion of Rebels—Mackenzie's Escape—Battle of St. Eustache, Lower Canada.

TUESDAY, the 5th of December, was an anxious day in Toronto. The alarm of the previous night had called to arms all the able-bodied men that could be mustered. There were young men of the town who had belonged to a rifle company that Col. FitzGibbon had organized, and was in the habit of drilling twice a week during the summer months for the past three years. This he did to encourage the young men to bear themselves in correct military style, to accustom them to discipline and the use of arms. The company numbered seventy. Col. FitzGibbon could always rely on these men, who had the greatest affection for him, and would at any time follow where he led. It was one of these young men that he had sent to ring the College bell to give the alarm of the approach of the rebels. That young man was John Hillyard Cameron.

Col. FitzGibbon in the afternoon of the 4th December, had asked six of his rifle corps to meet him in the evening at his room in the Government buildings. This he did to have them at hand in case of an emergency. He was an agreeable entertainer and made every one happy around him, but it was not for entertainment they met then, but because he had a most lively sense of the importance of showing a bold front in case of the rebels getting into the city. He entertained them by engaging in a game of chess. When Mr. Powell arrived in the city and reported to Fitz-Gibbon, he related how he had been taken prisoner and escaped, and the danger there was of an immediate attack on the city, Col. FitzGibbon set these men of his rifle corps to guard Government House and offices. The guard consisted of J. H. Hagarty (now Chief Justice), Thomas Galt (now Sir Thomas Galt), Ferguson Blair, John Hillyard Cameron, Thomas Hector and Walter McKenzie. They were in fact the Governor's body guard, and for the time being he had no other. Orders were given to batten and loophole the windows of Government House and the Secretary's office on the corner of King and Simcoe Streets, and to make them as defensible as possible. This was a new kind of work for these members of the rifle corps, most of whom were law students, to be engaged in, but they obeyed orders and did their duty. The Governor had to realize the situation, and after giving orders that his plate should be buried in the Government House grounds, a service which Mr. Alexander, his coachman (now an Usher of the Court at Osgoode Hall), duly executed, and giving orders that his family should seek refuge on a steamer on the bay, he left his comfortable quarters on this December night and accompanied Col. FitzGibbon to the City Hall, the only headquarters in the city. It was here that the arms and ammunition were stored, and it, above all other places, required protection. In the meantime Judge Jones, who had been awakened an hour before and had become aware of the threatened danger, had formed a picket and marched it out to the toll-bar on Yonge Street. As for Col. Fitz-Gibbon, he spent the night in arming and organizing the citizens. By sunrise on Tuesday morning, the citizens, who had been roused from their slumber, were formed in platoons in the market-square, with one gun, a six-pounder, mounted and loaded in front of the City Hall.

In a letter written by the Rev. William Ryerson to his brother, the Rev. Egerton Ryerson, on the 5th December, 1837, he described something of the night previous and the appearance of affairs in the early morning. He said:

"Last night about twelve or one o'clock the bells rang with great violence; we all thought it was the alarm of fire, but being unable to see any light we thought it was a false alarm, and we remained quiet until this morning, when visiting the market-place I found a large number of persons serving out arms to others as fast as they possibly could. Among others we saw the Lieutenant-Governor in his every-day suit, with one double-barreled gun in his hand, another leaning against his breast, and a brace of pistols in his leathern **belt**. Also Chief Justice Robinson, Judges Macaulay, Jones and McLean, the Attorney-General and Solicitor-General, with their muskets, cartridge **boxes** and bayonets, all standing in ranks as private soldiers, under the command of Col. FitzGibbon."

By 10 o'clock on Tuesday morning as many as three hundred men had assembled in the City Hall, to take part in defending the city, or to march out to meet the rebels, whichever course might be determined on. Col. FitzGibbon would have taken out men with the six-pounder gun and met the enemy if he had not been prevented doing so by the Governor. When he suggested this being done to Sir Francis, Sir Francis replied, "No, sir, I will not fight them on their ground, they must fight me on mine." If Col. FitzGibbon had had his way he would have dispersed the rebels without doubt, or captured them, as he did the Americans at the Beaver Dam in the war of 1812.

Sir Francis, though not a military man, thought he knew more than the experienced soldier, and thus the chance of taking Mackenzie was lost. Tuesday was spent in making further preparation for the defence of the city. The picket posted by Judge Jones had been withdrawn in the morning, and as the evening approached Col. Fitz-Gibbon undertook to form another to mount guard during the night. This also the Lieutenant-Governor prevented. When FitzGibbon urged, not only the importance, but the absolute necessity of not leaving the road open and unguarded, Sir Francis refused, saying: "We have not men enough to defend the city. **Let us** defend our posts, and it is my positive order that **you do** not leave this building (the City Hall) yourself." FitzGibbon determined to have his own way this time. Without the knowledge of the Governor he formed his picket of about thirty men, placed them under the command of Sheriff Jarvis, marched them out and posted them himself at a convenient spot, which is now the corner of Yonge and McGill Streets. To prove the necessity of the picket, they had not been in position **more** than an hour when the rebels, **eight** hundred strong, **under** Mackenzie and Lount, marched down Yonge **Street,** two hundred men armed with rifles being in the advance. As soon as the advance came opposite the picket, the picket fired a volley from both sides of the road. The rebels were thrown into a panic. The Lloydtown **pikemen** raised the cry "We **shall all be** killed," **threw down** their pikes, and retreated **toward the** main **body at the** tollgate, leaving several **dead** upon the **road side.** The attack of the picket **was so** sudden **and** unexpected that the rebels, who thought to take the city without a shot, fled precipitately to the north. The advantage gained by the driving back of this rebel party was important. The following day it was ascertained that they had been sent into the city to fire it in many places, to distract the small body of defenders, and to leave the road open for the main body of rebels to make triumphant entry into the Capital of the Province.

Sir Francis Head must have felt on this Tuesday, the 5th of December, that he had not sufficient men to cope with the rebels, if they had been bold enough to make an attack in force on the city that day. To gain time for more men to come to his rescue, he, in the forenoon of that day, sent a flag of truce to the rebel camp, asking what it was they wanted. Mr. Mackenzie replied, "Independence and a Convention to arrange details." He added that the Lieutenant-Governor's message must be in writing and said it must be forthcoming in one hour. It must have been humiliating to the Governor to be thus treated by the rebels. It could only have been the necessity of his position that induced the Governor to deal with the rebels and be bearded for his pains. The men selected to confer with the rebel chief under a flag of truce were two prominent men of the Reform party, Mr. Robert Baldwin and Dr. Rolph. Two others accompanied them, one of whom bore the flag. Surely the Governor could not have known that Dr. Rolph was head of the Rebel Executive, or he would not have been selected for such a mission. The case was different with Mr. Baldwin, for he was not connected with the Executive, or in any way connected with the rising, or in the slightest degree connected with the rebellion, and, in fact, did not know that it was proposed to have an armed rebellion. Dr. Rolph, on the contrary, knew all about it. Silas

Fletcher, a prominent actor in the rebellion, and for whose apprehension a reward of £500 was offered by the Lieutenant-Governor, on the 20th July, 1840, wrote to Mr. Mackenzie from Fredonia, New York, that "on the Saturday previous to the outbreak he had called to see Dr. Rolph at his house, and asked him, as he was in the Executive, whether any alteration was to be made, or ordered by him, as to the time of rising." The Doctor answered "No, by no means. I shall expect every man to be active and vigilant, so as to be able to get up the expedition and come on the 7th, and take the city. Fletcher further wrote Mr. Mackenzie, "On the same afternoon (Saturday, the 2nd,) I returned to Newmarket, and met with Thomas Lloyd and other friends on Sunday, who told me that Dr. Rolph had sent William Edmonstone on the same evening I had seen him, with orders to raise a sufficient number of men to come down and take the city within the next 48 hours, this is by the Monday night."

An incident connected with the flag of truce must not be passed over. Justice to the memory of all parties concerned requires that it should not escape observation, especially as in the discussion of the matter imputations have been made against some, which a close scrutiny of the circumstances may explain. It seems that after the deputation returned to the city and reported to the Governor that Mr. Mackenzie must have the Governor's demand in writing, the same parties were sent out again under the flag of truce to inform Mr. Mackenzie that the Governor could not yield to his counter demand. It has been asserted that on one of the occasions of the interview with Mr. Mackenzie, one of the deputation winked to Mr. Samuel Lount of the rebel party, who received the deputation, to walk aside, and that he then requested him not to heed the message but to go on with the proceedings. Samuel Lount, in his evidence before the commission on treason on December the 13th, 1837, put it in this way. He said: "When the flag of truce came up Dr. Rolph addressed himself to me. There were two other persons with it besides Dr. Rolph and Mr. Baldwin. Dr. Rolph said he brought a message from His Excellency the Lieutenant-Governor to prevent the effusion of blood, or to that effect. At the same time he gave me a wink to walk to one side, when he requested me not to heed the message, but to go on with our proceedings. What he meant was not to attend to the message. Mackenzie observed to me that it was a verbal message and that it had better be submitted to writing. I took the reply to the Lieutenant-Governor's message to be merely a put off. I heard all that was said by Dr. Rolph to Mr. Mackenzie, which is as above related."

. Lount did not say whether it was on the first or the second visit that Dr. Rolph said to go on with the proceedings. Without any information but Lount's statement it would seem that Lount referred to the first visit, but from what was said by Mr. Baldwin before the Commission it would appear that while it might have occurred at the second, it could not have occurred at the first visit. Mr. Alves, who was present, said that it was on the second visit, and P. C. H. Brotherton, another of the insurgents, made oath to the same effect, on the 12th December, 1837. Dr. Rolph denied the whole story, and Carmichael, the flag bearer, some years afterwards swore it was untrue. Rolph may no doubt have considered that having delivered his message and received the reply his mission was ended, and that he was then at liberty to advise the insurgents not to relax their preparations for an attack on the city. The conversation between Dr. Rolph and Lount did not take place within hearing of Mr. Baldwin, who knew nothing of the occurrence, if it happened. In the position Dr. Rolph stood to the rebel party it seems strange that he should have accepted the mission. The matter created a good deal of unnecessary controversy then and since. It is quite clear that Dr. Rolph was in an unfortunate position. He was no doubt a secret sympathizer of Mackenzie's rising, and when asked to be a bearer of messages from the Governor he was put in a doubtful position. Possibly the Governor selected him and Mr. Baldwin for the very reason that they had been prominent Reform leaders, and because he wished to commit them to his own side, and it may be that Dr. Rolph acted as has been charged merely to show his friends that he had not deserted them, as they might well suppose when he came as one of the representatives of the Governor.

On Tuesday the Governor had become alarmed for the safety of the arms at the City Hall. If the rebels had fired the city, as they threatened to do, the first building to go would probably be the City Hall. On Wednesday the arms were removed to the Parliament Buildings, which was thought to be a fitter place for their safe keeping. It was computed that on the afternoon of Tuesday there were as many as 500 men, young and old, available for the defence of the city. Perhaps that number could have been mustered, but they were not all reliable, for there were in the city certain persons, like Dr. Rolph, who sympathized with the rebels, but had not joined their ranks. If the rebels were to make an onslaught on the city, it was thought these men might be found numbered with the rebel force. All was uncertainty and confusion. It was not until late that night or in the early Wednesday morning that there was a ray of light. During the night a steamer moored at the Queen's wharf, from Hamilton, with "the men of Gore," under command of Sir Allan MacNab. What a thrill of joy passed through the hearts and minds of the people of the city! "The men of Gore, the men of Gore," was the cry everywhere. "We are saved!" It was now thought that there were enough reliable men in the city to withstand any attack the rebels might make. The number increased all day, recruits coming in from the country. By night-fall the city was strong enough not only to stand a siege, but to meet the enemy in the field.

No man was more pleased than Col. FitzGibbon at the arrival of these reinforcements. He had had an anxious night, expecting every moment to see fire brands applied by the rebels to the city. There were not sufficient men enrolled to guard every approach. During the night word was brought to Col. FitzGibbon that Sir Allan MacNab had arrived with his sixty men. Turning to the Governor, the Colonel said: "Now, sir, we are safe till morning, for with this reinforcement you can guard every approach to any distance from which we can be injured." Wednesday was an uneventful day, except for the coming of fresh arrivals and marshalling them into some kind of order. The position of the rebels on Wednesday was one demanding sympathy rather than condemnation. They had been led into a trap and determined to get out of it as quickly as possible. They had relied on getting assistance and support from the city, but had received none. It was in vain that Mr. Mackenzie assured them that if they would boldly march into the heart of the city, there six hundred good and true men would receive them. It was in vain that Mr. Mackenzie told them that the Government was friendless, that it had only been able to muster one hundred and fifty defenders, including the boys of Upper Canada College, and that the Lieutenant-Governor's family had been put on a steamer in the bay, ready to take flight. The Governor fearing for his family during Monday night, had, in fact, placed them on board the steamer

Transit, anchored in the bay. The rebel force, mostly made up of farmers, after the repulse by Sheriff Jarvis' picket felt more like farming than playing at war. The majority of the army of destruction returned to their houses. Although an additional force of two hundred arrived in the rebel camp during Tuesday night, Mackenzie's whole force during Wednesday did not exceed six hundred men. The force of Loyalists in the city was about equal, and was constantly increasing by a flow of vigorous men from the surrounding districts. Dr. Rolph becoming alarmed for his own safety, thought it prudent to leave the city. He was a fugitive, making his way by devious paths to the United States. The main body of the rebels still hovered about Yorkville, creating alarm in the neighbourhood, throwing into paroxysms of fear many delicate women and children, unaccustomed to see the public roads infested with bands of armed men. The people of Yorkville were literally between two fires, the Loyalists to the south and the rebels to the north. Dr. Horne, a prominent man, connected with the Bank of Upper Canada, lived in Yorkville. Anything connected with the Bank of Upper Canada, animate or inanimate, was thought to be fair game by Mackenzie's band of freebooters. They invaded Dr. Horne's house, demanded food, which was given them, and as a return set fire to the house and burnt it to the ground. On this Wednesday Mackenzie and Lount, and a small body of their men, intercepted the western mail on its arrival at the Peacock Inn on Dundas Street, seized the mail bags, the horses and their drivers, and landed them and the passengers, who were made prisoners of war, at the Montgomery rendezvous. Private letters in the mail bags were opened, money abstracted and general appropriation made of the contents. So much for Wednesday's work. But the day of retribution was at hand. That night, after consultation with Col. FitzGibbon, the Governor decided that the rebels should be attacked the next day.

By this time Col. Van Egmond had arrived in the rebel camp and a council of war was held, and some sort of arrangement made to direct the operations of the greatly diminished band. When he arrived in camp he had but a few followers. He would have had many more had not the day of rising been changed to suit the caprice of Dr. Rolph. The change of day had enabled the Loyalists to muster to meet the malcontents, and not only that, but the assembling of the Loyalists was a warning to many of the rebels that they would meet with stout opposition.

Van Egmond, after a survey of the situation, determined on a plan of action, which if successfully carried out, might still enable the rebels to sack Toronto. Thursday was the original day fixed for the attack on the city. One man had promised to bring down to Van Egmond a force of five hundred and fifty men. These and many others were on their way to his reinforcement, and he had hopes that they would arrive during the day. His policy then was to delay his attack till after night-fall, and in the meantime to occupy the Volunteer Militia by a demonstration, thus creating a panic amongst the men in the town. To accomplish this he despatched sixty of his men to the Don Bridge, which formed the eastern connection with the city, with orders to destroy it. By setting the bridge and the adjoining houses on fire it was thought the Loyalist force might be drawn off by this pretended flank attack in that direction, and their centre being exposed, he, with the remainder of his force, would march into the city and take it.

Van Egmond's plan was a good one, if it had been put in operation early in the morning; but unfortunately for the rebels there was a delay of two hours occasioned by the holding of the council of war and in patching up some differences that had arisen among them as to the plan of campaign. This delay gave the Loyalists in the town the advantage of forestalling the rebel leader by forming for an attack on the enemy's camp. On Wednesday night, after some vacillation on the part of Sir Francis Head as to whom should be confided the honour of leading the Volunteer Militia troops, it was finally settled that Col. FitzGibbon, the Adjutant-General, should have the chief command. Col. FitzGibbon at once gave out an order of distribution of forces for an attack on the rebel camp.

The following is his memorandum made for this purpose :—

December 7th, 1837.

ROUGH SKETCH OF DISTRIBUTION FOR THE ATTACK THIS MORNING.

Col. MacNab.
Lieutenant Nash ....1st Company..... Advance Guard.
     "   Coppinge ....2nd "   "
     "   Garrett ....3rd "   "
Major Draper.
Henry Sherwood.

Two Guns.

Capt. William Jarvis........1st Company......Battalion.
  "   Campbell ....2nd   "
  "   Nation...............3rd   "
  "   Taylor...............4th   "
  "   John Powell.........5th   "
Henry Sherwood............6th   "
Henry Draper ....7th   "
Donald Bethune ....8th   "
Col. Samuel McLean........Lieutenant Cox to aid.
Lieut.-Col. Geo. Duggan.
Major John Gamble.
Judge Macaulay.
Col. McLean.
Col. Jones............. . For the Left Battalion.
Col. John Macaulay.
Capt. Macaulay.
Capt. Durnford.

Artillery.

Capt. Mathias.
Major Carfrae.
Capt. Leckie.

Dragoons.

Three companies in front.
> One gun, Major Carfrae.

Four companies,
> The Men of Gore, under Col. MacNab.
> One gun.

Four companies,
> Right flank under Col. S. Jarvis.
> One company Men of Scarborough in the woods with Col. McLean (Allen).
> Left flank under Col. McLean (Archibald).

Two companies under Col. Jones.

When all was ready, which was about noon of Thursday, the 7th December, and before Van Edmond's party of sixty men, sent to fire the Don bridge, could reach their destination, the main body of the militia, under the direction of Col. FitzGibbon, Col. MacNab (afterwards Sir Allan MacNab) second in command, the right wing commanded by Col. S. Jarvis and the left by Col. Wm. Chisholm, assisted by Mr. Justice McLean, marched up Yonge Street with drums beating and flags flying to attack the rebels. It was a beautiful summer-like day when the body of nine hundred Loyalists marched out of the city. The writer of this narrative remembers the day and the scene, having witnessed it. The sun shone with brilliancy and warmth, as on an April day, notwithstanding a passing cloud sent down some wandering flakes of snow. The men, with but little attempt at military neatness of uniform, marched in column, their bayonets glistening in the sun; all seemed bent on one purpose, to crush the sedition. The step and mien of the men inspired confidence. The few people left in the town felt relieved, as they saw the militia vanishing in the distance to disperse the rebel bands that had been hovering round the town for the past four days and nights.

The happiness of the town's people was soon, however, interrupted by the news reaching the town that the Don bridge was on fire. Van Egmond's men were at their work, but it was too late to recall the troops who were already on their way to dislodge the misguided men assembled at Montgomery's under the flags of Mackenzie and Van Egmond. When the detachment of rebels had set fire to the Don bridge, they beat a sudden retreat, and the fire was put out by Loyalists in the neighbourhood.

When the volunteer militia, marching up Yonge Street at about one o'clock, came in sight of Mackenzie's men, posted on "Gallows Hill," near Montgomery's, they immediately began the attack. The rebels—who were inferior in number to the attacking body—then not numbering more than five hundred—saw a body of men superior in numbers, well armed and supplied with artillery, in front of them; they began to realize that the spirit of loyalty was dominant after all. The Loyalists at the word of command fired volley after volley of muskets into the rebel ranks. The two pieces of artillery that the militia had with them were skilfully managed, the rebels were but indifferently armed, some had rifles, some muskets, and some pikes. With such odds against them, the insurgents had to give way, and fled from the field, leaving thirty-six dead and three wounded behind them.

I have never been able to learn that any of the Loyalists were killed. Mackenzie, however, after the disaster, wrote of the battle and of the gallant deeds of his fellow-rebels in his usual turgid style. "Never," he said, "never did men fight more courageously. In the face of a heavy fire of grape and canister, with broadside following broadside of musketry in steady and rapid succession, they stood their ground firmly and killed and wounded a large number of the enemy, but at length were compelled to retreat." The engagement was a short one, but sufficient for the time being, at least, to cool the ardour of the men of York and to throw the responsibility for any further action in the way of insurrection upon the discontented outside of the Home District. By the Governor's orders Montgomery's house was set on fire and burnt to the ground. He also, in spite of the protests of Col. Fitz-Gibbon, ordered the burning of Gibson's house, two miles up the road from Montgomery's.

The affair at Montgomery's is sometimes called the battle of "Gallows Hill."

Immediately after the defeat of the insurgents, the Lieutenant-Governor, who had witnessed the engagement, returned to the town with the victors and at once issued a proclamation offering a reward of one thousand pounds to anyone who would apprehend and deliver up to justice William Lyon Mackenzie, and five hundred pounds to anyone who would apprehend and deliver up to justice David Gibson, Samuel Lount, Jesse Lloyd, or Silas Fletcher. The proclamation concluded: "The party of rebels, under the chief leaders, is wholly dispersed and flying before the loyal militia. The only thing to be done is to find them and arrest them." It was not so easy a matter to find and arrest Mackenzie. As soon as he saw his cause lost and the rebels dispersing in all directions, he mounted the fleetest horse to be found, and outriding his pursuers, made his way to the head of Lake Ontario, and thence through the Niagara district to Buffalo. The tempting reward of one thousand pounds set numerous parties, armed and unarmed, on his trail; his escape was miraculous. He was several days getting to the frontier, crossing streams barefooted, his horse having given out; wandering through woods, hiding in hay-ricks, sometimes in the house of friends, at other times in the house of enemies, still no one seemed desirous of preventing his escape. He had almost as many adventures as Prince Charlie in his wanderings and in the protection he received everywhere. Indeed, he received such friendship from Canadians of all classes and creeds that some years afterwards in narrating his escape he felt compelled to say:

"Why should such a people, as I tried and proved in those days, ever know hardship, or suffer from foreign or domestic misrule."

The two leaders of the Canada rebellion, Papineau and Mackenzie, being refugees in a foreign country, it now fell to the lot of their friends and accomplices in revolt to continue the struggle, if it were to be continued. About eighteen miles to the northwest of Montreal, in the County of Two Mountains, lies the village and parish of St.

Eustache. This place was a hotbed of rebellion. After the defeat of the insurgents at St. Charles, on the 25th day of November, and the triumphant return of the troops to Montreal, there was comparative quiet in the Province of Lower Canada. There were some insurrectionary demonstrations near the American frontier, but of no account. A party of sympathizers, coming to the aid of the Canadians in rebellion from the United States, were captured or dispersed at Four Corners, near Lake Champlain. The major spirit of rebellion left Lower Canada after St. Charles and took up its abode in Upper Canada, in the district around Toronto. We have seen how it fared at Gallows Hill on the 7th December. Its hydra head was, however, again raised at St. Eustache on the 14th day of December following. The people of that parish, headed by Dr. Chenier, a respectable and wealthy resident of the place, formed an insurgent body in the district, stole arms from the Indians of the Indian village and repaired to the village of St. Eustache. They seized upon the Convent there and turned it into a block house. The parish priest, M. Paquin, appealed to Chenier to abandon the rebellious enterprise of rebellion, and at the instance of Monsieur Paquin some rebels returned to their homes, but their places were filled by others from the neighbouring parish of Grand Brulé. Being joined by these new recruits the Chenier rebels engaged in all sorts of disorder, terrifying the people of the whole district.

The following is a free translation of what Carrier in his "Les Événements de 1837-1838" says about these disorders. He says: "The rebels then were under command of Dr. Chenier and a Swiss, a **stranger** in the country, named Amury Girod. They had **seized** by force from the Indians of Two Mountains their guns (muskets) and two cannon. They were joined by a large number of insurgents of St. Scholastique, St. Benoit, and had marched towards St. Eustache. The curé of St. Eustache, M. Paquin, M. Scott, M.P., one of the principal inhabitants of the country of Two Mountains, and M. Decelles, vicar of M. Paquin, tried to induce the peasants to promise to return to their homes, which most of them did. But others coming in great numbers from Grand Brulé, from St. Martin, and even from St. Laurent, replaced them, so that by the 29th November there were from 400 to 800 rebels in the parish of St. Eustache living by extortion, to the great damage of the merchants and farmers. The insurgents, says M. Paquin, made pillage their principal occupation; they went over all the farms, and by leave or by force levied contribution of all those who would not join them, and carried off cattle, horses and carriages. The greater part of these soldiers of the new form of religion acknowledged no law but their own, stole liquors from the merchant stores and were drunk day and night. Often not content only with stealing liquors, they removed goods and all that they could lay hands on, and when drunk grossly insulted the peaceably disposed. The chiefs, and above all Girod, were as bad as the rest; in this way they attached a great number of persons to their camp, who went there for the good things it afforded; for to protect

St. Eustache they gorged themselves with eating and drinking and the soldiers clothed and shod themselves by pillage. Beyond all other advantages, their chiefs offered to their soldiers the choice of the best lands, with absolution from tithes and seigniorial rents. These promises and the life led in the camp attracted a great number, and nearly all St. Eustache was in active insurrection.

"A great many were taken to camp by force. When the inhabitants refused their behests they threatened them with pillage, to burn their properties, and even to kill them. More than once these menaces were put into execution. Many people who refused saw their houses sacked, the insurgents went so far as sometimes to fire on them."

It was necessary that the rebellion should be crushed out in this quarter, and Sir John Colborne undertook the task. What he did is narrated by Capt. Beauclerk, whose statements of the affair of St. Denis and St. Charles have already been given. Here is Capt. Beauclerk's account of the battle of St. Eustache:—

"OPERATION AGAINST ST. EUSTACHE AND ST. BENOIT.

"Tranquillity having been restored on the Richelieu, and Montreal having been put in a state of defence by fortifying the houses and erecting temporary bulwarks at every avenue leading to the city, Sir John Colborne determined upon attacking the village of St. Eustache on the Du Chene River, in the populous and disturbed district of Grand Brulé, where the rebels had taken up a position. For this purpose the General mustered all his force amounting to 1,500 men, commanded by the Hon. Col. Maitland, consisting of the 32nd and 83rd Regiments, and the second under Col. Wetherall of the Royals, the Montreal Rifles, a large party of Cavalry and Volunteers, one corps of which was named after the Commander, 'The Globenski Corps.' With this force Sir J. Colborne left Montreal on the morning of the

13th Dec. The ground was covered with snow, which rendered it necessary to follow a beaten track, scarcely wide enough to admit of two to walk abreast. To lessen, therefore, the tediousness of the march, the brigades pursued different routes, but halted together at night, at the village of St. Martine's, making a distance of twelve miles. The following day the march was resumed and a rendezvous appointed within six miles of St. Eustache. The bridges had been destroyed, but sufficiently repaired by a party that preceded us, to admit of the uninterrupted progress of the troops, but an insurmountable obstacle at last presented itself. Our scouts reported that the ice in front of the village, and for some distance on both sides, was broken along the shore, and thus rendered impassable for the troops.

"The Globenski Corps, as being well acquainted with the line of country, was therefore detached from the 2nd Brigade to reconnoitre along the direct road to the village and at the same time to carry any out-posts they might fall in with. The main body by diverging to the right, and assisted by the Infantry, by cutting a road for the guns, now mounted on sledges, made the river about six miles below St. Eustache, not far from St. Rose, and having crossed over from Isle Jesus, proceeded to the village. The passage of the river proved to so large a body hazardous in the extreme, in consequence of the unsoundness of the ice, and as a precautionary measure the horses were detached from the guns and ammunition sledges, which were dragged by hand and the troops dispersed in every direction, to avoid the danger, which must otherwise have arisen, from the accumulated weight of parties congregating together. Nevertheless the ice gave way beneath several horses and a gun, but the water being shallow and shore near at hand, they were recovered. On the appearance of so large a force many of the rebels were seen retreating from the village, and, as appeared from their movements, were taking their cannon with them. Our Artillery immediately opened fire upon them, and when no longer within range turned upon the village and bombarded the church, the fortress of the rebels. Congreve rockets were at first fired, but laid aside, for one in its progress struck a rail, reverted upon the troops and exploded within a few feet of the General, fortunately without doing any injury. Col. Maitland's Brigade by this time had seized the brigades and store-houses in rear of the village, while Col. Weatherall, after a most tedious detour through fields three feet deep in snow, held a position in front of the church, protected by a turn in the street.

"To cover the Artillery, now attempting a breach in the church, two companies of the Royals, who occupied the surrounding houses, kept up an incessant fire at the windows of that edifice ; nevertheless many artillerymen were wounded, and little or no impression was made upon the building.

"Sir John Colborne now despatched a party of troops to reconnoitre. A house was fired by them, from which a dense smoke arose, and from its position immediately to the right and a little in front of the church, being to windward, hid it entirely from view. So favourable an opportunity for storming the church did not escape the practiced eye of our veteran General.

"The assembly was sounded and an order given, fix bayonets and advance at double, a manœuvre so promptly executed and on the part of the enemy so unexpectedly undertaken that the troops were under the walls and effected an entrance almost as soon as the besieged became acquainted with the movement. The rebels were found stationed in the gallery still defending themselves, and having cut away the staircase, every attempt to dislodge them for awhile proved utterly fruitless, but on a sudden the church was in flames and on the part of the rebels all was lost. The unfortunate and misguided people were then to be seen dispersing in every direction, few escaped. One hundred and twenty were made prisoners, but the estimated loss in killed and wounded was great. A large force, while retreating, was intercepted by the rear guard and the Globenski Corps proved a very efficient body.

"Col. **Gugy** of the Volunteers, a British subject of foreign extraction, also distinguished himself, as being the first man to enter the church, and in the attempt was severely wounded in the neck. This officer, moreover, from his perfect knowledge of the people and country, had rendered assistance in the military operations on the Richelieu. As at St. Charles, two of the rebel leaders, Girod and Pelletier, on the first appearance of the troops made their escape, under the pretence of procuring reinforcements, but the leader Dr. Chenier was among the slain. Besides the church, the nunnery and presbytery. as well as several houses adjacent, occupied by rebels, were destroyed, but the destructive element spreading far and wide, extended during the night even to the quarters of the troops, nor could it be arrested, although the military were ordered out, until about sixty houses were burnt to the ground. The effect of this general conflagration was considerably heightened by the temperature, then below zero, and the scene altogether was most brilliant.

"It may, at first sight, seem surprising, that such precaution should have been taken in the attack of a place defended by a force very inferior both in number and discipline, but considering the handful of troops then in Canada, the impossibility of increasing that force, since the navigation had closed, the extent of country and the impossibility of ascertaining the strength of the rebel force, the importance of not unnecessarily risking a single life, will, even though humanity were out of the question, be duly appreciated.

"December the 15th we were again under arms marching against St. Benoit. The Brigade had proceeded but a short distance, when a party of men advanced, bearing a flag of truce and demanded a parley. This Sir John refused and immediately made them prisoners, but the houses along our route having flags of truce suspended, met with respect, and such was universally the case. With the exception of the dwelling of a Scotch farmer and loyal subject, around which a stone wall was built by the rebels as a defence, no hostile appearance was discovered."

At St. Benoit the troops were received by the *habitants* bearing flags of truce, drawn up in line in front of the house of Girouard, one of the chief promoters of the rebellion. They surrendered unconditionally. Here the rebels displayed great cunning, for as positions of defence those supplicants had hitherto sought only those villages favourable to Government, but the horrors of war no sooner threatened their own homes than they endeavoured with the utmost diligence to avoid that devastation of which, when it affected the lives and property of others, they were utterly regardless. St. Benoit was nevertheless destroyed by fire, the extreme violence of its inhabitants in all the outrages of the rebellion, rendering this severe measure of retributive justice absolutely necessary. The General, however, had no intelligence of this event until after it transpired, nor were the perpetrators ever discovered. Thus by a decisive blow was the rebellion in Canada East to all appearance quelled, when Sir John returned to Montreal, followed by the Royals and 83rd. The remainder of the force under Col. Maitland advanced against St. Scholastique, but the villagers, like their neighbours of St. Benoit, having submitted to the will of Government, the Colonel returned to headquarters by St. Thérèse.

The French account of the Battle of St. Eustache in the main agrees with that of Capt. Beauclerk, though sufficient credit is not given in the military account of the battle to the valour displayed by Dr. Chenier. He was conspicuous for his bravery and daring during the whole siege. Before the conflict began, when M. Paquin, the parish priest, and others placed before him the danger he was bringing on himself and his followers by resisting the Queen's troops, he said that as for himself he disregarded the danger, "that he intended to die with arms in his hands." His purpose was fulfilled. When the church was set on fire, he, with arms in his hands, accompanied by seventy or eighty of his men who were in the church, sought to make a retreat through a small door in the rear of the church leading to the cemetery, where he fell and expired in the midst of the graves of those who had gone before. His compatriots, recognizing his worth and the sacrifices he made for them in the rebellion, have erected a statue to his memory in which he is represented standing, wearing the traditional French-Canadian sash, in which is a huge horse pistol, and a powder-horn hangs at his side.

Carrier says that one hundred French-Canadians were killed in the Battle of St. Eustache, and one hundred and five wounded. The French account seeks to throw discredit on the troops for the burning of houses and other property that took place after the Battle of St. Eustache. Captain Beauclerk, in his statement, explains that the extreme violence of the inhabitants in all the overt acts of the rebellion rendered this severe measure of retributive justice absolutely necessary. It has been generally supposed that these acts of retributive justice were committed by volunteers who had been subjected to most brutal treatment by the rebels. Carrier's account of the disorders shows this. Besides, there was the death of Lieut. Weir to avenge. His killing was regarded, by the volunteers and regulars alike; as an act of perfidious treachery.

Sir John Colborne, the commander of the forces, had no knowledge of the destruction of property by the troops, either regulars or volunteers, till after it was committed. There is not the least reason for saying that the escutcheon of the British soldier was in any way tarnished by what took place after St. Eustache, as it is only what often occurs in war when the enemy is driven from their stronghold.

The soldiers and volunteer militia, some of whom were French-Canadians, did their whole duty in overthrowing the rebels, and will ever deserve the thanks of the loyal people of Canada for the part they took in putting down the rebellion.

CHAPTER XV.

Bishop of Montreal Deplores the Rebellion and Its Result—Sends Out Circular to his Flock—Bishop of Quebec Gives Thanks that his Diocese Not in Rebellion—American Sympathizers—Meeting in Buffalo—Rochester Follows Buffalo—Doughty Deeds in Contemplation—Mackenzie Occupies Navy Island—Provisional Government for Canada Formed—Van Rensselaer Commander-in-Chief—Proclamation to Inhabitants of Upper Canada—Loyalists at Chippewa, Sir Allan MacNab in Command—Operations Before Navy Island—Burning of the Steamer *Caroline*—Evacuation of Navy Island—" Bois Blanc " Island at Mouth of Detroit River—Gen. Sutherland's Army of Invasion Occupies—Sutherland's Proclamation—Dr. Duncombe and Rebel Rising at Brantford and Scotland—Dispersed by MacNab—Sutherland's Failure at Bois Blanc—Sugar Island—Van Rensselaer Occupies Hickory Island in St. Lawrence—Rebels and Sympathizers Occupy Pelee Island, Detroit River—Invaders Attacked by British Troops and Dispersed—Projected Attack on Windsor and Fort Malden—Short Hills—Hunter's Lodges—Prescott, the Battle of the Windmill—Van Shultz.

AFTER a storm there comes a calm. The affairs of St. Eustache and St. Benoit served to convince the rebellious French-Canadians, for a time at least, that the better way for them would have been to listen to their spiritual pastors and masters rather than to agitators, who deserted them in time of trial. The Bishop of Montreal took advantage of the occasion to address **a circular in** which he said, " What misery, what desolation, **have** overspread many of **the** fairest fields since the demon of war **has** been let loose upon our beautiful **and**, till lately, happy country, wherein abundance and content reigned erewhile **with** order and security, until brigands and rebels, by means of sophistry and lies, misled a part of the people of this diocese. How now about the fine promises made of the wonderful things they would do for you? Was it the controlling spirit of a numerical majority of the people of this country, who according to the insurgents ought to have sway in all things, that directed their military operations? Did you find yourselves in a condition of greater freedom than before, while exposed to all sorts of vexations, threatened with fire raisings, loss of goods, deprivation of even life itself, if you did not submit to the frightful despotism of those insurgents, who by violent, not persuasive means, caused more than a moiety of all the dupes they had to take up arms against the victorious armies of our Sovereign?"

Inasmuch as the rebellion in Lower Canada was confined to a portion of the district of Montreal, and that not exceeding a circuit of thirty miles around the city of Montreal, the Bishop of Quebec gave thanks that his flock had listened to his admonitions and had abstained from taking up arms against lawful authority. He said: "For ourselves, during the disasters of which some parts of this Province have been the theatre, we have, in imitation of Moses, implored the Lord not to abandon His people in their extremity, and now we have the happiness to see, as well as yourselves, that God in His loving kindness listened to our humble supplications."

The case was different in Upper Canada. Mackenzie on reaching the land of the Stars and Stripes found plenty of sympathizers, who received him with open arms. Even while he was operating in the vicinity of Toronto he had on the 6th December, 1837, from his camp at Montgomery's, addressed a letter to the *Buffalo Express*, explaining the attempt he was making to secure the independence of Upper Canada, and soliciting aid for his enterprise. In this respect Mackenzie did not stand on so high a plane as Daniel O'Connell when battling for the independence of Ireland. O'Connell while anxious to secure the liberty of his country was ever ready to resent any attempt at foreign interference either in the way of arms or money. Mackenzie would have been glad to have had both.

On the 11th December a public meeting was held in Buffalo, the largest ever to that time held in that city, inviting assistance for the promoters of rebellion in Canada. The meeting broke up with cheers for Mackenzie, Papineau and Rolph. On the 12th December another meeting was held at which Mackenzie was present. At this meeting one Thomas Jefferson Sutherland offered his services as a volunteer to help the people of Canada to get rid of the "baneful domination of the Mother Country," as Mr. Hume was pleased to term it. Another American patriot requested a contribution of arms and ammunition to be sent to the Eagle tavern in Buffalo, for the benefit of the downtrodden people of Canada. That these meetings were composed mostly of Irish-Americans goes without saying.

Mr. Thomas Jefferson Sutherland got 97 of the citizens

of Buffalo to sign a document, himself heading the list of names attached, of which **the** following is a copy : " We, the young men residents of the City of Buffalo, whose names are hereunto subscribed, pledge to each other our mutual support and co-operation for the commendable purpose of aiding and assisting our Canadian brethren in their present struggle for liberty and those principles which have given to the world that Asylum which we have the honour of calling our home, and which pronounces to mankind the sacred dogma of equality."

"That Asylum which we have the honour of calling our home." That was it. Declared enemies of the United Kingdom, who had been given an asylum in the United States, aiding and abetting rebels in Canada in destroying the happy relations which existed between the Colony and the Empire. Rochester, another New York state town, followed the lead of Buffalo, beating drums, arming men, furnishing arms and inciting people to hasten to deliver Canada from the yoke of British tyranny.

Mackenzie, encouraged by the demonstrations in Buffalo and Rochester, took possession of Navy Island, about two miles above Niagara Falls on the Canadian side of the national boundary. When Mr. Mackenzie appropriated to himself this small piece of Canadian territory he had with him a gentleman of martial mien, whom Mackenzie had appointed Commander-in-Chief of the army, not exactly of the Republic, but of republicans and Canadian rebels, consorting together for the conquest of Canada. Mr. Mackenzie's General-Commander-in-Chief was Mr. Van Rensselaer of Buffalo. The name of Van Rensselaer was not unfamiliar to Canadians in connection with Queenston Heights and the war of 1812. Mr. Mackenzie and his General had only twenty-four men when they landed on Navy Island. They had been promised two hundred and fifty men, two pieces of artillery and some four hundred and fifty stand of arms, besides meat and drink in abundance to start with. It disheartened Mackenzie when he found his army of invasion reduced to twenty-four. So far he had been duped by his American friends. Still Mr. Mackenzie was not to be baulked, he had set out to pull down the Government of Canada, and this he did not yet despair of doing. His first act on taking possession of the Island was to formally establish a so-called Provisional Government for Upper Canada.

The Provisional Government composed of Canadian refugees having been duly established, the next step was, after the fashion of Hull and the Van Rensselaer of 1812, to issue a Proclamation calling on the people of Upper Canada to throw off their allegiance. Here is the Proclamation :—

"INHABITANTS OF UPPER CANADA !!

"For nearly fifty years has our country languished under the blighting influence of military despots, strangers from Europe, ruling us, not according to laws of our choice, but by the capricious dictates of their arbitrary power.

"They have taxed us at their pleasure, robbed our exchequer, and carried off the proceeds to other lands, they have bribed and corrupted ministers of the Gospel with the wealth raised by our industry; they have, in place of religious liberty, given rectories and clergy reserves to a foreign priesthood, with spiritual power dangerous to our peace as a people ; they have bestowed millions of our lands on a company for a nominal consideration, and left them to fleece and impoverish our country; they have spurned our petitions, involved us in their wars, excited feelings of national and sectional animosity in counties, townships and neighbourhoods, and ruled us, as Ireland has been ruled, to the advantage of persons in other lands, and to the prostration of our energies as a people.

"We are wearied of these oppressions, and resolved to throw off the yoke. Rise, Canadians! Rise as one man, and the glorious object of our wishes is accomplished.

"Our intentions have been clearly stated to the world in the Declaration of Independence, adopted at Toronto on the 31st of July last, printed in the *Constitution, Correspondent and Advocate* and the *Liberal*, which important paper was drawn up by Dr. John Rolph and myself, signed by the Central Committee, received the sanction of a large majority of the people of the Province, west of Port Hope and Cobourg, and is well known to be in accordance with the feelings and sentiments of nine-tenths of the people of this state.

"We have planted the standard of liberty in Canada, for the attainment of the following objects:

"Perpetual peace, founded on a government of equal rights to all, secured by a written constitution, sanctioned by yourselves in a convention to be called as early as circumstances will permit.

"Civil and religious liberty in its fullest extent, that in all laws made, or to be made, every person be bound alike, neither shall any tenure, estate, charter, birth, or place, confer any exemption from the ordinary course of legal proceedings and responsibilities whereunto others are subjected.

"The abolition of hereditary honours, of the laws of entail and primogeniture, and hosts of pensioners who devour our substance.

"A Legislature, composed of a Senate and Assembly chosen by the people.

"An Executive, to be composed of a Governor and other officers elected by the public voice.

"A judiciary, to be chosen by the Governor and Senate, and composed of the most learned, honourable and trustworthy of our citizens. The laws to be rendered cheap and expeditious.

"A free trial by jury, sheriffs chosen by you, and not to hold office as now at the pleasure of our tyrants. The freedom of the press. Alas for it, now. The free presses in the Canadas are trampled down by the hand of arbitrary power.

"The vote by ballot, free and peaceful township elections.

"The people to elect their Court of Request, Commissioners and Justices of the Peace, and also their militia officers, in all cases whatsoever.

"Freedom of trade—every man to be allowed to buy at the cheapest market and sell at the dearest.

"No man to be compelled to give military service unless it be his choice.

"Ample funds to be reserved from the vast natural resources of our country to secure the blessings of education to every citizen

"A frugal and economical Government, in order that the people may be prosperous and free from difficulty.

"An end forever to the wearisome prayers, supplications, and mockeries, attendant upon our connection with the lordlings of the Colonial Office, Downing Street, London.

"The opening of the St. Lawrence to the trade of the world, so that the largest ships might pass up to Lake Superior; and the distribution of the wild lands of the country to the industry, capital, skill and enterprise of worthy men of all nations.

"For the attainment of these important objects, the patriots now in arms under the standard of liberty, on Navy Island, U.C., have established a Provisional Government, of which the members are as follows (with two other distinguished gentlemen, whose names there are powerful reasons for withholding from public view), viz.:

"William L. Mackenzie, Chairman, *pro tem.*
"Nelson Gorham.   John Hawk.
"Samuel Lount.   Jacob Rymall.
"Silas Fletcher.   William H. Doyle.
"Jesse Lloyd.   A. G. W. G. Van Egmond.
"Thomas Darling.   Charles Duncombe.
"Adam Graham.

"We have procured the important aid of General Van Rensselaer, of Albany, of Colonel Sutherland, Colonel Van Egmond, and other military men of experience; and the citizens of Buffalo, to their eternal honour be it ever remembered, have proved to us the enduring principles of the Revolution of 1776, by supplying us with provisions, money, arms, ammunition, artillery and volunteers; and vast numbers are floating to the standard under which, heaven willing, emancipation will be speedily won for a new and gallant nation, hitherto held in Egyptian thraldom by the aristocracy of England.

"Brave Canadians! Hasten to join that standard, and to make common cause with your fellow-citizens now in arms in the Home, London and Western districts. The opportunity of the absence of the hired red coats of Europe is favourable to our emancipation. And short-sighted is that man who does not now see that, although his apathy may protract the contest, it must end in independence, freedom from European thraldom forever.

"Until independence is won, trade and industry will be dormant, houses and lands will be unsalable, merchants will be embarrassed, and farmers and mechanics harassed and troubled: that point once gained the prospect is fair and cheering, a long day of prosperity may be ours.

"The reverses in the Home district were owing, first, to accident, which revealed our design to our tyrants, and prevented a surprise; and. second, to the want of artillery. Three thousand five hundred men came and went, but we had no arms for one in twelve of them, nor could we procure them in the country.

"Three hundred acres of the best of the public lands will be freely bestowed upon any volunteer, who shall assist personally in bringing to a conclusion the glorious struggle in which our youthful country is now engaged against the enemies of freedom all the world over.

"Ten millions of these lands, fair and fertile, will, I trust, be speedily at our disposal, with the other vast resources of a country more extensive and rich in natural treasures than the United Kingdom or Old France.

"Citizens! Soldiers of Liberty! Friends of Equal Rights! Let no man suffer in his property, person, or estate—let us pass through Canada, not to retaliate on others for our estates ravaged, our friends in dungeons, our homes burnt, our wheat and barns burnt and our horses and cattle carried off; but let us show the praiseworthy example of protecting the houses, the homes, and the families of those who are in arms against their country and against the liberties of this continent. We will disclaim and severely punish all aggressions upon private property, and consider those as our enemies who may burn or destroy the smallest hut in Canada, unless necessity compel any one to do so in any cause for self defence.

"Whereas, at a time when the King and Parliament of Great Britain had solemnly agreed to redress the grievances of the people, Sir Francis Bond Head was **sent out to** this country with promises of conciliation and justice ; **and** whereas, the said Head hath violated his oath of office as a Governor, trampled upon every vestige of our rights and privileges, bribed and corrupted the Local Legislature, interfered with the freedom of elections, intimidated the freeholders, declared our country not entitled to the blessings of British freedom, prostrated openly the right of trial by jury, placed in office the most obsequious, treacherous and unworthy of our population, and sought to rule Upper Canada **by the** mere force of his arbitrary power ; imprisoned **Dr.** Morrison, **Mr.** Parker, and many others of our most respected citizens ; banishing in a most cruel manner the highly respected Speaker of our late House **of** Assembly, the Honorable Mr. Bidwell ; and causing the expatriation of that universally beloved and well tried eminent patriot, Dr. John Rolph, because they had made common cause with our injured people, and setting a vast price on the heads of several, as if they were guilty persons—for which crimes and misdemeanors he is deserving of being put upon his trial before the country —I do, therefore, hereby offer a reward of £500 for his apprehension, **so** that he may be dealt with as may appertain to justice.

"In Lower Canada, divine providence has blessed the arms of **the** Sons of Liberty—a whole people are there manfully struggling **for** that freedom without which property is but a phantom, and life scarce worth having a gift of. General Girard* is at the head of fifteen thousand determined democrats.

"The friends of freedom in Upper Canada have continued to act in strong and regular concert with Mr. Papineau and the Lower Canada patriots ; and it is a pleasing reflection that between us and the ocean, a population of six hundred thousand souls are now in arms, resolved to be free.

"The tidings that **worthy** patriots are in arms is spreading **through** the Union, and **the** men who were oppressed in England, Ireland, Scotland and the Continent, are flocking to our standard.

"We must be successful.

"I had the honour to address nearly three thousand of the citizens of Buffalo, two days ago, in the theatre. The friendship and sympathy **they** expressed is honourable to the great and flourishing Republic.

* The Swiss, Girod, is probably referred to.

" I am personally authorized to make known to you that from the moment that Sir Francis Bond Head declined to state in writing the objects he had in view, in sending a flag of truce to our camp in Toronto, the message once declined, our esteemed fellow-citizen, Dr. John Rolph, openly announced his concurrence in our measures, and now decidedly approves of the stand we are taking in behalf of our beloved country, which will never more be his until it be free and independent.

"Canadians ! My confidence in you is as strong and powerful in this, our day of trial and difficulty, as when, many years ago, in the zeal and ardour of youth, I appeared among you, the humble advocate of your rights and liberties. I need not remind you of the sufferings and persecutions I have endured for your sakes, the losses I have sustained, the risks I have run. Had I ten lives I would cheerfully give them up to procure freedom to the country of my children, of my early and disinterested choice. Let us act together, and warmed by the hope of success in a patriotic course, be able to repeat in the language so often happily quoted by Ireland's champion,

" ' The nations are fallen and thou still art young,
Thy sun is but rising when others have set ;
And though slavery's cloud o'er thy morning hath hung,
The full tide of Freedom shall beam round thee yet.'

" Militia men of 1812. Will ye again rally round the standard of our tyrants ? I can scarce believe it possible. Upper Canada Loyalists, what has been the recompense of your long tried and devoted attachment to England's aristocracy ? Obloquy and contempt.

"Verily we have learnt in the school of experience, and are prepared to profit by the lessons of the past. Compare the great and flourishing nation of the United States with our divided and distracted land, and think what we also might have been, as brave, independent lords of the soil. Leave then Sir Francis Bond Head's defence to the miserable serfs dependent on his bounty, and to the last hour of your lives the proud remembrance will be yours, ' We also were among the deliverers of our country.'

" Navy Island, December 13, 1837."

The proclamation had some effect. By the end of the month of December a body of men with munitions of war occupied Navy Island. Six hundred men had answered to the bugle call. After that date many more joined the standard of the Provisional Government, all bent on sharing with Mackenzie the spoil of Canada. But where was the General? Sad to say, he was dilatory, neglectful, ready to fight—but no fighter he. Mackenzie had commenced his compaign without an army, and now he found himself with an army but without a General ready to lead it.

The men under the command of Van Rensselaer clamoured to be allowed to cross over to the mainland on the Canada side, but the General would not move, for if he had he would have encountered on the Canadian shore a body of Canadian militia under Colonel, afterwards Sir Allan MacNab, quite able and willing to disarm any force that Mackenzie had it in his power to bring against them. Col. MacNab had more than a thousand men in and around Chippewa, infantry, cavalry, and artillery. Mackenzie's occupation of Navy Island lasted about a month, during which time there was cross-firing between the main shore of Canada and the Island. A great deal of ammunition was used, but not much damage done. It was long range shooting, and had but little effect. The rebel refugees and American citizens on the Island had twenty-four cannon, which they used to the best advantage, but for all that only lessened the number of the Loyalists by one or two. The greatest damage was done to the houses on the Canadian shore, and the inhabitants were kept in a constant state of anxiety. The guns of the Loyalists had not much effect on the Island occupants, owing to the distance and the wooded character of the Island. After about a fortnight's fighting,

Col. MacNab ordered Capt. Drew, of the Royal Navy, but a volunteer in this service, to organize such a force of armed vessels and boats for a flotilla as would protect the landing and transport of a thousand men from the Chippewa shore to the Island, with the object of clearing the Island of the rebels. While the expedition was being prepared, on the 29th December, Col. MacNab saw a small steamer, the *Caroline*, 48 tons burthen, engaged in carrying men, provisions and munitions of war from Buffalo to Navy Island in the interest of the rebels. Col. MacNab at once asked Capt. Drew if he could cut the boat out, and so cut off their supplies. Capt. Drew said it could be done, and was instructed to do so. There was no difficulty in getting volunteers for the service. Late that same night the expedition, comprising seven boats, with an average of nine men each, armed with pistols, cutlasses, and pikes, pushed off from the Chippewa shore to perform the duty assigned. The boats of the little naval brigade were under command of Capt. Drew, the several boats being officered by Lieuts. McCormick, Elmsley, and Christopher Breen, of the Royal Navy, Capt. John Gordon, of the steamboat *Britannia*, running on Lake Ontario, Lieut. Battersby, of London, Canada West, Mr. Harris, Master, R.N., and Mr. Lapenotiere. The expedition did not reach the Island till about midnight, and found that the vessel was moored at the wharf at Fort Schlosser, on the United States side of the river, instead of at the Island itself. This was embarrassing, as by seizing the vessel at the wharf, the Canadian volunteers would be invading American territory. But Capt. Drew had determined to risk the consequences. The boats went silently towards the fated vessel. When they reached the boat they boarded her, cleared her of her crew, set her on fire, detached her from her moorings and sent her adrift down the rushing river and over the Niagara Falls. This adventurous act of the Canadian Naval Brigade was well nigh bringing about a war between England and the United States, the Americans claiming that their territory had been unlawfully invaded by the Canadian force. The British Government, while regretting its occurrence, assumed the responsibility of the act and conferred the honour of knighthood on Col. MacNab. The Upper Canada House of Assembly tendered its thanks to the men engaged in the expedition and granted swords of honour to Col. MacNab and Capt. Drew.

In a fortnight after the burning of the *Caroline* Mr. Mackenzie, Van Rensselaer, and the force under his command evacuated Navy Island.

During the time that Mackenzie occupied Navy Island his friends on the mainland were not idle. Dr. Duncombe, a prominent Reformer in the West, had mustered four or five hundred men at Brantford to give battle to the Loyalists and Tories in that region. Col. MacNab having been informed of Dr. Duncombe's proceedings marched to Brantford with a detachment of 150 volunteers and 100 Indians, under command of Capt. Kerr. On their approach the rebels under Dr. Duncombe retreated to Scotland, a village a few miles to the south-west of Brantford. Col. MacNab followed them up. By the 14th of December he had nearly two thousand volunteers ready to face Dr. Duncombe's band and those who might choose to cast in their lot with him, who were expected from the London district. Col. MacNab's show of force overawed the rebels and they dispersed. Dr. Duncombe fled to the United States and made common cause with Mackenzie in the Republic.

Before leaving Navy Island, Gen. Van Rensselaer, Mr. Mackenzie's Commander-in-Chief, had determined to invade Canada with a force of American sympathizers and Canadian refugees. There was in Buffalo an individual of the name of Sutherland, who had, or professed to have had military experience. Upon him was conferred the rank of Brigadier-General of the second division of the army of invasion of Upper Canada. On December 28, 1837, Gen. Van Rensselaer issued the following order :

"Headquarters, Navy Island.

"Brig.-Gen. Sutherland will repair with all despatch to Detroit and its vicinity and promote every arrangement for making a descent upon Canada in favour of the Patriots, as he in his judgment may deem advisable, after consulting with the Canadian and American friends in that quarter."

Gen. Sutherland, on the 9th of January, 1838, called for volunteers. About sixty at once responded, and, under his command, took possession of Bois Blanc, an island in Canadian waters at the mouth of the Detroit River, not far from Fort Malden. His object was with these sixty men and eighteen others, whom he had embarked on the schooner *Anne*, to surprise Fort Malden, seize the arms stored there, and thus supplied to make another attempt to establish a footing in Upper Canada. Not to be outdone by his predecessors in the art of war, he, from his headquarters on Bois Blanc Island, issued another proclamation breathing sentiments of devotion to Canada and her political interests. Here is his manifesto:

"PROCLAMATION TO THE PATRIOTIC CITIZENS OF UPPER CANADA.

"You are called upon by the voice of your bleeding country to join the patriot forces and free your lands from tyranny. Hordes of worthless parasites of the British Crown are quartered upon you to devour your substance, to outrage your rights, to let loose upon your defenceless wives and daughters a brutal soldiery. Rally then around the standard of liberty, and a victory and a glorious future of independence will be yours."

It has always been a marvel to Canadians how it happens that there are so many citizens of the United States who in some way conceive that Canada is a bleeding country, when the fact is that she has always been contented and happy. There may at times be an ebullition of over-strong political feeling, but Canadians have always been able to harmonize their political differences without foreign interference.

Gen. Sutherland did not succeed in his enterprise. The schooner *Anne* lost her helmsman by a shot from the Canadian shore, drifted shoreward and was beached in three feet of water, much to the dismay of the sympathizers on Bois Blanc Island. The vessel was taken possession of by the Canadian militia, and Col. Radcliffe, in command of the boarding party, reported that he found on board "twenty-one persons (one killed, eight wounded, twelve prisoners), three pieces of cannon, about two hundred stand of arms, buff cross belts and ammunition." By Gen. Sutherland's orders those who made their escape retreated to Sugar Island on the American side of the boundary, further down the Detroit River, near where it enters Lake Erie.

At this time Gen. Sutherland had a rival in the Patriot forces in the person of Gen. Handy, of Illinois. This warrior had disputed with Sutherland who should command the western forces of the Patriot band. Gen. Handy was the commander of what was called the Patriot Army of the North-West, and was not disposed to yield command to Sutherland, who commanded the force gathered in Ohio and other volunteers from the east. The two generals quarrelled about the right to command. In true republican fashion it was left to the seven hundred men to decide who should have the honour of leading the men to the conquest of Canada and to elect their commander. The choice fell on Gen. Handy, and now let us see what he did. The net result of his operations was nothing beyond some ineffective measures taken by him with a view to the invasion of the Province from Sugar Island. He found, however, that he had neither men, arms or ammunition sufficient to cope with the Royal Canadian Militia, which stood ready to receive him on the Canadian shore. In this helpless condition he was forced to apply to the American authorities for friendly assistance to extricate him from his position. The Governor of Michigan went in a steamer to Sugar Island, took over the arms, and Gen. Handy and his force evacuated the island.

The evacuation of Sugar Island did not, however, end the attempt at invasion in the western part of the Province.

Before proceeding to describe the further attempts in the western part, we must turn to the East to watch the refugees' and American sympathizers' movements in the East. Near the end of February, Van Rensselaer made a show of force on Hickory Island, about two miles from Gananoque, where two companies of British regulars with a few militia were stationed. He had with him about two thousand five hundred men. The Loyalists were only about two hundred strong at Gananoque, and, had Van Rensselaer been a skilful general or brave soldier, he might have occasioned some trouble to the force at Gananoque. But as he was neither the one or the other his men lost confidence in him, deserted him in squads, and before two days were over Hickory Island was barren of sympathizers, and Canadians on the main shore could peacefully rest in their beds. The Canadians about Kingston, indeed, required rest. It had been reported in Kingston that Van Rensselaer with a great force was advancing to capture Fort Henry, Kingston's arsenal. The fort was garrisoned by civilians only, and the town itself was almost defenceless. There was, however, no lack of volunteers who came forward to serve their country in time of need. Sixteen hundred men were placed under arms, with a view of defending the old town of Kingston, but when Van Rensselaer evacuated Hickory Island, they were free to return to their homes and their families.

Turning again to the West, in March, 1838, American sympathizers made another attempt to take Canada, this time by way of Pelee Island, some forty miles south-east of Amherstburgh. About four hundred men mustered on this island with this object, not by their own strength alone, but with the hoped-for assistance from Canadians when they should reach the main shore. But it so happened they were not permitted to reach the main shore. British troops, consisting of five companies of regulars, with about two hundred militia and Indians, under command of Gen. Maitland, made a descent on the island, defeated the self-styled Patriots, killing about sixty of them, and making nine prisoners—Gen. Sutherland being one of the prisoners—and left the balance of the rebel force to their fate.

It would almost have been better if the exiled rebels and their friends in the United States could have penetrated the mainland of the Province for some little distance, for then they would have learned from the people themselves how futile it was for them to expect Canada to be subjugated and passed over to the United States. As it was, the border was kept constantly in a state of excitement by the reports spread abroad that the refugees and outpourings of the United States were, in formidable numbers, about to pounce on the inoffending people of Canada with a force that would crush them to atoms. There was some reason for these reports, as without doubt the organization for this purpose in the United States had by March, 1838, assumed formidable proportions.

About this time there was formed on the other side of the border an association called "The Canadian Refugee Relief Association." The object of this association was to focus all the refugees in the United States, to obtain new supplies of men from Canada, and with the American sympathizers then to invade Canada in force. The centre of the organization was in the State of Michigan. Gen. Handy was appointed Commander in Chief, and to promote the objects of the organization he signed blank commissions, and sent agents through the Province of Upper Canada to form revolutionary societies, and enroll all in whom he thought he could confide.

Mr. Lindsey, in his "Life and Times of W. L. Mackenzie," in referring to this organization, says: "In every square mile of settled country a person was appointed to grant commissions in the secret army of revolt. Handy's commissions were given to captains, and the Associations were left to elect their own colonels, couriers, and spies. One hundred in number were constantly kept in motion through the Provinces, taking intelligence daily to Handy. Each of them had a beat of ten miles, at either end of which he **communicated** with others, **and** this distance he regularly **made both ways every day.** Two hundred companies, of one hundred men each, were enrolled, making an aggregate force of 20,000 men in the Canadas, ready to rise whenever called upon, and through the system of couriers in operation they could have been called into operation with the least possible delay. The 4th of July, 1838, was fixed upon **for** striking the first blow. The Patriot standard **was to be raised at** Windsor opposite Detroit, and when this was accomplished the couriers were to be prepared to transmit **the** intelligence with **all possible** speed and a general rising was to take place. The first thing to be done was to seize all available public arms, ammunition, and provisions, and then the fortification of some prominent point designated was to be commenced."

To carry out the plan of invasion it was necessary for Gen. Handy to secure arms and ammunition in Michigan, to begin with. He depended upon the arsenal of the State to furnish him the supplies needed. He had gained the confidence of the guard of the arsenal, and the door was open to him, but with his usual bad luck the State authorities changed the guard the night before the day fixed for the descent on Canada, and the whole scheme was frustrated. There were many little intervening incidents connected with the insurrection, which are not of sufficient importance to be given a place in history. There is, however, one occurrence of local character which should be chronicled. This was an affair at Short Hills, in the County of Welland, that will bear recording. Here in June, 1838, some five or six hundred men, well armed and equipped, were terrorizing the country thereabout, and it became necessary to disperse them. "The Lancers," a javelin corps, of Toronto, under the command of Major McGrath, came across this body of men at Ooverholt's tavern, fired upon them, killed several and dispersed the rest, taking thirty-one of them prisoners. The band was composed of Canadians, who had been concerned in the insurrection under Dr. Duncombe in the London district, and at Montgomery's, back of Toronto.

Col. Kingsmill, who was in command on the frontier at

this time, had the disposition of the prisoners taken in the affair. Col. Kingsmill was a half-pay officer of the regular army, and did good service in protecting the Niagara frontier from the invasion of American sympathizers and otherwise.

Gen. Handy's failure to capture Fort Malden, and by this means gain a foothold in the western part of the Province of Upper Canada, was disappointing to all who were interested in the overthrow of British power in the colony. The question was asked, could not this be better accomplished in the eastern part of the Province, nearer the rebellious French-Canadians of Lower Canada and with their help? There was a man named Hunter, who lived near Whitby, in the east riding of the old County of York, now the County of Ontario, who had been active in promoting the rebellion in the Home district. He had been nearly taken as a rebel by the company of men from Port Hope and Peterborough coming to the assistance of Toronto, in December, 1837. Had it not been for an oven at Gate's tavern, ten or twenty miles east of Toronto, on the Kingston road, he would have fallen into the hands of the Loyalists. The oven afforded him a place of concealment, and when he escaped he went to the United States. Anxious to have his name handed down to posterity, he proceeded to form Lodges in the land of the Stars and Stripes, which were named Hunter's Lodges. There was a general convention of these Lodges held at Cleveland, Ohio, in September, 1838, which was attended by seventy delegates. The members of Hunter's Lodges took an oath, which commenced by swearing allegiance to Republican institutions, and ended by declaring that the aforesaid members would, "until death, attack, combat, and help to destroy, by all means that their superior officer should think proper, every power, or authority of Royal origin, upon this continent, and especially never to rest till all tyrants of Britain cease to have any dominion or footing whatever in North America." This was a pretty strong oath, but was greedily taken, not only by the exiled Canadians, but by the other members of the convention, whom Canadian refugees described as "Americans, men of poor fortunes."

"The Hunters," as they called themselves, now proceeded to active invasion, and by November, 1838, had assembled for an attack on Prescott, a town in the County of Grenville, on the frontier, opposite to the American town of Ogdensburg. On Sunday morning, the 11th of Nov., a large steamer, the *United States*, towing two schooners loaded with armed men, left Sackett's Harbour for Prescott. The number of armed men was about seven hundred, and all were under the command of Col. Von Shultz, a brave Pole, who had been appointed to the command of the expedition. The expedition was to have been commanded by a man of higher rank, General Bierge. If the advice of Von Shultz had been followed the expedition would have landed at Prescott and no doubt taken the town, but General Bierge and other officers overruled Von Shultz and demanded that the expedition should first land at Ogdensburg and increase their force by further recruits.

Von Shultz was opposed to this, for the simple reason that, in his belief, instead of getting recruits the expedition would lose many of its valiant men by desertion. Whether this actually happened or not is not known, but it is known that General Bierge suddenly fell sick, which his companions in arms imputed to cowardice.

In crossing the river one of the schooners, commanded by one Bill Johnson, who had for some time been alarming defenceless people on the Canadian shore, was in some way run ashore on a bar in the river, and the unfortunate Von Shultz was left with only one schooner and one hundred and seventy men with which to make a conquest of Canada.

Von Shultz however was not a man to turn back. He landed his men on the 12th of November, on the Canadian shore, and took possession of a windmill just below the town of Prescott, and there fortified himself. This move of Col. Von Shultz was not however effected without the loss of some men. Even on the landing he found himself opposed by the little British steamer *Experiment* of one gun, which poured shot into the schooner carrying Von Shultz's force, and into the steamer *United States*, which, with damaged engines, retired disabled across the river into American waters.

When Von Shultz and his men had secured a landing he felt secure. But matters turned out differently from what he expected. Capt. Sandom, commanding the Royal Navy in Upper Canada, having heard of Von Shultz's expedition and his setting out from Sackett's Harbour, immediately

THE SIEGE OF THE WINDMILL.

left Kingston with a detachment of forty men and a party of marines in the steamer *Victoria*, accompanied by the *Cobourg*, for the purpose of intercepting him if possible. Capt. Sandom and his men arrived at Prescott on the morning of the 13th of November, and after effecting the landing of his force, and being joined by a party of militia, the marines and militia made an attack on Von Shultz's fortified posts, and after an hour's firing drove them into the windmill.

The mill itself was a solid stone building of great strength, and Capt. Sandom feeling the risk of attempting to take it by land, except by a regular siege, decided to bombard it from the river, and accordingly brought his boat down the river and began an attack with his guns. By three in the afternoon, he found he could make no impression on the fortress, and he accordingly withdrew, posting pickets to prevent the escape of his prey, and awaited the arrival of heavier artillery.

Von Shultz and his men remained cooped up in the mill till the 16th, being all the time promised by those who had remained in safety on the American shore, watching the turn of events, that they would either reinforce or rescue him. But although thousands gathered on the shore to gaze, they did nothing. On the 16th, at noon, Col. Dundas, with four companies of the 83rd Regiment, two eighteen pounders, and a howitzer brought down from Kingston, appeared on the scene, planted his guns in good position, and began firing upon the windmill, first placing a company of the 83rd Regiment, supported by the militia on either flank to prevent the **escape of** the occupants. During the day the fire from Col. Dundas' battery was so effective that the mill became untenantable, and when darkness fell, under cover of the night, Von Shultz and a division of his men took refuge in the brush wood on the bank of the river, where he and his men were shortly taken prisoners.

It has been computed that one hundred and fifty men, killed and wounded on both sides, were lost in what is known in the annals of the rebellion as the battle of "The Windmill." One hundred and fifty-seven prisoners were taken, of whom eleven were executed, including the unfortunate Von Shultz, who never forgave Bill Johnson and the other leaders of the expedition for their desertion of him when endeavouring to hold his post against great odds. Von Shultz was a brave and generous man; he was a victim of more designing men who led him to the course which brought him to the gallows.

CHAPTER XVI.

American Sympathizers—Rebellion Carried On Without the Province—Foreign War Carried On by Irresponsible Americans—Determined to Avenge Prescott—Assemble at Detroit—Gen. Bierce's Proclamation—Lands at Windsor—Destroys Property—Met by Loyalists and Repulsed—Col. Prince—Mackenzie Dissatisfied with the American Allies—Will Rely on Himself and Canadians—Mackenzie Has no Faith in the United States—Regrets the Rebellion that he Had Stirred Up—Admits his Mistake—Should he Be Forgiven?—His Penitence Sincere—Trials, Imprisonments and Executions—Lord Durham, Governor—His Report—Constitution of 1841—Mackenzie, Papineau and Rolph Members of the Union House—Conclusion.

THE rebellion which had its beginning in 1837, within the limits of Canada, was after that year carried on from the United States. The only two risings in Upper Canada of local significance were those of Mackenzie and Dr. Duncombe respectively, the first in York and that of Duncombe at Brantford and Scotland. The year 1838 was a year of rebellion, historically speaking, but it was a rebellion carried on without, not within the Province. The seat of war, as it may be called, was on the American border, and in American territory. It was there the "Hunter's Lodges," "Patriot Societies," "Refugee Conventions," and all those who wished to make Canada a republic had their headquarters, and from thence all the supplies of arms and ammunition were obtained.

The American Government had great difficulty in preventing itself being drawn into the vortex of civil strife. Many men holding high positions in the state and municipal governments of the United States, made common cause with the Canadian insurrectionists, but the Federal Government, by the exercise of wholesome restraint and diplomacy, escaped being drawn into the struggle.

The struggle for the possession of Canada was thus more of a contest between sympathizing foreigners and the Loyalists of Canada, than between opposite factions in the Province. It was a foreign war carried on by irresponsible American citizens, mostly of foreign extraction, and Canadian refugees.

After the failure to capture the Province by way of Prescott and the "Windmill," the "Hunter's Lodge" determined to renew the attempt by way of Detroit. In the evening of the 3rd of December, 1838, a body of men numbering several hundred, well armed and provisioned, under the command of General Bierce who had superseded General Handy in the west, marched through the streets of Detroit, band playing and colours flying, ready for a fresh invasion of the Province of Upper Canada. This body of men was allowed to pass within sight of the sentinels stationed at the public arsenal without interruption. The warriors next morning crossed the Detroit River in the steamer *Champlain*, and landed on Canadian soil. No sooner had they landed than, following time-honoured precedent, the General issued his proclamation.

"Soldiers! the time has arrived that calls for action—the blood of our slaughtered countrymen cries aloud for revenge. The spirits of Lount, and Matthews, and Moreau, are yet unavenged. The murdered heroes of Prescott lie in an unhallowed grave in the land of tyranny. The manes of the ill-fated *Caroline's* crew can only be appeased by the blood of murderers.

"Arouse, then, soldiers of Canada! Let us avenge their wrongs! Let us march to victory or death; and ever, as we meet the tyrant foe, let our war cry be, 'Remember Prescott.'"

It was known in Detroit that this "Hunter's Lodge" army of invasion was to attack the town of Windsor the next morning. Just as was done on the American frontier opposite Prescott when Von Shultz made his abortive attempt to subjugate Canadians, several thousands of the citizens of Detroit lined the American shore to encourage the invaders, and, when, after landing, the so-called "Patriots" raised a tricoloured flag, displaying twin stars and the word "Liberty," the enthusiasm of the onlookers, on the American side of the river, knew no bounds. Their acclamations and hurrahs rent the air.

The invaders in pursuance of their enterprise, soon after landing, set fire to a building used as a barracks for the militia, and exchanged volleys with the occupants, several men being killed on both sides. They then set fire to the steamer *Thames*, which was frozen up in the river, and burned it to the edge of the ice. They then marched for the inhabited portion of the town, but being met by a force of militia under Col. Prince and Capt. Spark, were repulsed, driven out of the town and took refuge in the surrounding woods.

The invaders soon after were unpleasantly surprised

when they found that the British had marched their regular troops to within a convenient distance. They had not been long concealed in the woods, when Col. Broderick, with a detachment of Royal Artillery and a nine pounder, arrived on the ground from Amherstburgh. The Regulars and Militia made short work of the invaders and drove them ingloriously back to Detroit from whence they came. The United States steamer, *The Erie*, in the river, would not afford them any assistance in their efforts to regain American territory. They were obliged by begging, bribing and stealing, to get canoes or small boats of any kind to take them back to the land of the free.

In this raid twenty-five of the invaders lost their lives and forty-six were taken prisoners. Col. Prince, in his report on the proceedings, briefly and succinctly said: "Of the brigands and pirates twenty-one were killed, besides four, who were brought in just at the close and immediately after the engagement—all of whom I ordered to be shot upon the spot; *and it was done accordingly.*" This summary procedure was bitterly denounced by some—particularly the friends of the Americans who were shot, but on the other hand was warmly approved by those Canadians who had no sympathy with these invaders, who had entered their country with the design of laying waste their fair fields, burning and destroying their property and taking human lives in carrying out their nefarious purpose. Col. Prince's justice had a salutary and deterrent effect. There were no more raids after Windsor.

Mr. Mackenzie took no part in the raids either on Prescott or Windsor. He **was busy with** newspaper work, his favourite occupation, in New **York.** The failure of the " Hunter's Lodge " men to bring about the downfall of Canada, and the means adopted by these men, who evidently had no care for Canada or the Canadians, caused Mackenzie to lose confidence in his American friends. He did not, however, give up all hope of effecting the independence of Canada by the efforts of the Canadians themselves. In January, 1839, he wrote to a private friend that the sympathizers, "organization and union," apart from that of the Associations who aid them, is nothing. They have little influence, nor will it increase until a better system is adopted. He thought Canada could be redeemed if men went the right way about it. " I shall try," he said, " to get up such an organization here (in Rochester) and on the other side, and to make such use of that already in operation, as will probably somewhat change the aspect of Canadian affairs. The material is before us if we choose to make use of it."

This letter is but another proof of what a sanguine, visionary man Mackenzie was. It was this over-confidence in his own strength, which never forsook him during his stormy life, that led him into all the difficulties and troubles that seemed ever to surround him.

On the 12th **of** March, 1839, Mackenzie issued a confidential circular, calling a **special** convention, " to be composed of Canadians, **or persons connected** with Canada, who are favourable **to the attainment of** its political independence, and the entire separation of its government from the political power of Great Britain," to be held at Rochester. This convention duly met, and the outcome of it was that a Canadian Association was formed, a President, Secretary and Treasurer appointed, and the principles of the Association promulgated. These comprised the discarding of the notion of attempting to reform Canada by hostile invasion from the United States, and pledged the Association to "obtaining for the people of the North American Colonies the unrestricted power to choose their form of government, by means of conventions of delegates whose acts should afterwards obtain their concurrence."

Mr. Mackenzie lived long enough to realize that he, like many another man, in pursuing imagined "Liberty" was only following her pseudo-sister "License." In pursuit of this phantom he exiled himself for three years or more, becoming a citizen of the United States. The fact that he had been a rebel in Canada against the British Government was sufficient to ensure his honourable reception in the United States. His residence in that great country, however, cured him of his love for republican institutions. In the last number of the *Gazette*, a paper published by him in New York, the issue of December the 23rd, 1840, he said, "Over three years residence in the United States, and a closer observation of the condition of society here, have lessened my regrets at the results of the opposition raised to England in Canada, in 1837-1838. I have beheld the American people give their dearest and most valued rights into the keeping of the worst enemies of free institutions. I have seen monopoly and slavery triumph at the popular elections, and witnessed with pain, the bitter fruits of that speculative spirit of enterprise to which, as President Van Buren says in his late excellent message, his countrymen are so liable, and upon whom the lessons of experience are so unavailing. And, although the leaders of parties here may not say so to their followers, yet the conviction grows daily stronger in my mind that your brethren of this Union are rapidly hastening toward a state of society, in which President, Senate and House of Representatives, will fulfil the duties of Kings, Lords and Commons, and the power of the community pass from the democracy of numbers into the hands of an aristocracy, not of noble ancestry and ancient lineage, but of monied monopolists, land-jobbers and heartless politicians."

"Distance lends enchantment to the view." Mr. Mackenzie had only to leave Canada and cast his lot with those living under Republican institutions, to become thoroughly convinced that a limited monarchy gives more true liberty to the subject than the much vaunted Democracy. Mr. Mackenzie was a Scotchman, he had resided for a time in England before coming to Canada, he had seen all the phases of Colonial life, and that life had been to him a bitter one, yet experience proved to him that the British system of government was to be preferred to pure democracy. Nor was this all. Mackenzie as time went on saw the folly of his past proceedings. He deeply regretted having stirred up strife in Canada and became a penitent.

In 1842 he wrote from the United States to a friend in Canada, "The more I see this country, the more do I regret the attempt at revolution at Toronto and St. Charles." After having lived nine years in the United States he wrote, "I frankly confess that had I passed nine years in the United States before, instead of after the outbreak, I am sure I would have been the last man in America to be engaged in it."

As if to emphasize his regret at having been the fomenter of rebellion in Canada, and to place himself on record in the most public manner, as being his own accuser, in the early part of the year 1849, or about that time, he wrote to Earl Grey, the Colonial Secretary, in London: "A course of careful observation during the last eleven years has fully satisfied me that had the violent movement in which I and many others were engaged on both sides of the Niagara proved successful, that success would have deeply injured the people of Canada, whom I then believed I was serving at great risks. . . . I have long been sensible of the errors committed at that period. No punishment that power could inflict or nature sustain would have equalled the regrets I have felt on account of much I did and wrote and published. There is not a living man on this continent, who more sincerely desires that the British Government in Canada may long continue."

What stronger testimony than this is wanted to prove that the better and happier condition for Canada is to hold strongly to old Mother England? Here we have a Prince of Agitators, a man deeply dyed in revolution, acknowledging that he had been all wrong, and expressing his hope for the stability of that Empire which he had so earnestly sought to rob of her colony.

One is almost inclined to forgive Mr. Mackenzie for his revolutionary propaganda after such expressions of contrition as have been quoted.

But, alas! the consequences of the rebellion were so serious—so many lives were sacrificed, so many women made widows, so many children fatherless, and so much property destroyed in the civil war—that the leaders in it cannot be altogether forgiven, though all would wish to forget this unfortunate episode in Canadian history. It is safe to say that as many as a thousand lives were sacrificed in the rebellion. The greater proportion of the lives lost was among the insurrectionary class, American sympathizers and Canadian refugees. The loss in the ranks of the Loyalists was comparatively small. There were several executions for treason in Upper Canada. The most prominent of those executed for treason in that Province were Lount and Matthews at Toronto, and Von Shultz at Kingston. After the rebellion had finally collapsed, the rebels taken prisoners in Upper Canada were brought to trial before competent tribunals. The result was that ten were executed and fifty-eight transported. More than 800 persons were made prisoners in Upper Canada and dealt with by Court Martial and the Civil Courts. The prisons in Lower Canada were filled with prisoners.

On the 31st of March, 1838, the Earl of Durham was appointed High Commissioner for the investigation of certain important questions pending in the Provinces of Lower and Upper Canada, respecting the form of the future government of the Provinces; and by the same Commission was appointed Governor-General and Commander-in-Chief of the Provinces.

It was a misfortune that the Commission had not been appointed at an earlier period. Before the insurrection broke out, in the preceding year, the Queen, in her speech at the opening of the Imperial Legislature, called the attention of the two houses of Parliament to the troubled state of affairs in Canada.

The Constitutional Act of 1791 was well enough in its day, but by the incoming of the year 1837 had outgrown its usefulness. The fact was recognized by the Imperial Government, and, in 1840, an Imperial Act was passed, superseding the Act of 1791, and uniting the Provinces of Upper and Lower Canada. The Union of the Provinces was always opposed by the inhabitants of Lower Canada, the politicians of that Province being apprehensive that with the rapid growth of Upper Canada, the latter Province would have a numerical majority so large as to be able to control the legislation of the two Canadas, and thus destroy the French-Canadian influence. Notwithstanding the opposition of Lower Canada, and the not too ready willingness of Upper Canada, the Union had to be brought about. The Earl of Durham was appointed High Commissioner, as stated, on the 31st of March, 1838, and made his report to the British Government on the 31st of January, 1839. The report was the foundation of the Act of Union of 1840.

It is too lengthy to give in full, but a synopsis of it will aid in coming to a conclusion as to the merits or demerits of the Rebellion of 1837. The Report makes a large folio volume, though containing but thirty-eight paragraphs. The substance of the Report is as follows:—

Paragraph 1. This paragraph is preliminary, and states that the suspension of the Constitution gave him (Lord Durham) an essential advantage over his predecessors. It not merely relieved him from the burthen of constant discussions with the Legislative bodies, but it enabled him to turn his attention to the real grievances of the Province, etc., etc.

Paragraph 2. He himself, he found, as well as most people in England, had had a very erroneous view of the parties at issue in Lower Canada. The quarrel he had been sent to heal, had been a quarrel between the Executive Government and the popular branch of the Legislature. The latter body had apparently been contending for popular rights, free government, etc. The Executive defending prerogative of the Crown and the institutions which had been established as checks on the unbridled exercise of popular power.

"I had in common with most of my countrymen imagined that the original and constant source of the evil was to be found in the defects of the political institutions of the Province, that a reform of the Constitution, or perhaps merely the introduction of a sounder practice into the administration of the Government would remove all cause of contest and complaint." In this he refers to his despatch of the 9th August, 1838, to the Principal Secretary of State, in which he gave in detail, the impressions produced on his mind by the state of things he found actually to exist in Lower Canada. That experience, derived from his residence in the Province, had completely changed his views of the relative value of the causes which had been assigned for the existing disorders. "From the peculiar circumstance in which I was placed, I was enabled to make such effectual observations as convinced me that there had existed in the Constitution of the Province, in the balance of political power, in the spirit and practice of the administration, in every department of the Government defects that were quite sufficient to account for a great degree of mismanagement and dissatisfaction. I found a deeper than political

cause, a cause that penetrated deep into **its** social fabric. . . .
I expected to find a contest between a Government and a people, I
found two nations warring in the bosom of **a** mighty state, I found a
struggle not of principle, but of races," **etc.**

Paragraph 3. Animosities between **French** and English. Every
contest is one of French and English in the outset, or becomes so
ere it has run its course. Exasperation of the races against each
other. Refers to the divisions in Quebec and Montreal, and that the
Eastern Townships remained comparatively quiet, not coming into
contact with the French. British population in some cases voted
French from local causes, and still Government influence as a general
rule could not influence the French, they stick together. A large part
of the Catholic Canadians, a few of the principal proprietors of the
seigniorial families and some of those who are influenced by commercial connexion support the Government against revolutionary
violence, a middle party exercising influence, it is English or French.

Paragraph 4. Grounds of quarrel as put forward not the
real grounds. The grounds put forward only as a mask to conceal the
real grounds, which were *national animosity*. French politicians in
the majority have invoked the principle of popular control and
democracy. The English parade their loyalty. When we look **to** the
rights of each party the analogy to our own politics seems lost, if not
actually reversed ; the French appear to have used their democratic
aims for Conservative purposes, rather than those of liberal and
enlightened government, and the sympathies of the friends of reform
are naturally enlisted on the side of sound amelioration, which the
English minority in vain attempted to introduce into the antiquated
laws of the Province.

Paragraph 5. Papineau's influence on the legislative body. The
English complained of the Assembly, referred to the establishment of
the Registry Office, and desired to commute the feudal tenures; and yet
it was amongst the able and most influential leaders of the English
that I found some of the opponents of some of the proposed reforms.
The French anxious to disclaim any hostility to these reforms, but
Papineau restrained the Assembly from considering them. The mass
of the population opposed to the feudal tenure. There is every
reason to believe that **a great** number of the peasants who fought at
St. Denis and **St.** Charles imagined that the principal result **of success**
would be **the** overthrow **of** tithes and feudal burthens ; **and in** the

Declaration of Independence, which Nelson issued, two of the objects of the insurrection were stated to **be the** abolition of feudal tenures and the establishment of Registry Offices.

Paragraphs 6 and 7. Independent spirit **of** the English population. Dissimilarity of races. The ignorance **of** the French *habitants*, etc. The two races inimical **to** each other, **not** like French and English, but French-Canadian **and** English, the French clinging to old laws and customs, not modern. "We must bear **in** mind," he says, "what kind of French and English they are that are brought in contact, and in what proportions they meet."

Paragraph 8. Enlarges on the ignorance of the French peasant. His general character. How he was kept down by the old French regime. He had no desire to raise more than for his immediate wants. No general provision had been made for education. Not surprising that they made little advance in improvements. Whatever energy displayed was in the fur trade. They (the French) remained an old and stationary society in a new and progressive world. In all essentials they are French, but French in every respect dissimilar to old France in the present day.

Paragraph 9. Enlarges on social conditions. Notaries in villages and priest and doctor. Seminaries and colleges. Although common schools defective, seminaries and colleges effective. The most instructed population is confined to a small body of educated persons. To this singular state of things is attributable the extraordinary influence of the Canadian demagogues.

Paragraph 10. English population progressive, etc. In the early history of the Province, under English rule, Canadians were excluded from power, and all offices of trust and emolument mostly in hands of English strangers.

Paragraph 11. The superiority **of** English farms and reclaiming them, thus giving cause of jealousy to the French settlers.

Paragraphs 12 and 13. Working classes not divided by collision of interest, but national prejudices.

Paragraphs 14, 15, 16 and 17. Effects of difference of language.

Paragraphs 19 and 20. **No** social intercourse between races.

Paragraph **21**. Intermarriages rare.

Paragraph **22. Marked division of** society.

Paragraph 23. No combination for public objects.

Paragraph 24. Political strife the result of such social feeling. Superior intelligence of English, but greater refinement of French.

Paragraphs 25 and 26 Collisions. between Executive and Assembly.

The Union Act of 1840, based on the report of Lord Durham, had the effect of bringing the Upper and Lower Canadians into more intimate relations. It was designed to harmonize the two races, and did good work in bringing that about. I will not enlarge on this topic, however, which is more for the politician and the general historian to discourse upon than for a writer of the Rebellion of 1837. Before concluding the narrative, however, it may be proper to say something of the leaders of the rebellion, after peace had been restored and the affairs of the Provinces well under way under the new Constitutional Act of 1840.

Messrs. Papineau, Mackenzie and Rolph, after their exile of many years, returned to Canada, to take part in the government of the country they had affected to believe was hopelessly sunk in the slough of despond, and was the victim of British tyranny. In 1851, Mr. Mackenzie presented himself to the electors of the County of Haldimand, and was elected for that county against that stalwart reformer, George Brown. Rolph regained the confidence of his old constituency of Norfolk, and held office as Commissioner of Crown Lands in the Government of the United Province. Mr. Papineau yielded to the temptation of again becoming a representative of the people and secured a place in Parliament. None of these gentlemen ever attained the influence they possessed in their more happy ante-rebellion days. The political atmosphere by which they were surrounded was entirely different from what it was when Papineau had only but to speak, and all Lower Canada answered to his call, and when Mackenzie piped to his many dancers in Upper Canada. As for Mr. Papineau he ever retained his French-Canadian nationality, and never concealed his discontent with the Union, which he had bitterly opposed in Lower Canada. He had the respect of all his countrymen. Some who had been his lieutenants in former days were now in office, while he maintained that self-same haughty independence, which was a prominent characteristic of his nature. Those who were opposed to him could not help admiring his conscientiousness and devotion to principle. He accepted the Union as it was, but had no regard for the Unionists.

Mr. Mackenzie on his return from the United States, in the performance of his duties in Parliament, was the same active representative that he had been when member for York, but his critical mind had to submit to the altered state of things, which afforded him little scope for his ruling passion.

The remembrance of the rebellion did for some years rankle in the breasts of those who were called upon to defend the Provinces in a time of internal disorder and foreign aggression. For those Americans, who, in despite of neutrality laws, and in defiance of the peaceful relations then existing, and which ought at all times to exist between the two great nations, Great Britain and the United States, sought to embroil these countries in war, there was no excuse whatever.

The Canadian insurgents, on the contrary, could claim that they acted in the honest belief that the institutions of their country required reforming, which could only be brought about by rebellion. This was an entirely mistaken idea. It nevertheless influenced the minds of many good men who would never have thought of rebelling but for the overdrawn pictures of misgovernment in public affairs, designed by disappointed politicians and professional agitators.

Most of the men who took part in the rebellion have long since left the stage of life, but some are living who took part in the struggles of that period. In writing this narrative I have sought to avoid personalities or individualising as far as possible, and at the same time to present to the reader an intelligent account of the civil strife.

> "If I unwittingly . . . . .
> Have aught committed that is hardly borne
> By any in this presence, I desire
> To reconcile me to his friendly peace."

www.ingramcontent.com/pod-product-compliance
Lightning Source LLC
Chambersburg PA
CBHW032024220426
43664CB00006B/352